SECURITY

A New Framework for Analysis

Barry Buzan
Ole Wæver
Jaap de Wilde

LYNNE
RIENNER
PUBLISHERS

BOULDER
LONDON

Published in the United States of America in 1998 by
Lynne Rienner Publishers, Inc.
1800 30th Street, Boulder, Colorado 80301

and in the United Kingdom by
Lynne Rienner Publishers, Inc.
3 Henrietta Street, Covent Garden, London WC2E 8LU

Library of Congress Cataloging-in-Publication Data
Buzan, Barry.
    Security:a new framework for analysis/by Barry Buzan, Ole
Wæver, and Jaap de Wilde.
    Includes bibliographical references and index.
    ISBN 1-55587-603-X (hc:alk. paper).
    ISBN 1-55587-784-2 (pb:alk. paper)
    1. Security, International.   2. National security.
3. Regionalism.   4. International economic relations.   I. Wæver,
Ole, 1960– . II. Wilde, Jaap de. III. Title.
KZ5588.B89   1997
303.48'2—dc21   97-21300
                                        CIP

British Cataloguing in Publication Data
A Cataloguing in Publication record for this book
is available from the British Library.

Printed and bound in the United States of America

5 4 3 2

Contents

Preface

This book sets out a new and comprehensive framework of analysis for security studies. Establishing the case for the wider agenda, it both answers the traditionalist charge that the wider agenda makes the subject incoherent and formulates security to incorporate the traditionalist agenda. It examines the distinctive character and dynamics of security in five sectors: military, political, economic, environmental, and societal. It rejects the traditionalists' case for restricting security to one sector, arguing that security is a particular type of politics applicable to a wide range of issues. And it offers a constructivist operational method for distinguishing the process of securitization from that of politicization—for understanding who can securitize what and under what conditions.

The original motive for the book was to update regional security complex theory (Buzan 1991; Buzan et al. 1990), reflecting the widespread feeling in the mid-1990s that the post–Cold War international system was going to be much more decentralized and regionalized in character. We wanted to bring security complex theory in line with the wider post–Cold War security agenda so we could use it to analyze the emergent international (dis)order. Our question was, How could security complex theory be blended with the wider agenda of security studies, which covered not only the traditional military and political sectors but also the economic, societal, and environmental ones? This question was a natural outgrowth of the contradiction, already evident in *People, States and Fear* (Buzan 1991), between an argument for a wider conception of security on the one hand and a presentation of security complex theory cast largely in traditional military-political terms on the other. The question also followed naturally from our two earlier books (Buzan et al. 1990; Wæver et al. 1993), the first of which was based on state-centric security complex theory and the second of which sought to unfold the societal component of the wider security agenda.

Traditional security complex theory has considerable power to explain and predict both the formation of durable regional patterns of security relations and the pattern of outside intervention in these regions. But could this same logic be extended into the newer sectors as the relative importance of military-political security declined after the end of the Cold War? In pursuing this question, we found it necessary to take up the challenge that the wider security agenda is intellectually incoherent. As a consequence, the project became more ambitious, evolving into a general consideration of how to understand and analyze international security without losing sight of the original purpose.

Much of the conceptualization and writing of the book has been a genuinely joint enterprise, with all of the authors making substantial inputs into every chapter. But different parts do have distinctive individual stamps. Barry Buzan was the main drafter of Chapters 1, 3, 5, and 9; was largely responsible for the sectoral approach; and took overall responsibility for editing and coordinating the work. Ole Wæver was the main drafter of Chapters 2, 6, 7, and 8, as well as the third section of Chapter 9, and was the primary supplier of the securitization approach to defining the subject. Jaap de Wilde, the newest member of the Copenhagen research group, was the main drafter of Chapter 4 and the first two sections of Chapter 8, made substantial inputs into Chapters 5 and 9, and restrained the other two from taking a too unquestioning position toward realist assumptions.

We have received a great amount of help with this project. First and foremost, our thanks to the Fritz Thyssen Stiftung, whose generous grant made it possible for Buzan to devote his main attention to this book during the years 1995–1996, for us to assemble a team of experts who provided continual critical scrutiny, and for the support of the cost of a research assistant. Next, thanks to Håkan Wiberg and the staff at the Copenhagen Peace Research Institute, who provided a supportive, stimulating, and congenial atmosphere in which to work. Thanks also to our consultants— Mohammed Ayoob, Owen Greene, Pierre Hassner, Eric Helleiner, Andrew Hurrell, and Thomas Hylland-Eriksen—who lent us both their expertise and their wider judgment. All of the consultants made extensive written comments at various stages of the drafting of the book. This final version owes much to their input, although they bear no formal responsibility for what is written here. And thanks to Eva Maria Christiansen and Mads Vöge, our research assistants, who handled most of the logistical tasks and sometimes worked unreasonable hours without complaint. Finally, our thanks to people who volunteered comments along the way and whose insights have helped to shape our arguments: Didier Bigo, Anne-Marie le Gloannec, Lene Hansen, Helge Hveem, Emile Kirschner, Wojciech Kostecki, Grazina Miniotaite, Bjørn Møller, Marie-Claude Smouts, Michael Williams, and an anonymous reviewer for Lynne Rienner Publishers.

Barry Buzan
Ole Wæver
Jaap de Wilde

CHAPTER 1

Introduction

The purpose of this book is to set out a comprehensive new framework for security studies. Our approach is based on the work of those who for well over a decade have sought to question the primacy of the military element and the state in the conceptualization of security. This questioning has come from diverse sources rarely coordinated with each other. Some has come from the policy side, representing organizations (including the state) trying either to achieve recognition for their concerns or to adapt themselves to changed circumstances. Other questions have come from academia: from peace research, from feminists, from international political economy, and from security (and strategic) studies. Their move has generally taken the form of attempts to widen the security agenda by claiming security status for issues and referent objects in the economic, environmental and societal sectors, as well as the military-political ones that define traditional security studies (known in some places as strategic studies).

As a consequence, two views of security studies are now on the table, the new one of the wideners and the old military and state-centered view of the traditionalists.[1] It is time to compare these two views and assess their costs and benefits. Doing so requires both unifying concepts and a method for pursuing the wider agenda in a coherent fashion. It also requires us to provide a classification of what is and what is not a security issue, to explain how issues become securitized, and to locate the relevant security dynamics of the different types of security on levels ranging from local through regional to global. Identifying security issues is easy for traditionalists, who, broadly speaking, equate security with military issues and the use of force. But it is more difficult when security is moved out of the military sector. There are intellectual and political dangers in simply tacking the word *security* onto an ever wider range of issues.

In this chapter, the next section surveys the debate between the new and the traditional approaches to security studies. The following two sections define the concepts that structure the analysis in this book. The first sets out our understanding of levels of analysis (spatial locations from macro to micro, where one can find both sources of explanation and outcomes), and the second addresses sectors (views of the whole that select a

1

particular type of interaction). The rest of the chapter deals with regions, looking at how they relate to levels of analysis, outlining "classical" security complex theory as we have used it to this point, and unveiling some of the problems with trying to extend security complex thinking into the nontraditional sectors (economic, societal, environmental).

The "Wide" Versus "Narrow" Debate About Security Studies

The "wide" versus "narrow" debate grew out of dissatisfaction with the intense narrowing of the field of security studies imposed by the military and nuclear obsessions of the Cold War. This dissatisfaction was stimulated first by the rise of the economic and environmental agendas in international relations during the 1970s and 1980s and later by the rise of concerns with identity issues and transnational crime during the 1990s. The issue-driven widening eventually triggered its own reaction, creating a plea for confinement of security studies to issues centered around the threat or use of force. A key argument was that progressive widening endangered the intellectual coherence of security, putting so much into it that its essential meaning became void. This argument perhaps masked a generally unspoken political concern that allowing nonmilitary issues to achieve security status would have undesirable and counterproductive effects on the entire fabric of social and international relations (more on this in Chapter 9).

Those arguing explicitly for widening include Ullman (1983); Jahn, Lemaitre, and Wæver (1987); Nye and Lynn-Jones (1988); Matthews (1989); Brown (1989); Nye (1989); Crawford (1991); Haftendorn (1991); Tickner (1992); and Wæver et al. (1993), most taking off from the urgency of new, often nonmilitary sources of threat. There has also been a strong thread in international political economy linking patterns in the economic and military sectors (Gilpin 1981; Crawford 1993, 1995; Gowa 1994; Mansfield 1994). Buzan (1991) is a widener, but he has been skeptical about the prospects for coherent conceptualizations of security in the economic (see also Luciani 1989) and environmental (see also Deudney 1990) sectors. Buzan has argued for retaining a distinctively military subfield of strategic studies within a wider security studies (1987; 1991, chapter 10). Ullman (1983) and Buzan (1991, chapter 3) have specifically widened the definition of threat away from a purely military to a more general formulation. The other two authors of this book are also wideners, de Wilde from a liberal-pluralist background and Wæver self-defined as a postmodern realist.

The defense of the traditionalist position got underway as the Cold War unraveled. Until rather late one could still find arguments for restricting the field to "anything that concerns the prevention of superpower nuclear war"

(Lebow 1988: 508). But as the main task of the strategic community—analysis of East-West military confrontation—evaporated, a period of disorientation occurred. The function, and therefore the status and funding, of the entire edifice of strategic studies built up during the Cold War seemed to be at risk; consequently, the military focus of strategic analysis seemed extremely vulnerable to pressure from the wideners. Indicative of this period was the 1989 issue of *Survival* (31:6) devoted entirely to "nonmilitary aspects of strategy."

Traditionalists fought back by reasserting conventional arguments about the enduring primacy of military security (Gray 1994b). In varying degrees, they accepted the need to look more widely at nonmilitary causes of conflict in the international system and made little explicit attempt to defend the centrality of the state in security analysis at a time when so many nonstate actors were playing vigorously in the military game. Most traditionalists insist on *military* conflict as the defining key to security and are prepared to loosen their state centrism. But some—Jahn, Lemaitre, and Wæver (1987) and Ayoob (1995)—hold the *political* sector as primary and Ayoob the *state* as the focal point, and ease the link to military conflict. Some traditionalists (Chipman 1992; Gray 1992) have argued that there was simply a return to the natural terrain of the subject after the artificial nuclear narrowing of the Cold War, but the key strategy was to allow widening only inasmuch as it could be linked to concerns about the threat or actual use of force between political actors. As Chipman (1992: 129) put it:

> The structuring element of strategic analysis must be the possible use of force. . . . Non-military aspects of security may occupy more of the strategist's time, but the need for peoples, nations, states or alliances to procure, deploy, engage or withdraw military forces must remain a primary purpose of the strategic analyst's inquiries.

Although he is clearly trying to keep the lid on the subject, Chipman's statement is interesting because it explicitly moves away from strict state centrism by acknowledging that peoples and nations, as well as states and alliances, can be strategic users of force in the international system.

Stephen Walt gives perhaps the strongest statement on the traditionalist position. He argues that security studies is about the phenomenon of war and that it can be defined as "the study of the threat, use, and control of military force." Against those who want to widen the agenda outside this strictly military domain, he argues that doing so

> runs the risk of expanding "Security Studies" excessively; by this logic, issues such as pollution, disease, child abuse, or economic recessions could all be viewed as threats to "security." Defining the field in this way would destroy its intellectual coherence and make it more difficult to

devise solutions to any of these important problems. (Walt 1991: 212–213)

Walt (1991: 227; see also Dorff 1994; Gray 1994a) does allow "economics and security" into his picture but only as they relate to military issues rather than as economic security per se.

The traditionalists' criticism that wideners risk intellectual incoherence can be a powerful point. The wider agenda does extend the range of knowledge and understanding necessary to pursue security studies. More worryingly, it also does two other things. First, given the political function of the word *security*, the wider agenda extends the call for state mobilization to a broad range of issues. As Deudney (1990) has pointed out, this may be undesirable and counterproductive in the environmental sector, and the argument could easily be extended into other sectors. Second, the wider agenda tends, often unthinkingly, to elevate "security" into a kind of universal good thing—the desired condition toward which all relations should move. But as Wæver (1995b) has argued, this is a dangerously narrow view. At best, security is a kind of stabilization of conflictual or threatening relations, often through emergency mobilization of the state. Although security in international relations may generally be better than insecurity (threats against which no adequate countermeasures are available), a secure relationship still contains serious conflicts—albeit ones against which some effective countermeasures have been taken. Even this degree of relative desirability can be questioned: liberals, for example, argue that too much economic security is destructive to the workings of a market economy. Security should not be thought of too easily as always a good thing. It is better, as Wæver argues, to aim for desecuritization: the shifting of issues out of emergency mode and into the normal bargaining processes of the political sphere.

The main purpose of this book is to present a framework based on the wider agenda that will incorporate the traditionalist position. Our solution comes down on the side of the wideners in terms of keeping the security agenda open to many different types of threats. We argue against the view that the core of security studies is war and force and that other issues are relevant only if they relate to war and force (although in Buzan's view [1991, chapter 10] such an approach would fit nicely with the idea of *strategic studies* remaining a militarily focused specialism within the new security studies). Instead, we want to construct a more radical view of security studies by exploring threats to referent objects, and the securitization of those threats, that are nonmilitary as well as military. We take seriously the traditionalists' complaint about intellectual incoherence but disagree that the retreat into a military core is the only or the best way to deal with such incoherence. We seek to find coherence not by confining security to the military sector but by exploring the logic of security itself to find out what differentiates security and the process of securitization from that which is merely political. This solution offers the possibility of breaking free from the existing dispute between the two approaches.

The need is to construct a conceptualization of security that means something much more specific than just any threat or problem. Threats and vulnerabilities can arise in many different areas, military and nonmilitary, but to count as security issues they have to meet strictly defined criteria that distinguish them from the normal run of the merely political. They have to be staged as existential threats to a referent object by a securitizing actor who thereby generates endorsement of emergency measures beyond rules that would otherwise bind. These criteria are explained in detail in Chapter 2, and they show how the agenda of security studies can be extended without destroying the intellectual coherence of the field.

Levels of Analysis

For more than three decades, the debate about levels of analysis has been central to much of international relations theory (Buzan 1994c; Onuf 1995). Levels also run through all types of security analysis, whether in debates about preferred referent objects for security (individuals versus states) or about the causes of war (system structure versus the nature of states versus human nature). Since our project started with questions about the relationship between regional security theory and the multisectoral security agenda, it, too, depends on an understanding of levels of analysis. In the following chapters, we use levels of analysis extensively to locate the actors, referent objects, and dynamics of interaction that operate in the realm of security.

By levels, we mean objects for analysis that are defined by a range of spatial scales, from small to large. Levels are locations where both outcomes and sources of explanation can be located. Theories may suggest causal explanations from one level to another—for example, top down from system structure to unit behavior (e.g., market to firms, anarchy to states) or bottom up from human nature to the behavior of human collectivities, whether firms, states, or nations. But nothing is intrinsic to levels themselves that suggests any particular pattern or priority of relations among them. Levels are simply ontological referents for where things happen rather than sources of explanation in themselves.

In the study of international relations, the five most frequently used levels of analysis are as follow:

1. *International systems,* meaning the largest conglomerates of interacting or interdependent units that have no system level above them. Currently, this level encompasses the entire planet, but in

earlier times several more or less disconnected international systems existed simultaneously (Buzan and Little 1994).

2. *International subsystems,* meaning groups of units within the international system that can be distinguished from the entire system by the particular nature or intensity of their interactions with or interdependence on each other. Subsystems may be territorially coherent, in which case they are regional (the Association of Southeast Asian Nations [ASEAN], the Organization of African Unity [OAU]), or not (the Organization for Economic Cooperation and Development, the Organization of Petroleum Exporting Countries), in which case they are not regions but simply subsystems.

3. *Units,* meaning actors composed of various subgroups, organizations, communities, and many individuals and sufficiently cohesive and independent to be differentiated from others and to have standing at the higher levels (e.g., states, nations, transnational firms).

4. *Subunits,* meaning organized groups of individuals within units that are able (or that try) to affect the behavior of the unit (e.g., bureaucracies, lobbies).

5. *Individuals,* the bottom line of most analysis in the social sciences.

Levels provide a framework within which one can theorize; they are not theories in themselves. They enable one to locate the sources of explanation and the outcomes of which theories are composed. Neorealism, for example, locates its source of explanation (structure) at the system level and its main outcome (self-help) at the unit level. Bureaucratic politics locates its source of explanation (process) at the subunit level and its outcome (irrational behavior) at the unit level. Up to a point, levels also enable one to locate many of the actors, forums, and other elements involved in international relations. Some organizations (the UN) and structures (the global market, international society) operate at the system level; others (the North Atlantic Treaty Organization, the European Union [EU], the North American Free Trade Agreement [NAFTA], ASEAN) are clearly subsystemic. But it is not always possible to locate actors clearly within a given level. A lobby group such as the national farmers' union may sit clearly at the subunit level, but transnational organizations such as Greenpeace or Amnesty International cross levels. They may act in part on the subunit level and in part on the subsystem and system ones. The same can be said for multinational firms.

Because the levels-of-analysis debate in international relations has been closely associated with neorealism, it has tended to reflect that theory's state centrism, picturing subunits as within states and subsystems and systems as made up of states. On this basis, the levels-of-analysis scheme has been criticized for reinforcing the state centrism and inside-outside assumptions typical of international relations (Walker 1993; Onuf 1995). In this view, the scheme is not just an innocent, abstract typology but presents a specific ontology that obscures and discriminates against those transnational units that do not fit clearly into the scheme. If one wants to see political time and space structured along different lines, the levels-of-analysis scheme in its neorealist form will be seen as problematic. There is no necessity for levels to privilege states—the unit level can encompass much more than states. Since in this project we are trying to open up a greater diversity of security units, and since one can argue that by necessity any unit has an inside and an outside (Wæver 1994, forthcoming-b), we do not accept the far-reaching version of the critique. But we do accept the reminder that in international relations one should be aware of the tendency for the levels-of-analysis scheme to reinforce state-centric thinking.

Sectors

What does it mean to adopt a more diversified agenda in which economic, societal, and environmental security issues play alongside military and political ones? Thinking about security in terms of sectors simply grew up with little reflection during the later decades of the Cold War as new issues were added to the military-political agenda. The practice of resorting to sectors is common but is seldom made explicit. Realists from Morgenthau to Waltz talk in terms of *political* theory, thereby assuming that sectors mean something analytically significant. It has become common when discussing international relations to qualify the identity of systems in terms of particular sectors of activity within them, as in "the international economic system" or "the international political system." Michael Mann (1986, chapter 1) thinks about power in terms of distinctions among ideology, economic, military, and political power. Indeed, the entire division of social and other sciences into disciplines is based largely on a preference for thinking in terms of sectors—a practice reflected in the general discourse, which often assumes that economy, society, and politics can somehow be separated without thinking too hard about how to do so. Embracing the wider security agenda means we need to consider what sectors mean.

One way of looking at sectors is to see them as identifying specific types of interaction. In this view, the military sector is about relationships of forceful coercion; the political sector is about relationships of authority, governing status, and recognition; the economic sector is about relationships of trade, production, and finance; the societal sector is about relationships of collective identity; and the environmental sector is about relationships between human activity and the planetary biosphere. Buzan (1991: 19–20) set out sectors in security analysis as follows.

> Generally speaking, the military security concerns the two-level interplay of the armed offensive and defensive capabilities of states, and states' perceptions of each other's intentions. Political security concerns the organizational stability of states, systems of government and the ideologies that give them legitimacy. Economic security concerns access to the resources, finance and markets necessary to sustain acceptable levels of welfare and state power. Societal security concerns the sustainability, within acceptable conditions for evolution, of traditional patterns of language, culture and religious and national identity and custom. Environmental security concerns the maintenance of the local and the planetary biosphere as the essential support system on which all other human enterprises depend.

In more recent work (Wæver et al. 1993: 24–27), we modified this statement to move away from its implicit (and sometimes explicit) placement of the state as the central referent object in all sectors. If a multisectoral approach to security was to be fully meaningful, referent objects other than the state had to be allowed into the picture. The present book extends this line of argument much further.

Sectors serve to disaggregate a whole for purposes of analysis by selecting some of its distinctive patterns of interaction. But items identified by sectors lack the quality of independent existence. Relations of coercion do not exist apart from relations of exchange, authority, identity, or environment. Sectors might identify distinctive patterns, but they remain inseparable parts of complex wholes. The purpose of selecting them is simply to reduce complexity to facilitate analysis.

The use of sectors confines the scope of inquiry to more manageable proportions by reducing the number of variables in play. Thus, the economist looks at human systems in terms that highlight wealth and development and justify restrictive assumptions, such as the motivation of behavior by the desire to maximize utility. The political realist looks at the same systems in terms that highlight sovereignty and power and justify restrictive assumptions, such as the motivation of behavior by the desire to maximize power. The military strategist looks at the systems in terms that highlight offensive and defensive capability and justify restrictive assumptions, such as the motivation of behavior by opportunistic calculations of coercive advantage. The environmentalist looks at systems in terms of the ecological underpinnings of civilization and the need to achieve sustainable development. In the societal sector, the analyst looks at the systems in terms of patterns of identity and the desire to maintain cultural independence. Each is looking at the whole but is seeing only one dimension of its reality.

The analytical method of sectors thus starts with disaggregation but must end with reassembly. The disaggregation is performed only to achieve simplification and clarity. To achieve understanding, it is necessary to reassemble the parts and see how they relate to each other, a task we undertake in Chapter 8.

Regions

Our interest in regions as a focus for security analysis stems not only from our previous work on regional security complex theory but also from an interest in the widespread assumption that in the post–Cold War world, international relations will take on a more regionalized character. The reasoning behind this assumption is that the collapse of bipolarity has removed the principal organizing force at the global level. The remaining great powers are no longer motivated by ideological rivalries, and they all show conspicuous signs of wanting to avoid wider political engagements unless their own interests are immediately and strongly affected. This situation creates weak leadership at the global level and, consequently, leads to the assumption that more than before, regions will be left to sort out their own affairs. Reinforcing this tendency is the fact that the weakening of the commitment to global engagement among the great powers is matched by ever rising power capabilities in most parts of the world. The long period of European and Western power advantage is being steadily eroded by the diffusion of industrial, military, and political capability among an ever wider circle of states and peoples.

In terms of level of analysis, regions are a special type of subsystem.[2] Geographical clustering does seem to be a sufficiently strong feature of international subsystems to be worth studying in its own right: Why should states tend to form regional clusters, and do other units behave in the same way? One has only to think of the EU, NAFTA, ASEAN, the South Asian Association for Regional Cooperation, the South Pacific Forum, the Southern African Development Community, the OAU, and others to see the importance of territorially defined subsystems. Regions are objects of analysis in themselves, particular locations where one can find outcomes and sources of explanation. Why does this type of territorial subsystem (or any particular instance of it) come into being and sustain itself as a feature of the wider international system?

Perhaps the best general explanation of regional state systems can be derived from the thinking of Hans Mouritzen (1995, 1997). He starts with the simple but seldom considered fact that the units (states) are fixed rather than mobile. In contemporary international relations theory, it is taken for granted that the main political units are not mobile, but this was not always so. For thousands of years prior to the fifteenth century, barbarian tribes were a major feature of the international system. These tribes could and did move over long distances. In those times, it was not uncommon to find one morning that one had a great power as a neighbor where there had been no neighbor before. Mouritzen argues that if units are mobile, each unit's average environment will, after a reasonable time, constitute the system as such rather than any particular segment of that system. By contrast, if the units are nonmobile, each unit will face a relatively stable regional environment consisting of the major units in its geographical proximity; each unit will be characterized by a specific *location* in the system's structure (Mouritzen 1980: 172, 180).

The failure to account for the effect of nonmobile units explains in part why the subsystem level has been relatively neglected in international relations theory. Hollis and Smith (1991: 7–9), for example, do not even mention it in their scheme. Identifying the mechanism that forms regions underpins the argument for paying attention to the regionalizing aspect of the subsystem level in the analysis of international security.

This discussion relates mostly to states, where the mobility/immobility question is relatively clear. Mouritzen's argument, with its focus on the military and political sectors, provides additional justification for classical, state-centric security complex theory and also gives us clues about how to begin thinking about security relations in other sectors. In the societal sector, for example, one might expect units such as nations to display immobility logic similar to that of states and thus to find regional formations among them. But in the economic sector, units such as firms and criminal gangs may be highly mobile. There, in an echo of the barbarians, one might expect to find system-level logic working more strongly and therefore expect little in the way of regional formations.

"Classical" Security Complex Theory

This section summarizes "classical" security complex theory as developed up to 1991 and can be skipped by those familiar with Buzan (1991, chapter 5). Security complex theory was first sketched by Buzan in the first edition of *People, States and Fear* in 1983 (pp. 105–115). The theory was applied to South Asia and the Middle East (Buzan 1983), then elaborated and applied in depth to the case of South Asia (Buzan and Rizvi 1986), and later applied to Southeast Asia (Buzan 1988). Väyrynen (1988), Wriggins (1992), and Ayoob (1995) have applied versions of the theory to several regional cases, and Wæver (1989b, 1993), Buzan and colleagues (1990), Buzan and Wæver (1992), and Wæver and colleagues (1993) have used it to study the post–Cold War transformation in Europe. The most recent updates to the theory have been presented in Buzan (1991, chapter 5).

The logic of security regions stems from the fact that international security is a relational matter. International security is mostly about how human collectivities relate to each other in terms of threats and vulnerabilities, although sometimes it addresses the ways such collectivities relate to threats from the natural environment. The emphasis on the relational nature of security is in line with some of the most important writings in security studies (Herz 1950; Wolfers 1962; Jervis 1976), which have stressed relational dynamics such as security dilemmas, power balances, arms races, and security regimes. Little of interest can be said about the security of an isolated object (e.g., the security of France); thus, security must be studied in a wider context.

The widest context, the global level, is useful for studying the great powers, and also for thinking about systemic referent objects (the global environment, the world economy, international society). In the traditional (i.e., military-political) mode of security analysis, global security is integrated insufficiently to make much sense for most units: The securities of Togo and the Kurds might be deteriorating, whereas those of Argentina and Israel are improving and those of Sweden and Japan remain unchanged—without any of these situations being affected by the others. The rationale behind classical security complex theory was that for most of the actors at the unit level, military-political security falls into some in-between-sized clusters, and the theory claimed the most relevant scale was the regional one. Whether this rationale remains true within a multisectoral approach to security is one of the issues we address in this book.

Classical security complex theory posits the existence of regional subsystems as objects of security analysis and offers an analytical framework for dealing with those systems. Also, like most other traditionalist work in this area, the theory has focused primarily on the state as the key unit and on the political and military sectors. This framework was designed to highlight the relative autonomy of regional security relations and to set those relations within the context of the unit (state) and system levels. One of its purposes was to provide area specialists with the language and concepts to facilitate comparative studies across regions, which is a notable weakness in the existing literature. Another purpose was to offset the tendency of power theorists to underplay the importance of the regional level in international security affairs. This tendency was exacerbated by the rise of neorealism in the late 1970s (Waltz 1979), which focused almost exclusively on the power structure at the system level. It seems reasonable to expect this bias to decline with the demise of strong bipolarity at the system level and the advent of a more diffuse international power structure.

All of the states in the system are enmeshed in a global web of security interdependence. But because most political and military threats travel more easily over short distances than over long ones, insecurity is often associated with proximity. Most states fear their neighbors more than distant powers; consequently, security interdependence across the international system as a whole is far from uniform. The normal pattern of security interdependence in a geographically diverse, anarchic international system is one of regionally based clusters, which we label *security complexes*. Security interdependence is markedly more intense among the states inside such complexes than among states outside them. Security complexes are about the relative intensity of interstate security relations that lead to distinctive regional patterns shaped by both the distribution of power and historical relations of amity and enmity. A security complex is defined as *a set of states whose major security perceptions and concerns are so interlinked that their national security problems cannot reasonably be analyzed or resolved apart from one another.* The formative dynamics and structure of a security complex are generated by the states within that complex—by their security perceptions of, and interactions with, each other. Individual security complexes are durable but not permanent features of the international system. The theory posits that in a geographically diverse, anarchic international system, security complexes are a normal and expected feature; if they are not present, one wants to know why.

Because they are formed by local groupings of states, classical security complexes not only play a central role in relations among their members; they also crucially condition how and whether stronger outside powers penetrate the region. The internal dynamics of a security complex can be located along a spectrum according to whether the defining security interdependence is driven by amity or enmity. At the negative end lies conflict formation (Senghaas 1988; Väyrynen 1984), in which interdependence arises from fear, rivalry, and mutual perceptions of threat. In the middle lie security regimes (Jervis 1982), in which states still treat each other as potential threats but have made reassurance arrangements to reduce the security dilemma among them. At the positive end of the spectrum lies a pluralistic security community (Deutsch et al. 1957: 1–4), in which states no longer expect or prepare to use force in their relations with each other. Regional integration will eliminate a security complex with which it is coextensive by transforming it from an anarchic subsystem of states to a single, larger actor within the system. Regional integration among some members of a complex will transform the power structure of that complex.

The theory assumes that security complexes, like the balance of power, are an intrinsic product of anarchic international systems. Other things being equal, one should therefore expect to find them everywhere in the system. Two conditions explain why a security complex may not be present. First, in some areas local states have so few capabilities that their power projects little, if at all, beyond their own boundaries. These states have domestically directed security perspectives, and there is insufficient security interaction among them to generate a local complex. The second condition occurs when the direct presence of outside powers in a region is strong enough to suppress the normal operation of security dynamics among the local states. This condition is called *overlay,* which normally involves extensive stationing of armed forces in the area overlain by the intervening great power(s) and is quite distinct from the normal process of intervention by great powers into the affairs of local security complexes. Intervention usually reinforces the local security dynamics; overlay subordinates them to the larger pattern of major power rivalries, and may even obliterate them. The best examples of overlay are the period of European colonialism in what is now the Third World and the submergence of European security dynamics by superpower rivalry after World War II. Under overlay, one cannot see the local security dynamics with any clarity and therefore cannot identify a local complex; one only knows what the local dynamics were before overlay.

Security complexes are subsystems—miniature anarchies—in their own right, and by analogy with full systems they have structures of their own. Since security complexes are durable rather than permanent features of the overall anarchy, seeing them as subsystems with their own structures and patterns of interaction provides a useful benchmark against which to identify and assess changes in the patterns of regional security.

Essential structure is the standard by which one assesses significant change in a classical security complex. The three key components of essential structure in a security complex are (1) the arrangement of the units and the differentiation among them (this is normally the same as for the international system as a whole, and if so it is not a significant variable at the regional level), (2) the patterns of amity and enmity, and (3) the distribution of power among the principal units. Major shifts in any of these components would normally require a redefinition of the complex. This approach allows one to analyze regional security in both static and dynamic terms. If security complexes are seen as structures, one can look for outcomes resulting from either structural effects or processes of structural change.

The changes bearing on any given local security complex are usually numerous and continuous. Power relativities are in constant motion, and even patterns of amity and enmity shift occasionally. The key question is, do such changes work to sustain the essential structure or do they push it toward some kind of transformation? Four broad structural options are available for assessing the impact of change on a security complex: maintenance of the status quo, internal transformation, external transformation, and overlay.

Maintenance of the status quo means the essential structure of the local complex—its distribution of power and pattern of hostility—remains fundamentally intact. This outcome does not mean no change has taken place. Rather, it means the changes that have occurred have tended, in the aggregate, either to support or not seriously to undermine the structure.

Internal transformation of a local complex occurs when its essential structure changes *within* the context of its existing outer boundary. Such change can come about as a result of regional political integration, decisive shifts in the distribution of power, or major alternations in the pattern of amity and enmity.

External transformation occurs when the essential structure of a complex is altered by either the expansion or contraction of its existing outer boundary. Minor adjustments to the boundary may not significantly affect the essential structure. The addition or deletion of major states, however, is certain to have a substantial impact on both the distribution of power and the pattern of amity and enmity.

Overlay means one or more external powers moves directly into the regional complex with the effect of suppressing the indigenous security dynamic. As argued earlier, this situation is distinct from the normal process of intervention by great powers into the affairs of regional security complexes.

Once the regional level has been established, the full range of layers that comprise a comprehensive analytical framework for security can be sketched out. At the bottom end lies the domestic security environment of individual states and societies. Next come the regional security complexes. One would expect security relations to be relatively intense within these complexes and relatively subdued among them, but in some instances significant interplay can occur across the boundaries of indifference that mark off one complex from another. Thus relations among security complexes also comprise a layer within the framework, one that becomes important if major changes in the pattern of security complexes are underway. At the top end, one finds the higher, or great-power, complex that constitutes the system level. One would expect security relations among the great powers to be intense and to penetrate in varying degrees into the affairs of the local complexes. The method of analysis within this framework is first to understand the distinctive security dynamic at each layer and then to see how the patterns at each layer interact with each other.

In one sense, security complexes are theoretical constructs the analyst imposes on "reality." But within the theory they have ontological status: They reflect an observable patterning of global politics and so cannot be constructed merely at random. One can argue about the correct interpretation of the dividing lines, but one cannot simply use the term *security complex* to describe any group of states (Norden, the Warsaw Pact, the Non-Proliferation Treaty members). A distinctive territorial pattern of security interdependence must exist that marks off the members of a security complex from other neighboring states. And this pattern has to be strong enough to make the criteria for inclusion and exclusion reasonably clear.[3] Thus, there is a European security complex but not a Nordic one (because Norden is part of a larger pattern of security interdependence), a Middle Eastern complex but not a Mediterranean one (because the Mediterranean states are parts of several other regional complexes). South Asia is a clear example of a security complex centered on the rivalry between India and Pakistan, with Burma acting as the border with the complex in Southeast Asia, Afghanistan delineating the border with the Middle East complex, and China looming as an intervening great power.

One value of classical security complex theory is that it draws attention away from the extremes of national and global security and focuses it on the region, where these two extremes interplay and where most of the action occurs. Security complex theory also links studies of internal conditions in states, relations among states of the region, relations among regions, and relations between regions and globally acting great powers. More ambitiously, and as demonstrated in our 1990 book (Buzan et al.), security complex theory can be used to generate definitive scenarios and thus to structure the study of, as well as predictions about, possibilities for stability and change. The theory offers descriptive concepts for both static and dynamic analysis and provides benchmarks for locating significant change within the structure of international security relations. Once the structure of any given complex has been identified, it can be used to narrow possible options for change. The theory is prescriptive to the extent that it identifies appropriate (and inappropriate) realms for action and organization and suggests a range of states of being (conflict formation, security regime, security community) that can serve as frameworks for thinking about policy objectives.

Moving Beyond Classical Security Complex Theory

The classical approach to regional security analysis looks for patterns of security interdependence that are strong enough to mark off a group of units from its neighbors (Buzan, Jones, and Little 1993, chapter 5). Security complexes are formed from the inside out, by the interactions among their constituent units. Because classical security complex theory was formulated for thinking about the political and military sectors, states were its referent objects. Security regions therefore had the following characteristics:

1. They were composed of two or more states.
2. These states constituted a geographically coherent grouping (because threats in these sectors travel more easily over short distances than over long ones).
3. The relationship among these states was marked by security interdependence, which could be either positive or negative but which had to be significantly stronger among them than between them and outside states.
4. The pattern of security interdependence had to be deep and durable (i.e., much more than a one-time interaction), although not permanent.

In other words, security regions were a type of international political subsystem and were relatively autonomous microversions of the larger international political system within which they were embedded. Because the units of analysis were states, security regions tended to be a fairly large-scale phenomenon. Most security complexes were subcontinental or continental in size: South Asia, the Middle East, Southern Africa, Europe, South America, and the like.

One of the ways in which this book moves beyond classical security complex theory (CSCT) is by opening the analysis to a wider range of sectors. To what extent are regional patterns discernible when one no longer sticks to the state and privileges the political and military sectors? Will the security dynamics in the nontraditional sectors generate significant regional formations, or will their security logics place their main focus on higher (system) or lower (subunit) levels? Will the other sectors show dynamics that are mainly global, mainly local, a mess, or what? The answers to these questions will hinge on whether the relevant units are fixed or mobile and on whether threats and vulnerabilities are strongly shaped by distance. If units are not fixed or if threats are not shaped by distance, regionalizing logic may be weak. Even if we find "regions" in several or all sectors, will they line up—for example, are the regions in the environmental sector at all like those in the political sector? Will environmental sectors cluster, for example, around seas (the Mediterranean, the Baltic, the Black Sea, the Sea of Japan, and so on) and rivers (the Nile, Euphrates, and Jordan), whereas the political and societal sectors will be mainly land-based and continental? Discovering the answers to these questions is the work of Chapters 3 through 7, and putting the findings together is that of Chapter 8.

Logically, there are two possible ways of opening security complex theory to sectors other than the military-political and to actors other than states:

1. *Homogeneous complexes.* This approach retains the "classical" assumption that security complexes are concentrated within specific sectors and are therefore composed of specific forms of interaction among similar types of units (e.g., power rivalries among states). This logic leads to different types of complexes that occur in different sectors (e.g., military complexes made up predominantly of states, a societal complex of various identity-based units, and the like).

2. *Heterogeneous complexes.* This approach abandons the assumption that security complexes are locked into specific sectors. It assumes that the regional logic can integrate different types of actors interacting across two or more sectors (e.g., states + nations + firms + confederations interacting across the political, economic, and societal sectors).

There is no reason to choose between these alternatives. In principle, both are possible, and the analyst needs to determine which alternative best fits the case under study.

Heterogeneous security complexes have the advantage of linking actors across sectors, thus enabling the analyst to keep the entire picture in a single frame and also to keep track of the inevitable spillovers between sectors (military impacts on economic developments and the like). A, B, C, and D could be nations, a state, and a supranational institution such as the EU, and the security dynamics of Europe can perhaps best be understood as a constellation of security fears and interactions among nations, states, and the EU (Wæver et al. 1993, chapter 4; Wæver 1996b, forthcoming-a). A similar logic might be applied to the Middle East, where the security complex contains both states and nations (e.g., Kurds, Palestinians).

Homogeneous, or sector-specific, security complexes (which would include the classical political-military, state-dominated model) require the construction of separate frames for each sector. They offer the possibility of isolating sector-specific security dynamics (politico-military, economic, societal, and so forth), but they also present the challenge of how to reassemble the separate frames into a holistic picture and the danger that linkages across sectors will be lost or obscured. Looking at security complexes sector by sector, one might find patterns that do not line up. In the chapters that follow, we take the sector-by-sector approach on the grounds that we need to explore the as yet poorly understood security dynamics of sectors and because it seems to be the best way to set out the framework. This should not be read as privileging the homogeneous approach over the heterogeneous one, as becomes apparent in Chapter 8.

Each of the sector chapters contains a subsection that asks, where are the security dynamics of this sector predominantly located, and what are the trends? Are they regional, global, or maybe local? Two types of considerations affect how we answer those questions. First is the cause-effect nature of the issues around which securitization takes place: the "facilitating conditions" for securitization. Second is the process of securitization itself. Facilitating conditions are sometimes clearly located on a level and sometimes not. Issues are clearly global when they have global causes and effects—for example, planetary temperature change, sea-level rises, and the like. They are local when they have local causes and effects—for example, pollution of water by industrial waste or sewage discharge. Water pollution may occur in many places worldwide, but that does not make it a global-level issue in the sense we use that term here but rather a case of parallel local issues. The difference is not whether pollution is felt locally—sea-level rises are too—but that one case could take place without the other. Rising sea level, in contrast, is an integrated phenomenon; it is impossible for it to rise in one region and not in another. But in principle its causes could be local, caused, for example, by energy consumption in one country.

It is possible to mix levels and have, for example, local causes and global effects (the earlier example) or global causes and local effects (such as holes in the ozone layer). This situation, however, is all about the level of the *issue,* not necessarily of its securitization. As in classical security complex theory, the more important criterion is which actors are actually linked by their mutual security concerns. If the Middle Eastern powers become locked into a security rivalry and thus form a security complex, it is irrelevant whether some analyst can argue that the "real" threat to those powers is Russia or the United States. If the actors make their major securitizations so the Middle East becomes tied together, it constitutes a regional security complex.

More generally in this investigation, the criterion for answering the levels question is ultimately political: what constellation of actors forms on this issue. The nature of the issue—causes and effects—can often be an indicator of the likely level, but it is not what ultimately answers the question. In the process of securitization, the key issue is for whom security becomes a consideration in relation to whom. For example, a water shortage could become securitized at the global level, but the major battles will more likely be regional. Upstream and downstream powers and other potential beneficiaries from a particular river or lake will see each other as both threats and potential allies, which might play into other rivalries and constellations in the region and thus become tied into a more general regional security complex. This result is not determined purely by the nature of the issue: If all downstream nations could join together and push for global regulations on water usage, they could securitize the issue at the global level. The outcome that materializes is a result of politics, and our answer to the levels question thus must pay attention to the actual securitizations and not only to the objective qualities of the issue itself. The defining feature is the size of the political security constellation that is formed around the issue.

Because we opt for the homogeneous, sector-specific approach in Chapters 3 through 7, there is a problem in pinning down the meaning of region and, more generally, of levels. In line with the scheme presented in the section Levels of Analysis, we would have preferred to think of regions and units in terms appropriate to specific sectors. Thus, in the military and political sectors the units would be states and regions would be sets of adjacent states, but, say, in the societal sector, units might be nations and regions sets of adjacent nations. The problem with this approach is that unit and region can mean very different things in different sectors: The politico-military unit Nigeria, for example, might contain several societal "regions." We therefore adopt a state-centric frame for the purpose of getting a fixed scale against which to measure levels. Thereby, we achieve consistency in the meaning of *region* by using the political, state-defined sense of the term as a standard measure no matter which sector we are discussing. We do this not to determine or privilege the state as an actor but merely to achieve consistency in discussions. Other units exist, but only one is chosen as the instrument of measurement.

Thus, by *region* we mean a spatially coherent territory composed of two or more states. *Subregion* means part of such a region, whether it involves more than one state (but fewer than all of the states in the region) or some transnational composition (some mix of states, parts of states, or both). *Microregion* refers to the subunit level within the boundaries of a state.

The second way in which we move beyond CSCT is by taking an explicitly social constructivist approach to understanding the process by which issues become securitized. CSCT addressed this issue simply in terms of patterns of amity and enmity (which entailed some constructivist deviation from objectivist, material realism—amity and enmity are generated by the actors and are not reflections of material conditions); adopting the wider agenda requires a more sophisticated approach. That approach is the subject of Chapter 2, which makes the case for understanding security not just as the use of force but as a particular type of intersubjective politics. Chapter 2 attempts to clarify two analytical issues: (1) how to identify what is and what is not a security issue, or, put another way, how to differentiate between the politicization and the securitization of an issue; and (2) how to identify and distinguish security actors and referent objects. These clarifications aim to meet the criticism of the broad security agenda which holds that opening up the agenda risks securitizing everything, therefore voiding the security concept of any meaning. We hope to show how the essential meaning of security can be carried across sectors (thus achieving the desired aim of broadening) without so diluting the concept that its distinctive meaning is destroyed.

Each of Chapters 3 through 7 covers one of the principal sectors that define the attempt to construct a broader agenda for international security studies. These chapters have a common structure: each asks what the security agenda is within the sector, what types of actors are distinctive to the sector, what logic of threats and vulnerabilities operates within the sector, and how the security dynamics within the sector divide among the local, regional, and global scales. Each of these chapters is a lens that isolates a specific sector for analytical purposes and tries to uncover its distinctive security dynamics. The assumptions are that these dynamics may be different and that the overall character of security relations will change as the dominant focus of security concerns shifts among sectors. Investigating whether we should expect a strong regional logic in the nontraditional sectors is one of the main purposes of the inquiry.

Chapter 8 attempts the reaggregation, first in terms of how the security dynamics in the five sectors align with each other but mainly in terms of the reintegration of sectors by actors in the policymaking process. Chapter 9 reflects on the approach used to pull security studies into a coherent framework, compares the new framework with the traditional one, and looks at implications for security complex theory.

Notes

1. A possible third contender is the newly launched "critical security studies," committed to seeking alternatives to realist, statist, and positivist orthodoxies. Some of what follows might be seen as fitting that description, but we have no prior commitment to antistate or antirealist positions, and we are driven more by methodological collectivism than by methodological individualism. More on critical security studies in Chapter 2.

2. We are aware that in some other literatures the term *region* has a different meaning from ours. The term was originally introduced at the subunit level. In nineteenth-century France, a political movement formulated regionalism as an ideal for political organization that was located in the middle of the continuum between centralized government and political autonomy. This politicized notion of the region lives on in separatist movements. Also, contemporary journals like *Regional Politics and Policy* (published since 1990), *International Regional Science Review* (since 1975), *Journal of Regional Science* (since 1958), and *Regional Studies* (since 1967) are devoted primarily to the situation of ethnic minorities in specific subunit regions and to issues of administration and planning at different political levels—that is, political centralization and decentralization. Additionally, there is a Europe of the regions: The contemporary map of the EU is subdivided not only into states but also into thousands of smaller units (a Swissification of Europe) and also increasingly into a variety of transnational "regions" (the Baltic Sea region, the Alpe-Adriatic, and the like), which in our terminology would appear as subregions and transregions, respectively. In this study, region refers to what that other literature sometimes calls macroregions (cf. Joenniemi 1993, 1997).

3. The security complex is not objective in the sense of "independent of actors." In much traditional security analysis, region is defined "objectively" purely in terms of geography or history (cf. current debates about whether Russia is a part of Europe). In this sense, a region is simply an arena for security and one that is not influenced by security policies—the analyst observes "objective" reality and tells the actors to which region they belong. In contrast, security complexes are specifically defined by security interactions among units. Since we argue that security is not an objective issue but a product of the behavior of actors, security complexes are not objective in the traditional sense. Nor is the security complex to be seen as a discursive construction by the actors. We are not (in this context) interested in whether the actors define themselves as a region or whether they claim that their true region is something larger or smaller. Security complexes do not require that their members think in terms of the concept *security complex* (cf. note 6, Chapter 2). Analysts apply the term *security complex* (and therefore designate a region) based upon the contingent, historically specific, and possibly changing constellation generated by the interdependent security practices of the actors. On this basis, lines can be drawn on a map, and the theory can be put into operation.

CHAPTER 2

Security Analysis:
Conceptual Apparatus

What Is Security?

What quality makes something a security issue in international relations? It is important to add the qualification "in international relations," because the character of security in that context is not identical to the use of the term in everyday language. Although it shares some qualities with "social security," or security as applied to various civilian guard or police functions, international security has its own distinctive, more extreme meaning. Unlike social security, which has strong links to matters of entitlement and social justice, international security is more firmly rooted in the traditions of power politics. We are not following a rigid domestic-international distinction, because many of our cases are not state defined. But we are claiming that international security has a distinctive agenda.[1]

The answer to what makes something an international security issue can be found in the traditional military-political understanding of security. In this context, security is about survival. It is when an issue is presented as posing an existential threat to a designated referent object (traditionally, but not necessarily, the state, incorporating government, territory, and society). The special nature of security threats justifies the use of extraordinary measures to handle them. The invocation of security has been the key to legitimizing the use of force, but more generally it has opened the way for the state to mobilize, or to take special powers, to handle existential threats. Traditionally, by saying "security," a state representative declares an emergency condition, thus claiming a right to use whatever means are necessary to block a threatening development (Wæver 1988, 1995b).

When we consider the wider agenda, what do the terms *existential threat* and *emergency measures* mean? How, in practice, can the analyst draw the line between processes of politicization and processes of securitization on this basis? Existential threat can only be understood in relation to the particular character of the referent object in question. We are not dealing here with a universal standard based in some sense on what threatens individual human life. The essential quality of existence will vary greatly across different sectors and levels of analysis; therefore, so will the nature of existential threats.

In the military sector, the referent object is usually the state, although it may also be other kinds of political entities. It is also possible to imagine circumstances in which threats to the survival of the armed forces would elevate those forces to referent object status in their own right, perhaps serving to justify a coup against the existing government and its policy (whether of disarmament or of hopeless conflict). Traditional security studies tends to see all military affairs as instances of security, but this may not be the case. For many of the advanced democracies, defense of the state is becoming only one, and perhaps not even the main de facto, function of the armed forces. Their militaries may be increasingly trained and called upon to support routine world order activities, such as peacekeeping or humanitarian intervention, that cannot be viewed as concerning existential threats to their states or even as emergency action in the sense of suspending normal rules.

In the political sector, existential threats are traditionally defined in terms of the constituting principle—sovereignty, but sometimes also ideology—of the state. Sovereignty can be existentially threatened by anything that questions recognition, legitimacy, or governing authority. Among the ever more interdependent and institutionalized relations characteristic of the West (and increasingly of the international system as a whole), a variety of supranational referent objects are also becoming important. The European Union (EU) can be existentially threatened by events that might undo its integration process. International regimes, and international society more broadly, can be existentially threatened by situations that undermine the rules, norms, and institutions that constitute those regimes.

In the economic sector, the referent objects and existential threats are more difficult to pin down. Firms are most commonly existentially threatened by bankruptcy and sometimes by changes to laws that make them illegal or unviable (as after communist revolutions). But in the market economy firms are, with few exceptions, expected to come and go, and only rarely do they try to securitize their own survival. National economies have a greater claim to the right of survival, but rarely will a threat to that survival (national bankruptcy or an inability to provide for the basic needs of the population) actually arise apart from wider security contexts, such as war. Unless the survival of the population is in question, the huge range of the national economy doing better or doing worse cannot be seen as existentially threatening. As in the political sector, supranational referent objects from specific regimes to the global market itself can be existentially threatened by factors that might undermine the rules, norms, and institutions that constitute them.

In the societal sector, as we have defined it, the referent object is large-scale collective identities that can function independent of the state, such as nations and religions. Given the peculiar nature of this type of referent object, it is extremely difficult to establish hard boundaries that differentiate existential from lesser threats. Collective identities naturally evolve and change in response to internal and external developments. Such changes may be seen as invasive or heretical and their sources pointed to as existential threats, or they may be accepted as part of the evolution of identity. Given the conservative nature of "identity," it is always possible to paint challenges and changes as threats to identity, because "we will no longer be us," no longer the way we were or the way we ought to be to be true to our "identity." Thus, whether migrants or rival identities are securitized depends upon whether the holders of the collective identity take a relatively closed-minded or a relatively open-minded view of how their identity is constituted and maintained. The abilities to maintain and reproduce a language, a set of behavioral customs, or a conception of ethnic purity can all be cast in terms of survival.

In the environmental sector, the range of possible referent objects is very large, ranging from relatively concrete things, such as the survival of individual species (tigers, whales, humankind) or types of habitat (rain forests, lakes), to much fuzzier, larger-scale issues, such as maintenance of the planetary climate and biosphere within the narrow band human beings have come to consider to be normal during their few thousand years of civilization. Underlying many of these referent objects are baseline concerns about the relationship between the human species and the rest of the biosphere and whether that relationship can be sustained without risking a collapse of the achieved levels of civilization, a wholesale disruption of the planet's biological legacy, or both. The interplay among all of these factors is immensely complicated. At either the macro or the micro extreme are some clear cases of existential threat (the survival of species, the survival of human civilization) that can be securitized. In between, somewhat as in the economic sector, lies a huge mass of problems that are more difficult, although not impossible, to construct in existential terms.

Securitization

"Security" is the move that takes politics beyond the established rules of the game and frames the issue either as a special kind of politics or as above politics. Securitization can thus be seen as a more extreme version of politicization. In theory, any public issue can be located on the spectrum ranging from nonpoliticized (meaning the state does not deal with it and it is not in any other way made an issue of public debate and decision) through politicized (meaning the issue is part of public policy, requiring government decision and resource allocations or, more rarely, some other form of communal governance) to securitized (meaning the issue is presented as an existential threat, requiring emergency measures and justifying actions outside the normal bounds of political procedure). In principle, the placement of issues on this spectrum is open: Depending upon circumstances, any issue can end up on any part of the spectrum.[2] In practice, placement varies substantially from state to state (and also across time). Some states will politicize religion (Iran, Saudi Arabia, Burma) and some will not (France, the United States). Some will securitize culture (the former USSR, Iran) and some will not (the UK, the Netherlands). In the case of issues (notably the environment) that have moved dramatically out of the nonpoliticized category, we face the double question of whether they have merely been politicized or have also been securitized. This link between politicization and securitization does not imply that securitization always goes through the state; politicization as well as securitization can be enacted in other fora as well. As will be seen later, it is possible for other social entities to raise an issue to the level of general consideration or even to the status of sanctioned urgency among themselves.

In this approach, the meaning of a concept lies in its usage and is not something we can define analytically or philosophically according to what would be "best." The meaning lies not in what people consciously think the concept means but in how they implicitly use it in some ways and not others. In the case of security, textual analysis (Wæver 1988, 1995b, 1995c) suggests that something is designated as an international security issue because it can be argued that this issue is more important than other issues and should take absolute priority. This is the reason we link the issue to what might seem a fairly demanding criterion: that the issue is presented as an existential threat. If one can argue that something overflows the normal political logic of weighing issues against each other, this must be the case because it can upset the entire process of weighing as such: "If we do not tackle this problem, everything else will be irrelevant (because we will not be here or will not be free to deal with it in our own way)." Thereby, the actor has claimed a right to handle the issue through extraordinary means, to break the normal political rules of the game (e.g., in the form of secrecy, levying taxes or conscription, placing limitations on otherwise inviolable rights, or focusing society's energy and resources on a specific task). "Security" is thus a self-referential practice, because it is in this practice that the issue becomes a security issue—not necessarily because a real existential threat exists but because the issue is presented as such a threat.

Of course, places do exist where secrecy or violation of rights is the rule and where security arguments are not needed to legitimize such acts. The earlier illustrations were for a liberal-democratic society; in other societies there will also be "rules," as there are in any society, and when a securitizing actor uses a rhetoric of existential threat and thereby takes an issue out of what under those conditions is "normal politics," we have a case of securitization. Thus, the exact *definition* and *criteria* of securitization is constituted by the intersubjective establishment of an existential threat with a saliency sufficient to have substantial political effects. Securitization can be studied directly; it does not need indicators. The way to study securitization is to study discourse and political constellations: When does an argument with this particular rhetorical and semiotic structure achieve sufficient effect to make an audience tolerate violations of rules that would otherwise have to be obeyed? If by means of an argument about the priority and urgency of an existential threat the securitizing actor has managed to break free of procedures or rules he or she would otherwise be bound by, we are witnessing a case of securitization.

Even if the general logic of securitization is clear, we have to be precise about its threshold. A discourse that takes the form of presenting something as an existential threat to a referent object does not by itself create securitization—this is a *securitizing move,* but the issue is securitized only if and when the audience accepts it as such. (Accept does not necessarily mean in civilized, dominance-free discussion; it only means that an order always rests on coercion as well as on consent. Since securitization can never only be imposed, there is some need to argue one's case.) We do not push the demand so high as to say that an emergency measure has to be adopted, only that the existential threat has to be argued and just gain enough resonance for a platform to be made from which it is possible to legitimize emergency measures or other steps that would not have been possible had the discourse not taken the form of existential threats, point of no return, and necessity. If no signs of such acceptance exist, we can talk only of a securitizing move, not of an object actually being securitized. The distinction between a securitizing move and successful securitization is important in the chapters that follow.

Securitization is not fulfilled only by breaking rules (which can take many forms) nor solely by existential threats (which can lead to nothing) but by cases of existential threats that legitimize the breaking of rules. Still, we have a problem of size or significance. Many actions can take this form on a small scale—for example, a family securitizing its lifestyle as dependent on keeping a specific job (and therefore using dirty tricks in competition at the firm) or the Pentagon designating hackers as "a catastrophic threat" and "a serious threat to national security" (*San Francisco Chronicle,* May 23, 1996: A11), which could possibly lead to actions within the computer field but with no cascading effects on other security issues. Our concept of international security has a clear definition of what we are interested in, but it does not tell us how we sort the important cases from the less important ones. We do not want to sort by arbitrarily assigning degrees of importance to referent objects and sectors, for instance, defining state as more important than environment or military as more securitylike than identity. Doing so would undermine the logic of both widening the security agenda and taking a securitization approach to that agenda. It would constrain arbitrarily and a priori what we can see and thus make it impossible to capture the extent to which the security agenda has actually changed or been widened.

A better measure of importance is the scale of chain reactions on other securitizations: How big an impact does the securitizing move have on wider patterns of relations? A securitizing move can easily upset orders of mutual accommodation among units. The security act is negotiated between securitizer and audience—that is, internally within the unit—but thereby the securitizing agent can obtain permission to override rules that would otherwise bind it. Typically, the agent will override such rules, because by depicting a threat the securitizing agent often says someone cannot be dealt with in the normal way. In the extreme case—war—we do not have to discuss with the other party; we try to eliminate them. This self-based violation of rules is the security act, and the fear that the other party will not let us survive as a subject is the foundational motivation for that act. In a securitized situation, a unit does not rely on the social resources of rules shared intersubjectively among units but relies instead on its own resources, demanding the right to govern its actions by its own priorities (Wæver 1996b). A successful securitization thus has three components (or steps): existential threats, emergency action, and effects on interunit relations by breaking free of rules.

The distinguishing feature of securitization is a specific rhetorical structure (survival, priority of action "because if the problem is not handled now it will be too late, and we will not exist to remedy our failure"). This definition can function as a tool for finding security actors and phenomena in sectors other than the military-political one, where it is often hard to define when to include new issues on the security agenda. Must new issues affect the military sector or be as "dangerous" as war (Deudney 1990)? To circumvent these restrictive ties to traditional security, one needs a clear idea of the essential quality of security in general.

That quality is the staging of existential issues in politics to lift them above politics. In security discourse, an issue is dramatized and presented as an issue of supreme priority; thus, by labeling it as *security,* an agent claims a need for and a right to treat it by extraordinary means. For the analyst to grasp this act, the task is not to assess some objective threats that "really" endanger some object to be defended or secured; rather, it is to understand the processes of constructing a shared understanding of what is to be considered and collectively responded to as a threat. The process of securitization is what in language theory is called a speech act. It is not interesting as a sign referring to something more real; it is the utterance itself that is the act. By saying the words, something is done (like betting, giving a promise, naming a ship) (Wæver 1988; Austin 1975: 98ff.).

Sectors and Institutionalization of Security

What we can study is this practice: Who can "do" or "speak" security successfully, on what issues, under what conditions, and with what effects? It is important to note that the security speech act is not defined by uttering the word *security*. What is essential is the designation of an existential threat requiring emergency action or special measures and the acceptance of that designation by a significant audience. There will be instances in which the word *security* appears without this logic and other cases that operate according to that logic with only a metaphorical security reference. As spelled out later, in some cases securitization has become institutionalized. Constant drama does not have to be present, because it is implicitly assumed that when we talk of *this* (typically, but not necessarily, defense issues), we are by definition in the area of urgency: By saying "defense" (or, in Holland, "dikes"), one has also implicitly said security and priority. We use this logic as a definition of security because it has a consistency and precision the word as such lacks. There is a concept of international security with this specific meaning, which is implied in most usages of the word.

Our claim is that it is possible to dig into the practice connected to this concept of security in international relations (which is distinct from other concepts of security) and find a characteristic pattern with an inner logic. If we place the survival of collective units and principles—the politics of existential threat—as the defining core of security studies, we have the basis for applying security analysis to a variety of sectors without losing the essential quality of the concept. This is the answer to those who hold that security studies cannot expand its agenda beyond the traditional military-political one without debasing the concept of security itself.

Sectors are "views of the international system through a lens that highlights one particular aspect of the relationship and interaction among all of its constituent units" (Buzan, Jones, and Little 1993: 31). Given that the analytical purpose of sectors is to differentiate types of interaction (military, political, economic, societal, and environmental), it seems reasonable to expect (1) that one will find units and values that are characteristic of, and rooted in, particular sectors (although, like the state, they may also appear in other sectors); and (2) that the nature of survival and threat will differ across different sectors and types of unit. In other words, security is a generic term that has a distinct meaning but varies in form. Security means survival in the face of existential threats, but what constitutes an existential threat is not the same across different sectors. One purpose of the following chapters is to unfold this sectoral logic of security more fully.

Securitization can be either ad hoc or institutionalized. If a given type of threat is persistent or recurrent, it is no surprise to find that the response and sense of urgency become institutionalized. This situation is most visible in the military sector, where states have long endured threats of armed coercion or invasion and in response have built up standing bureaucracies, procedures, and military establishments to deal with those threats. Although such a procedure may seem to reduce security to a species of normal politics, it does not do so. The need for drama in establishing securitization falls away, because it is implicitly assumed that when we talk of this issue we are by definition in the area of urgency. As is the case for defense issues in most countries and for the dikes in the Netherlands, urgency has been established by the previous use of the security move. There is no further need to spell out that this issue has to take precedence, that it is a security issue—by saying "defense" or "dikes," one has also implicitly said "security" and "priority." This can be shown by trying to inquire about the rationale for decisions in these areas. Behind the first layers of ordinary bureaucratic arguments, one will ultimately find a—probably irritated—repetition of a security argument so well established that it is taken for granted.

Some security practices are not legitimized in public by security discourse, because they are not out in the public at all (e.g., the "black programs" in the United States, which are not presented in the budget), but this is actually a very clear case of the security logic. In a democracy, at some point it must be argued in the public sphere why a situation constitutes security and therefore can legitimately be handled differently. One could not take something out of the budget without giving a reason for the use of such an extraordinary procedure. When this procedure has been legitimized through security rhetoric, it becomes institutionalized as a package legitimization, and it is thus possible to have black security boxes in the political process. The speech act reduces public influence on this issue, but in democracies one must legitimize in public why from now on the details will not be presented publicly (because of the danger of giving useful information to the enemy and the like). In all cases, the establishment of secret services has some element of this logical sequence. Not every act is presented with the drama of urgency and priority, because it has been established in a general sense that this is an entire field that has been moved to a form of treatment legitimate only because this area has been defined as security.

In well-developed states, armed forces and intelligence services are carefully separated from normal political life, and their use is subject to elaborate procedures of authorization. Where such separation is not in place, as in many weak states (Nigeria under Abacha, the USSR under Stalin) or in states mobilized for total war, much of normal politics is pushed into the security realm.[3] The prominence of institutionalized military security underpins not only the claim of those who want to confine security studies to the military sector but also the de facto primacy of the state in security affairs. But nothing is necessary about this particular construction; it comes out of a certain history and has formidable institutional momentum but is not fixed for all time. Where the threat profiles warrant them, one can see other types of institutionalized security structures, such as those concerned with flood control in the Netherlands. One of the difficulties facing those attempting to securitize environmental issues is that the threats are both new (or newly discovered) and controversial regarding their existential urgency. Consequently, they do not (yet) have institutions, and they find themselves operating in a political context dominated by security institutions designed for other types of threat.

Although in one sense securitization is a further intensification of politicization (thus usually making an even stronger role for the state), in another sense it is opposed to politicization. Politicization means to make an issue appear to be open, a matter of choice, something that is decided upon and that therefore entails responsibility, in contrast to issues that either could not be different (laws of nature) or should not be put under political control (e.g., a free economy, the private sphere, and matters for expert decision). By contrast, securitization on the international level (although often not on the domestic one) means to present an issue as urgent and existential, as so important that it should not be exposed to the normal haggling of politics but should be dealt with decisively by top leaders prior to other issues.

National security should not be idealized. It works to silence opposition and has given power holders many opportunities to exploit "threats" for domestic purposes, to claim a right to handle something with less democratic control and constraint. Our belief, therefore, is not "the more security the better." Basically, security should be seen as negative, as a failure to deal with issues as normal politics. Ideally, politics should be able to unfold according to routine procedures without this extraordinary elevation of specific "threats" to a prepolitical immediacy. In some cases securitization of issues is unavoidable, as when states are faced with an implacable or barbarian aggressor. Because of its prioritizing imperative, securitization also has tactical attractions—for example, as a way to obtain sufficient attention for environmental problems. But desecuritization is the optimal long-range option, since it means not to have issues phrased as "threats against which we have countermeasures" but to move them out of this threat-defense sequence and into the ordinary public sphere (Wæver 1995b).

When considering securitizing moves such as "environmental security" or a "war on crime," one has to weigh the always problematic side effects of applying a mind-set of security against the possible advantages of focus, attention, and mobilization. Thus, although in the abstract desecuritization is the ideal, in specific situations one can choose securitization—only one should not believe this is an innocent reflection of the issue *being* a security threat; it is always a political choice to securitize or to accept a securitization.

Subjective, Objective, and Intersubjective Security

Extracting the essential quality of international security takes one some way toward pinning down a general but nonetheless still fairly confined meaning of the concept that can operate both within and beyond the traditional military-political understanding of that concept. But this does not solve all of the problems. Commentators on security at least as far back as Arnold Wolfers (1962: 151) have noted that security can be approached both objectively (there is a real threat) and subjectively (there is a perceived threat) and that nothing ensures that these two approaches will line up. This distinction turns out to be crucial in formulating an international security concept for a multisectoral agenda.

Our argument is that securitization, like politicization, has to be understood as an essentially intersubjective process. Even if one wanted to take a more objectivist approach, it is unclear how this could be done except in cases in which the threat is unambiguous and immediate. (An example would be hostile tanks crossing the border; even here, "hostile" is an attribute not of the vehicle but of the socially constituted relationship. A foreign tank could be part of a peacekeeping force.) It is not easy to judge the securitization of an issue against some measure of whether that issue is "really" a threat; doing so would demand an objective measure of security that no security theory has yet provided. Even if one could solve the measurement problem, it is not clear that the objectivist approach would be particularly helpful. Different states and nations have different thresholds for defining a threat: Finns are concerned about immigration at a level of 0.3 percent foreigners, whereas Switzerland functions with a level of 14.7 percent (Romero 1990).[4]

Regardless of whether an analyst finds that an actor's disposition toward high or low thresholds leads to correct assessments, this disposition has real effects. And other actors need to grasp the logic this unit follows. When states or nations securitize an issue—"correctly" or not—it is a political fact that has consequences, because this securitization will cause the actor to operate in a different mode than he or she would have otherwise. This is the classical diplomatic (and classical realist) lesson, which holds that good statesmanship has to understand the threshold at which other actors will feel threatened and therefore more generally to understand how the world looks to those actors, even if one disagrees (Carr 1939; Kissinger 1957; Wæver 1995d).

In some cases, however, it *does* matter how others judge the reasonableness of a securitization, because this influences how other actors in the system will respond to a security claim. What may seem a legitimate securitization within a given political community may appear paranoid to those outside it (e.g., Western perceptions of Soviet concerns about pop music and jeans). Conversely, outsiders may perceive that a political community undersecuritizes a "real" threat and thus endangers itself or free rides (e.g., U.S. perceptions of Danish defense policy during the Cold War). The way the securitization processes of one actor fit with the perceptions of others about what constitutes a "real" threat matters in shaping the interplay of securities within the international system. Both within and between actors, the extent of shared intersubjective understandings of security is one key to understanding behavior.

In any case, it is neither politically nor analytically helpful to try to define "real security" outside of the world of politics and to teach the actors to understand the term correctly. Such rationalist universalism will easily be "right" on its own terms, but it will be of very little help in political analysis. It is more relevant to grasp the processes and dynamics of securitization, because if one knows who can "do" security on what issue and under what conditions, it will sometimes be possible to maneuver the interaction among actors and thereby curb security dilemmas.

The distinction between subjective and objective is useful for highlighting the fact that we want to avoid a view of security that is given objectively and emphasize that security is determined by actors and in this respect is subjective. The label *subjective,* however, is not fully adequate. Whether an issue is a security issue is not something individuals decide alone. Securitization is intersubjective and socially constructed: Does a referent object hold general legitimacy as something that *should* survive, which entails that actors can make reference to it, point to something as a threat, *and* thereby get others to follow or at least tolerate actions not otherwise legitimate? This quality is not held in subjective and isolated minds; it is a social quality, a part of a discursive, socially constituted, intersubjective realm. For individuals or groups to speak security does not guarantee success (cf. Derrida 1977a; Wæver 1995b). Successful securitization is not decided by the securitizer but by the audience of the security speech act: Does the audience accept that something is an existential threat to a shared value? Thus, security (as with all politics) ultimately rests neither with the objects nor with the subjects but *among* the subjects (cf. Arendt 1958, 1959; Wæver 1990; Huysmans 1996).

Social Power and Facilitating Conditions

This relationship among subjects is not equal or symmetrical, and the possibility for successful securitization will vary dramatically with the position held by the actor. Security is thus very much a structured field in which some actors are placed in positions of power by virtue of being generally accepted voices of security, by having the power to define security (Bigo 1994, 1996, forthcoming). This power, however, is never absolute: No one is guaranteed the ability to make people accept a claim for necessary security action (as even the Communist elites of Eastern Europe learned; see Wæver 1995b), nor is anyone excluded from attempts to articulate alternative interpretations of security. The field is structured or biased, but no one conclusively "holds" the power of securitization.[5] Therefore, it is our view (contra Bigo) that one can not make the actors of securitization the fixed point of analysis—the practice of securitization is the center of analysis. In concrete analysis, however, it is important to be specific about who is more or less privileged in articulating security. To study securitization is to study the power politics of a concept.

Based on a clear idea of the nature of security, securitization studies aims to gain an increasingly precise understanding of who securitizes, on what issues (threats), for whom (referent objects), why, with what results, and, not least, under what conditions (i.e., what explains when securitization is successful).

The impossibility of applying objective standards of securityness relates to a trivial but rarely noticed feature of security arguments: They are about the future, about alternative futures—always hypothetical—and about counterfactuals. A security argument always involves two predictions: What will happen if we do not take "security action" (the threat), and what will happen if we do (How is the submitted security policy supposed to work?). A security theory that could tell politicians and citizens what actually constitute security problems and what do not would demand that such predictions should be possible to make on a scientific basis, which means society would have to be a closed, mechanical, and deterministic system. Even this condition, however, would not be enough, because a second complication is that securityness is not only a matter of degree—"how threatening"—but is also a qualitative question: Do we choose to attach the security label with its ensuing effects? Actors can choose to handle a major challenge in other ways and thus not securitize it. The use of a specific conceptualization is always a choice—it is politics, it is not possible to decide by investigating the threat scientifically.

An objective measure for security can never replace the study of securitization, because the security quality is supplied by politics, but this does not mean a study of the features of the threat itself is irrelevant. On the contrary, these features rank high among the "facilitating conditions" of the security speech act. Facilitating conditions are the conditions under which the speech act works, in contrast to cases in which the act misfires or is abused (Austin 1975 [1962]). Conditions for a successful speech act fall into two categories: (1) the internal, linguistic-grammatical—to follow the rules of the act (or, as Austin argues, accepted conventional procedures must exist, and the act has to be executed according to these procedures), and (2) the external, contextual and social—to hold a position from which the act can be made ("The particular persons and circumstances in a given case must be appropriate for the invocation of the particular procedure invoked" [Austin 1975 (1962): 34]).

A successful speech act is a combination of language and society, of both intrinsic features of speech and the group that authorizes and recognizes that speech (Bourdieu 1991 [1982]; Butler 1996a, b). Among the internal conditions of a speech act, the most important is to follow the security form, the grammar of security, and construct a plot that includes existential threat, point of no return, and a possible way out—the general grammar of security as such plus the particular dialects of the different sectors, such as talk identity in the societal sector, recognition and sovereignty in the political sector, sustainability in the environmental sector, and so on (cf. Wæver 1996b). The external aspect of a speech act has two main conditions. One is the social capital of the enunciator, the securitizing actor, who must be in a position of authority, although this should not be defined as official authority. The other external condition has to do with threat. It is more likely that one can conjure a security threat if certain objects can be referred to that are generally held to be threatening—be they tanks, hostile sentiments, or polluted waters. In themselves, these objects never make for necessary securitization, but they are definitely facilitating conditions.

After thus subdividing the social, external speech-act conditions into actor authority and threat related, we can sum up the facilitating conditions as follows: (1) the demand internal to the speech act of following the grammar of security, (2) the social conditions regarding the position of authority for the securitizing actor—that is, the relationship between speaker and audience and thereby the likelihood of the audience accepting the claims made in a securitizing attempt, and (3) features of the alleged threats that either facilitate or impede securitization.

Actor and Analyst in Securitization Studies

Approaching security from a speech-act perspective raises questions about the relationship between actors and analysts in defining and understanding the security agenda. As analysts, we define security as we have done here because it is the only way that makes coherent sense of what actors do. We have identified a particular sociopolitical logic that is characteristic of security, and that logic is what we study. Although analysts unavoidably play a role in the construction (or deconstruction) of security issues (viz., the long argument between peace research and strategic studies or the U.S. debate about the securityness of the Vietnam War), it is not their primary task to determine whether some threat represents a "real" security problem.

Objective security assessment is beyond our means of analysis; the main point is that actors and their audiences securitize certain issues as a specific form of political act. Actors who securitize do not necessarily say "security," nor does their use of the term *security* necessarily always constitute a security act. We use our criteria to see if they take the form of "politics of existential threats," with the argument that an issue takes priority over everything else and therefore allows for a breaking of the rules. As a first step, the designation of what constitutes a security issue comes from political actors, not analysts, but analysts interpret political actors' actions and sort out when these actions fulfill the security criteria. It is, further, the analyst who judges whether the actor is effective in mobilizing support around this security reference (i.e., the attempted securitizers are "judged" first by other social actors and citizens, and the degree of their following is then interpreted and measured by us). Finally, to assess the significance of an instance of securitization, analysts study its effects on other units. The actor commands at only one very crucial step: the performance of a political act in a security mode.

Thus, it is the actor, not the analyst, who decides whether something is to be handled as an existential threat. This does not make analysts hostage to the self-understanding of actors for the duration of the analysis. In all subsequent questions of cause-effect relationships—what are the effects of these security acts, who influenced decisions, and so on—we do not intend to give actors any defining role. Thus, a concept such as *security complex* is defined not by whether actors label themselves a complex (they do not!) but by analysts' interpretation of who is actually interconnected in terms of security interaction.[6] (Security complex is basically an analytical term; security is a political practice that we have distilled into a specific, more precise category on the basis of the way the concept is used.) The speech-act approach says only that it is the actor who by securitizing an issue—and the audience by accepting the claim—makes it a security issue. At that level, the analyst cannot and should not replace the actor.

This point does not suggest that we feel obliged to agree with this securitizing act. One of the purposes of this approach should be that it becomes possible to evaluate whether one finds it good or bad to securitize a certain issue. One rarely manages to counter a securitizing attempt by saying as an analyst, "You are not really threatened, you only think so." But it is possible to ask with some force whether it is a good idea to make this issue a security issue—to transfer it to the agenda of panic politics—or whether it is better handled within normal politics. As witnessed in the discussion about environmental security, even environmentalists have had strong second thoughts about the effects of putting the environmental agenda in security terms. The securitization approach serves to underline the responsibility of talking security, the responsibility of actors as well as of analysts who choose to frame an issue as a security issue. They cannot hide behind the claim that anything in itself constitutes a security issue.

The relationship of analyst to actor is one area in which our approach differs from that taken by many scholars with whom we share some theoretical premises. An emerging school of "critical security studies" (CSS) wants to challenge conventional security studies by applying postpositivist perspectives, such as critical theory and poststructuralism (Krause and Williams 1996, 1997). Much of its work, like ours, deals with the social construction of security (cf. also Klein 1994; Campbell 1993), but CSS mostly has the intent (known from poststructuralism as well as from constructivism in international relations) of showing that change is possible because things are socially constituted.

We, in contrast, believe even the socially constituted is often sedimented as structure and becomes so relatively stable as practice that one must do analysis also on the basis that it continues, using one's understanding of the social construction of security not only to criticize this fact but also to understand the dynamics of security and thereby maneuver them. This leads us to a stronger emphasis on collectivities and on understanding thresholds that trigger securitization in order to avoid them. With our securitization perspective, we abstain from attempts to talk about what "real security" would be for people, what are "actual" security problems larger than those propagated by elites, and the like. To be able to talk about these issues, one has to make basically different ontological choices than ours and must define some emancipatory ideal. Such an approach is therefore complementary to ours; it can do what we voluntarily abstain from, and we can do what it is unable to: understand the mechanisms of securitization while keeping a distance from security—that is, not assuming that security is a good to be spread to ever more sectors.

There are other differences between the two approaches (much of CSS takes the individual as the true reference for security—human security—and thus in its individualism differs from our methodological collectivism and focus on collectivities; cf. Chapter 9), but the political attitude and its corresponding view of constructivism and structuralism is probably the most consistent one. The analyst in critical security studies takes on a larger burden than the analyst in our approach; he or she can brush away existing security construction disclosed as arbitrary and point to some other issues that are more important security problems. Our approach links itself more closely to existing actors, tries to understand their modus operandi, and assumes that future management of security will have to include handling these actors—as, for instance, in strategies aimed at mitigating security dilemmas and fostering mutual awareness in security complexes. Although our philosophical position is in some sense more radically constructivist in holding security to always be a political construction and not something the analyst can describe as it "really" is, in our purposes we are closer to traditional security studies, which at its best attempted to grasp security constellations and thereby steer them into benign interactions. This stands in contrast to the "critical" purposes of CSS, which point toward a more wholesale refutation of current power wielders.

The Units of Security Analysis: Actors and Referent Objects

The speech-act approach to security requires a distinction among three types of units involved in security analysis.

1. *Referent objects:* things that are seen to be existentially threatened and that have a legitimate claim to survival.
2. *Securitizing actors:* actors who securitize issues by declaring something—a referent object—existentially threatened.
3. *Functional actors:* actors who affect the dynamics of a sector. Without being the referent object or the actor calling for security on behalf of the referent object, this is an actor who significantly influences decisions in the field of security. A polluting company, for example, can be a central actor in the environmental sector—it is not a referent object and is not trying to securitize environmental issues (quite the contrary).

The most important and difficult distinction is that between referent objects and securitizing actors, and this distinction requires some discussion. We deal with functional actors in the sector chapters.

The referent object for security has traditionally been the state and, in a more hidden way, the nation. For a state, survival is about sovereignty, and for a nation it is about identity (Wæver et al. 1993, chapter 2). But if one follows the securitization approach outlined earlier, a much more open spectrum of possibilities has to be allowed. In principle, securitizing actors can attempt to construct anything as a referent object. In practice, however, the constraints of facilitating conditions mean actors are much more likely to be successful with some types of referent objects than with others. Security action is usually taken on behalf of, and with reference to, a collectivity. The referent object is that to which one can point and say, "It has to survive, therefore it is necessary to . . ."

Size or scale seems to be one crucial variable in determining what constitutes a successful referent object of security. At the micro end of the spectrum, individuals or small groups can seldom establish a wider security legitimacy in their own right. They may speak about security to and of themselves, but few will listen. At the system end of the scale, problems also exist in establishing security legitimacy. For example, attempts have been made to construct all of humankind as a security referent—most notably in terms of shared fears of nuclear annihilation during the Cold War but also in the context of environmental fears. Another system-scale attempt was the failed move by socialists in 1914 to mobilize in the name of the international working class. Thus far, however, the system level has rarely been able to compete with the middle scale, although this does not mean it will not become more attractive in the future as international circumstances change.

In practice, the middle scale of limited collectivities has proved the most amenable to securitization as durable referent objects. One explanation for this success is that such limited collectivities (states, nations, and, as anticipated by Huntington, civilizations) engage in self-reinforcing rivalries with other limited collectivities, and such interaction strengthens their "we" feeling. Because they involve a reference to a "we," they are social constructs operative in the interaction among people. A main criterion of this type of referent is that it forms an interpretative community—it is the context in which principles of legitimacy and valuation circulate and within which the individual constructs an interpretation of events. The referent is a social context with the dignity of a "site of judgment" (Foucault 1979). If rivalry is a facilitating condition for successful securitization, middle-level collectivities will always have an advantage over the system level in this respect. Somehow, the system-level candidates are still too subtle and indirect to trigger the levels of mass identity necessary for securitization. Lacking the dynamic underpinning of rivalry, their attempt at universalist political allegiance confronts the middle-level collectivities and loses.[7]

The apparent primacy of the middle-level, limited collectivities opens the way for an attack on our approach from traditional state-centric security analysts (and perhaps also from certain types of liberals). Their argument goes like this: Security, by definition, is and should be about the state, and the state is and should be about security, with the emphasis on military and political security. A hard-line liberal might say the state has no legitimate functions other than security. When security is expanded beyond the state, we have problematic securitizations such as environmental security; when the state expands beyond security, we have problems such as the conflation of economic security with protectionism. It is possible to take the state-security position and argue politically against all attempts to "do" security with reference to other referent objects on the ground that only through the state can the process of securitization be controlled democratically and kept in check.

We acknowledge that there is some analytical truth, as well as a legitimate political position, in this tight link between state and security. But the logic of our approach forces us to reject the use of such a narrow and self-closing definitional move. We have constructed a wider conceptual net within which the state-centric position is a possible but not a predetermined outcome. In using this scheme, one may still find that the state is the most important security referent; if so, this finding would carry much more force than if it were made true by definition and would also remain open to change. We do not say security is only about the state (although there is much truth to the argument that the state is the ideal security actor) nor that security is equally available to all—states and other social movements. Security is an area of competing actors, but it is a biased one in which the state is still generally privileged as the actor historically endowed with security tasks and most adequately structured for the purpose. This explanation acknowledges the difference between a state-centric approach and a state-dominated field.

But whereas the middle level in general, and the state in particular, might enjoy primacy in the selection of referent objects, that is not the end of the story. Being a middle-level, limited collectivity is insufficient for achieving status as a referent object. This is probably best illustrated in the case of economic security, where one would think firms are the natural limited collectivity units. But by their very nature, firms rarely have a strong claim to a right of survival. If the survival of a firm is threatened, the firm will not be able to legitimize action beyond the normal, legal rules of the game. We rarely see middle-level security policy in this field except when economic arguments can be linked to what in economic terms is the secondary unit—the state—which *can* claim a natural right to survive, to defend its existence, and to take extraordinary measures (protectionism and the like) on a national issue (such as maintaining the capability for military mobilization) if deemed necessary.

Nor do system-level referent objects always lose out. Thus far they have done so in the military and political sectors, where the security of humankind has generally had less appeal than that of the state. But the story is different in other sectors. The environment is becoming an interesting case, because groups are using a securitizing logic that exactly follows the format prescribed in the previous section: The environment has to survive; therefore, this issue should take priority over all others, because if the environment is degraded to the point of no return all other issues will lose their meaning. If the normal system (politics according to the rules as they exist) is not able to handle this situation, we (Greenpeace and especially the more extremist ecoterrorists) will have to take extraordinary measures to save the environment. Sustainability might be the environmentalists' equivalent of the state's sovereignty and the nation's identity; it is the essential constitutive principle that has to be protected. If this idea catches on, the environment itself may be on the way to becoming a referent object—an object by reference to which security action can be taken in a socially significant way. We discuss this more fully in Chapter 4.

Once this door is opened, one can see other plausible candidates for security referent objects at the system level. Humankind as a whole achieved some status as a referent object in relation to nuclear weapons and could do so again—perhaps more successfully—in relation to environmental disasters, such as new ice ages or collisions between the earth and one or more of the many large rocks that occupy near-earth space. The level of human civilization could also become the referent object in relation to environmental threats. In the economic sector, system-level referents may be more effective vehicles for security discourse than limited collectivities, such as the firm and the state. Already, systems of rules or sets of principles, such as "the liberal world economy" and "free trade," have some status as referent objects in the economic sector. A similar practice could grow in the political sector around international society or democracy (the latter as an extension of the democracy = peace hypothesis). Our position is that no principled, logical exclusion of referent objects should take place at the system level; therefore, we investigate the issue in each of the sector chapters.

Also, the individual is again a factor in security debate. As argued by Ken Booth (1991, 1994, 1995), much of security analysis blanks out the effects on actual human beings of the issues discussed; thus, his argument is an attempt to securitize concrete individuals in their competition with aggregate categories. Emma Rothschild (1995) has argued that historically, a major part of liberal thought had the individual as the referent of security; thus, there is a respectable philosophical tradition to build on. In the 1980s, with projects like the Brandt and Palme Commissions, security thought drifted back toward the individual, and Rothschild argues convincingly that regardless of whether it is intellectually coherent or ethically ideal, securitization of the individual is a real political practice of our times. (In this book, the individual will reappear primarily in the political-sector chapter, because it is usually a question of establishing the *principle* of, for example, human rights rather than of specific individuals appearing one by one as securitized referent objects.[8])

To conclude, one can study security discourse to learn what referent objects are appealed to and can study outcomes to see which hold security legitimacy so an appeal to their necessary survival is able to mobilize support. Traditionally, the middle level has been the most fruitful generator of referent objects, but lately more has been heard about system- and micro-level possibilities (Rothschild 1995). Referent objects must establish security legitimacy in terms of a claim to survival. Bureaucracies, political regimes, and firms seldom hold this sense of guaranteed survival and thus are not usually classed as referent objects. Logically, they could try to establish a claim to survival and thus to security legitimacy, but empirically this is not usually possible. In practice, security is not totally subjective. There are socially defined limits to what can and cannot be securitized, although those limits can be changed. This means security analysis is interested mainly in successful instances of securitization—the cases in which other people follow the securitizing lead, creating a social, intersubjective constitution of a referent object on a mass scale. Unsuccessful or partially successful attempts at securitization are interesting primarily for the insights they offer into the stability of social attitudes toward security legitimacy, the process by which those attitudes are maintained or changed, and the possible future direction of security politics. In these larger patterns, desecuritization is at least as interesting as securitization, but the successful acts of securitization take a central place because they constitute the currently valid specific meaning of security.

Critics will undoubtedly protest our abdication of the critical use of objective security measures as a way to question dominant definitions (cf. McSweeney 1996). When a threat is not securitized, should one not be able to show that this *is* a threat? Yes, the securitization perspective, which basically removes the objective ground from the dominant discourse, opens the possibility of problematizing both actual securitization and the absence of securitization, but it cannot do so by proving that something "is" a security problem—at least not without shifting from the role of analyst to securitizing actor. Thus, it is not advisable to add to our basic securitization perspective that there are also objective security problems (to hold against false securitizations and the lack thereof). Doing so would introduce an incompatible ontology that would ultimately undermine the basic idea of security as a specific social category that arises out of, and is constituted in, political practice.

What one *can* add are arguments about the likely effects.[9] One can try to show the effects of either excessive securitization—security dilemmas—or of *not* securitizing—the inability to handle an issue effectively unless it is securitized. Only within society and by one's own participation in political practice can one contribute to securitization or desecuritization, which is a different matter from the threat "being" a security problem. Things can be facilitators of securitization—it is made easier if one can point to matters associated with threats, but the ultimate locus of securityness is social rather than technical, and it is between a securitizing actor and its audience in reference to something they value.

A *securitizing actor* is someone, or a group, who performs the security speech act. Common players in this role are political leaders, bureaucracies, governments, lobbyists, and pressure groups. These actors are not usually the referent objects for security, because only rarely can they speak security through reference to the need to defend their own survival. Their argument will normally be that it is necessary to defend the security of the state, nation, civilization, or some other larger community, principle, or system. Only occasionally will actors such as governments or firms be able to speak successfully of security on their own behalf.

The notion of an "actor" is in itself problematic. To say precisely who or what acts is always tricky, because one can disaggregate any collective into subunits and on down to individuals and say, "It is not really 'the state' that acts but some particular department—or in the last instance individuals." But to disaggregate everything into individuals is not very helpful, because much of social life is understandable only when collectivities are seen as more than the sum of their "members" and are treated as social realities (methodological collectivism).

Identifying actors is thus more complicated than identifying referent objects. The former involves a level-of-analysis problem: The same event can be attributed to different levels (individual, bureaucracy, or state, for instance). Unlike the case with the referent object, a speech act is often not self-defining in terms of who or what speaks, and the designation "actor" is thus in some sense arbitrary. Ultimately, individuals can always be said to be the actors, but if they are locked into strong roles it is usually more relevant to see as the "speaker" the collectivities for which individuals are designated authoritative representatives (e.g., parties, states, or pressure groups)—for example, France-materialized-as-de Gaulle rather than the person de Gaulle. If one wants to downgrade the role of the analyst in defining actors, one option is to let other actors settle the matter. Other states treated de Gaulle as acting on behalf of France and held France responsible for his acts; thus, in the world of "diplomatics" France was constituted as the actor (Manning 1962; Wæver forthcoming-c). How to identify the securitizing actor is in the last instance less a question of who performs the speech than of what logic shapes the action. Is it an action according to individual logic or organizational logic, and is the individual or the organization generally held responsible by other actors? Focusing on the organizational logic of the speech act is probably the best way to identify who or what is the securitizing actor.

The difference between actor and referent object in any specific case will also usually mean there is a separate category of "audience," those the securitizing act attempts to convince to accept exceptional procedures because of the specific security nature of some issue. One danger of the phrases *securitization* and *speech act* is that too much focus can be placed on the acting side, thus privileging the powerful while marginalizing those who are the audience and judge of the act (Huysmans 1996).

One use of the distinction between actors and referent objects is to avoid reifying some security units—for example, nations. When we say in the chapter on societal security (and in Wæver et al. 1993) that societal security is often about nations and their survival, we do not want to say that "a nation acts to defend itself," which would represent reifying and anthropomorphic terminology. Someone—some group, movement, party, or elite—acts with reference to the nation and claims to speak or act on behalf of the nation.

The distinction between securitizing actor and referent object is less of a problem in the context of the state and therefore has not previously been clearly noted. The state (usually) has explicit rules regarding who can speak on its behalf, so when a government says "we have to defend our national security," it has the right to act on behalf of the state. The government *is* the state in this respect. No such formal rules of representation exist for nations or the environment; consequently, the problem of legitimacy is larger in these areas than in the case of the state. When someone acts in the name of a nation, certain discursive rules are imposed on the actor, because he or she has to speak in terms of identity, in terms that follow the logic of "nation," and these terms shape the discourse and action in a way that differs from that appropriate to other referent objects. But only in the weakest sense does this mean the nation is "acting." The rules for what one can do in the name of a nation are less rigid than those for a state; therefore, it will be easier to talk of the state acting than of the nation doing so. This is a matter of degree rather than necessarily a qualitative difference. Consequently, the analyst who writes about a fringe neo-Nazi group that tries to mobilize people to defend "our national survival" against the threat posed by immigrants will feel uncomfortable phrasing this as "the nation acting." It feels more correct to make the distinction between who actually does the acting and what those actors are referring to as that which should survive and then see how successful they are in asserting a claim to speak for that higher entity.

These arguments show why it is important to distinguish between securitizing actors and referent objects. But the distinctions are contextual rather than intrinsic to specific units: In many cases, the securitizing actors will be different from the referent object, but in others—most notably the state—the referent object will in a sense speak for itself through its authorized representatives. In all cases, however, the analyst is obliged to question the success or failure of the securitizing speech act. Even governments can fail at securitization, as happened to Britain over the Suez, the United States in Vietnam, and the European Communist regimes domestically in the late 1980s.

In applying the distinction among referent objects, securitizing actors, and functional actors to the five sector chapters that follow, it is important first to clarify the referent object(s) in each sector. In some cases, this will constitute most of the exercise. To map societal security around the world, it is probably more interesting—and at least logically primary—to know where people are mobilized in the name of nations, civilizations, religions, or tribes than to know where mobilization is effected by political parties, where by state elites, where by social movements, where by churches, and where by intellectuals. In the military sector, the referent object may almost always be the state, and the securitizing actor may in some sense also be "the state," but a number of functional actors may also influence decisions. If so, one would need to spend more space tracking down these functional actors. Thus, the sector chapters will vary in terms of the weight of analysis given to the three types of security unit. In an ideal situation—perhaps in more complete future case studies based on this approach—all three types will be covered fully, in particular the articulation of referent objects and securitizing actors.

Regions and Other Constellations of Securitization

In the part of this work aimed at tracing security complexes, the approach is to look at the pattern of security connectedness. The investigation proceeds in three steps: (1) Is the issue securitized successfully by any actors?

(2) If yes, track the links and interactions from this instance—how does the security action in this case impinge on the security of others, and where does this then echo significantly? (3) These chains can then be collected as a cluster of interconnected security concerns. When this case along with the patterns from all of the other cases (of the sector in the case of homogeneous sector–specific analysis or across sectors in the case of heterogeneous security complex analysis; cf. Chapters 1 and 8) are aggregated, we can see the level on which the processes of securitization and the patterns of interaction are concentrated.

Our general assumption, and one of the key motivations for this project, is that the post–Cold War world will exhibit substantially higher levels of regionalization and lower levels of globalization than was the case during the Cold War. One of our purposes is to adapt security complex theory to deal with this more complicated world. In the sector chapters that follow, however, we keep this question open. It may be that the security logic of some sectors inherently inclines toward regionalization, whereas in other sectors it does not. This is what we need to investigate in these chapters. And we do so in basically the same way as is done in classical security complex theory: by combining the concerns of major actors into a constellation, a knot of mutual security relations.

One final problem in thinking about security regions is how to tie such thinking into the discussion of actors and referent objects in the previous section. Is a security complex defined by actors or referent objects? As just argued, the security complex is actually a constellation of security concerns; the different instances of securitization as such form the nodes among which the lines can be drawn and the complex mapped. Because referent objects are the more basic, enduring, and salient features on the security landscape, the answer to our earlier question is the referent objects. Some might object that according to our scheme referent objects do not act and therefore cannot be the units in subsystems that are defined by interactions. This is an illusion. Security actors speak and act in the name of referent objects, and they generally see threats as emanating from other referent objects. There is thus a real sense in which India and Pakistan, Turkey and the Kurds, or Chile and ITT interact.

Since referent objects are the socially constituted units, they are often actors for each other, even if some analytical theories point to other links in the chains as the actors. For instance, states are to some extent real as states and they act as states even if the literal acting is done by statesmen, because states ascribe intentions and responsibility to each other as states (Manning 1962; Wæver forthcoming-c). This reflection is structured by the motivation of security complex analysis, which is to reach a dynamic analysis of security situations. We want to be able to grasp the connections between the security of A and that of B, the security dilemmas as well as mutually reinforcing security loops. Therefore, it is essential that we organize the regional analysis around nodes that are simultaneously that which is (claimed to be) threatened and that which is (depicted as) the source of threat.

In classical security complex theory (CSCT), the definition was phrased in terms of primary security concerns; in the current framework, it must be instances of securitization that connect and form the complex. In both cases, the core is obviously the articulation of threats by the major actors. Unfortunately, there is little conceptual literature on threats. In discussions of the concept of security, some participants claim an actor-based threat is a precondition for something to be a security problem (Deudney 1990). It is difficult to see what justifies this as a logical step, although it could be an empirical connection, a structural proclivity making threats attributed to actors more easy to securitize. We do not, however, want to define security problems such that actors *have* to be the problem. Probably, they usually are.

It follows from our general securitization perspective that what interests us is the *attribution* of security problems to specific sources rather than the actual origins of what appear as security problems. As argued by attribution theory, there is a general psychological tendency to overestimate the degree of choice for *alter* while emphasizing necessity as to *ego* (Hart 1978; Jervis 1976). One will therefore generally tend to "actorize" the other side—that is, fashion the other as a willful chooser rather than a chain in a series of events. In most cases, the fact that the other is a strategic actor with several choices is an amplifying factor in any threat perception and therefore assists in pushing an issue across the security threshold. Because the other is an actor, not just a wheel in a machine, it has the potential of outwitting us, of having intentions, or of bending or suppressing our will to replace it with its own (cf. Clausewitz 1983 [1832]; Wæver 1995b).

This focus on actors could seem to point to securitizing actors rather than to referent objects. This deduction, however, is probably false. What the attribution argument implies is not that we should focus on those units *we* see as actors but rather that whatever is presented as the cause of security problems is most likely also actorized. If securitizing actor "a" on behalf of community "A" claims A is threatened by B, he or she will present B as an actor, as responsible for the threat, as an agent who had a choice. Therefore, we do not have to define security complexes in terms of what we have labeled *actors* in our analytical framework: The actors might operate with other actors and thereby point to the bigger, more abstract categories—the referent objects. On the other hand, threats do not need to be attributed to the same categories as those the other side acted with reference to. Actual events are likely to be varied and complex, requiring a pragmatic approach that allows us to find the specific units of the case.

For instance, Churchill as a securitizing actor could have securitized Nazism as a threat. This does not necessarily mean a countersecuritization is performed either by Nazism as actor or with Nazism as referent object. Instead, Hitler could securitize England (the referent object of Churchill, so far so good) as the threat in the name of Germany, all Germans, and the Aryan race. What constitutes the threat for one is not necessarily the referent object for the other. This procedure was much easier in CSCT where security was conducted for and by India, which was also the (perceived) threat to Pakistan and vice versa. The argument from attribution theory gives us reason to believe that most threats will be linked to actors and that what we analyze as referent objects will often be constructed by other actors as actors. If, however, one draws the map too finely, a number of actors will be securitizing slightly different referent objects (the German race, the German people, Germany, Aryans)—differences that are important when one is trying to look into the politics of securitizing moves—whereas we in security complex analysis need to find the main patterns of interaction and therefore need to bundle together the various versions of securitizing "Germany" as one node.

When generating the security complex, the best way to define the points between which the security arrows go might be to point to conglomerates of a referent object and the corresponding securitizing actor. In the extreme case, this means we have referent objects with stable spokespersons. A stable combination of referent object and "voice" points to the classical concept of the state as a clear instance. But even the state and sovereignty as referent object is appealed to by other than the one official voice. There are several actual securitizing actors, and the state as well as the other actors occasionally securitize other referents, such as the nation, the European Union (EU), or some principles of international society. In the case of France, Japan, and Sudan, the name makes a relatively clear reference to a dense network of correlated referent objects and securitizing actors. The different securitizing actors are connected by competing for the representation of the same referent object; the different referent objects are unified by their mutual substitutability for each other. There is more a chain of family resemblances than a clear-cut criterion or one primary unit. In each case, a conglomerate of actors and referent objects is unified by the density of overlapping security discourse and usually also nominally by a name: the security of "France" (which can mean several different referent objects and a large number of possible actors), of Europe and the EU, and of "the environment." (See the further discussion on pp. 171–175.)

The key question in security analysis is, who can "do" security in the name of what? For a time, experts could get away with analyzing only "states," and the system was then the sum of the states. Regional security meant the sum of national securities or rather a particular constellation of security interdependence among a group of states. The approach developed here offers more types of units to choose from, but the basic idea of security complexes can be carried over into a world of multiple units.

Notes

1. The history of the word *security* is complex (Kaufmann 1970; Der Derian 1993; Delumeau 1986; Corze 1984), but in the 1940s it was established in international affairs with a fairly distinct meaning (Rosenberg 1993). Much of this meaning was so easily installed because it rested on an old argument that had used the word *security* much less systematically—an argument about "necessity" previously contained primarily in the concept of *raison d'état* (Butterfield 1975). Especially from the mid-nineteenth century, when the state enters a juridical self-limitation and self-control, this "is balanced by the designation of a range of 'governmental acts' which are immune to legal challenge. This juridical reserve area of executive power is . . . the qualification which . . . calculations of security impose as a condition for the political feasibility of a liberal democracy" (Gordon 1991: 33; cf. Foucault 1991 [1978]). The classical argument, which holds that in extreme cases the government can use all means necessary, becomes concentrated as a specific, exceptional case (Wæver 1988, 1995b). This meaning of security evolved separately from the use of security in various domestic contexts (although connections definitely exist; see Kaufman 1970). This international type of security starts to spread to new referents and new actors; therefore, we want to retain a focus on international security because it has a distinct meaning, but we do not exclude the possibility that we will meet this kind of security increasingly in domestic contexts.

2. This argument does not imply that private issues could not in some sense be political, an argument made forcefully by feminists. To claim such is a politicizing move.

3. The concept of strong and weak states is elaborated and defined in Buzan (1991: 96–107) and rests on the degree of sociopolitical cohesion within the state, which is high for strong states and low for weak ones. The concept should not be confused with the distinction between strong and weak powers, which is about their capabilities vis-à-vis other powers.

4. Baldwin (1997) is the most sophisticated and consistent attempt to define security and to structure security studies according to the idea that the purpose and task is to assist decisionmakers in correctly assessing the relative attention to devote to different threats.

5. The importance of "cultural capital" to the ability to perform a speech act has been argued by Pierre Bourdieu (1991 [1982]). A speech act is not only linguistic; it is also social and is dependent on the social position of the enunciator and thus in a wider sense is inscribed in a social field. However, Bourdieu made this argument to counter a tendency of some poststructuralists and philosophers of everyday language to make the purely linguistic, internal features of a speech act completely determining (Bourdieu 1996). He has accepted the critique by Judith Butler (1996a, b) that since the speech act needs to include an idea of—with his own phrase—the "social magic" whereby some are accepted as holding authority and others are not, it has to be indeterminate, open for surprises. This is not purely a question of a formal *position* of authority (Austin's example in which "I declare you man and wife" is an effective speech act only when performed by a properly authorized authority; 1975 [1962]: 8–15). There is a performative force to the speech act; to use Bourdieu's own concepts, it has a magical efficiency, it makes what it says. A speech act is interesting exactly because it holds the insurrecting potential to break the ordinary, to establish meaning that is not already within the context—it reworks or produces a context by the performative success of the act. Although it is important to study the social conditions of successful speech acts, it is necessary always to keep open the possibility that an act that had previously succeeded and for which the formal resources and position are in place may fail and, conversely, that new

actors can perform a speech act they had previously not been expected to perform (Butler 1996a, b; Derrida 1977a [1972], 1977b, 1988). Therefore, the issues of "who can do security" and "was this a case of securitization" can ultimately be judged only in hindsight (Wæver et al. 1993: 188). They cannot be closed off by finite criteria for success.

6. This stands in contrast to some other studies of regions where one is interested in the *construction* of regions by actors (Neumann 1994; Joenniemi and Wæver 1992; Joenniemi 1997). Both approaches to regions are relevant, but for different purposes.

7. For those interested in pinpointing our position within the field of international relations theory, this is probably the passage to pick. We do not take the state or sovereignty as representing fixed limits, but we are skeptical of individualism as the traditional alternative to state centrism. We therefore form a picture of a world of multiple units, which might be called postsovereign realism. The units can be overlapping (in contrast to the exclusivity of sovereign territorial states), but this does not necessarily lead to any benign transnationalism in which the focus is on the multiple identities of individuals relativizing all units and collectivities. Although each individual in a world of overlapping units is a "member" of several units, instead of focusing on any such softening effects produced by overlap, we study how the units can continue to conduct power politics; think, for example, of the work of Susan Strange (state-firm diplomacy; 1994) and Robert Kaplan (a very anarchic anarchy after sovereignty; 1994). Each unit has a possibility of becoming the reference for security action, but since the different units overlap and are placed at different levels, there is no fixed line between domestic and international—what is internal to one unit can be interunit when one thinks of other units. More importantly a distinction exists between individual and collective security. This argument is important for the present project, because if domestic and international were fixed, there would be a risk of generating a cozy Western view of politics: Domestic politics is normal and without security, whereas the extreme is relegated to the international space. In other parts of the world, domestic is not cozy. This fact can be grasped by focusing on those units and collectivities that are mobilized in such contexts: These domestic security relations are interunit because in these places the most powerful referent objects are smaller than the state.

8. One can contemplate cases in which concern seems to focus on a particular individual: one girl in Sarajevo or Salman Rushdie. To a large extent, these individuals are given such prominence and more resources are spent on them than on most others because they are taken to represent principles. Action for some specific individual always depends on a construction of that person as representing some category, as deserving protection because he or she belongs to a particular social category—for example, leader, representative, free intellectual, or revealing test case.

9. The analyst can also intervene to countersay actors in relation to the use of the *word* security. Sloppy talk of "economic security" or "environmental security" can be questioned by arguing that the security act has not really been performed and that the securitizing actor has not managed to establish a case for treating the threat as existential. Whether the threat really is or is not existential in relation to the referent object is impossible to decide from the outside, but we can study the discourse and see if the issue has been securitized in this sense. This is primarily an intervention into the debate among observers over the appropriateness of the use of the security label. When intervening in direct policy debates over a securitization, the mode of argumentation will typically be in terms of comparing the likely effects of having the issue securitized or desecuritized.

CHAPTER 3

The Military Sector

The Military Security Agenda

This chapter covers the core subject of traditional security studies, and we hope to show how the method unfolded in Chapter 2 allows us both to incorporate that agenda and to add some new insights. The military sector is the one in which the process of securitization is most likely to be highly institutionalized. This is not necessarily so, but it reflects the particular historical condition of the contemporary international system. It is also worth noting that, contrary to the traditionalist position, not everything in the military sector is necessarily about security. Given the criteria for securitization set out in Chapter 2, it is easy to see that for some states an increasing number of military functions are not security issues at all. In the mid-1990s, most Western European states face little in the way of existential military threats. But they maintain substantial armed forces and often use those forces in roles that have much more to do with political and economic relations than with military ones. If Danish or Japanese troops participate in peacekeeping organizations (PKOs) in Africa, this has nothing to do with existential threats to Denmark or Japan and everything to do with the normal politics of those countries' international roles. For states living in security communities, rather substantial parts of their military activities may fall into the political rather than the security sphere.

In the military sector, the state is still the most important—but not the only—referent object, and the ruling elites of states are the most important—but not the only—securitizing actors. This situation exists not only because states generally command far greater military resources than other actors but also because governing elites have evolved legally and politically as the prime claimants of the legitimate right to use force both inside and outside their domain.

The modern state is defined by the idea of sovereignty—the claim of exclusive right to self-government over a specified territory and its population. Because force is particularly effective as a way of acquiring and controlling territory, the fundamentally territorial nature of the state underpins the traditional primacy of its concern with the use of force. Throughout history, the right to govern has been established by the capability to assert and defend that claim against armed challengers from within and without. The agenda of military security is thus focused largely around states, although as is shown later other referent objects and securitizing actors are also in play. The main exception to this rule occurs when the state itself either fails to take root or spirals into disintegration. This situation can lead to prolonged periods of primal anarchy, as is currently the case in Afghanistan and various parts of Africa, in which the state is only a shadow and reality is one of rival warlords and gangs.

Military security matters arise primarily out of the internal and external processes by which human communities establish and maintain (or fail to maintain) machineries of government. The process of government is, of course, about much more than the use of force. The terms and conditions of political legitimacy, and the extent to which those terms are accepted both between rulers and ruled and among different sets of rulers, are at least as important as military considerations. In practice, the military security agenda revolves largely around the ability of governments to maintain themselves against internal and external military threats, but it can also involve the use of military power to defend states or governments against nonmilitary threats to their existence, such as migrants or rival ideologies.

Although the political and military sectors are conceptually distinct, the partial interchangeability of force and consent in the process of government links them together. Like the state itself, this linkage must face in two directions: inward, into the domestic construction and life of the state, and outward, to its position in and relation to the other members of the international system. Threats against which military responses may be effective can arise either inside or outside the state—or sometimes, as in the case of "fifth columns," both. The securitization of such threats may reflect a genuine fear of attack (e.g., South Korean perceptions of the North), a desire by ruling elites to consolidate their domestic and international legitimacy (e.g., apartheid, South Africa's anticommunism), or both. The amity-enmity component of security complex theory reflects the outcomes of these securitization processes.

Among the principal domestic functions of government are the maintenance of civil order and peace, as well as administration and law. The maintenance of the territorial integrity of the state might be added, but territory is not always securitized, and on occasion governments freely negotiate substantial reorganizations, as in the recent splittings up of Czechoslovakia and the former Soviet Union. When the perceived threat is internal, military security is primarily about the ability of the ruling elite to maintain civil peace, territorial integrity, and, more controversially, the machinery of government in the face of challenges from its citizens (Ayoob 1995). The typical forms of such challenges are militant separatist, revolutionary, terrorist, or criminal organizations or movements, although some governments also securitize unarmed challengers to their authority or jurisdiction in order to use force against them.

It is noteworthy that the most extreme modern form of the state, the European or Westphalian state, has consolidated itself by a progressive disarming of the citizenry and a movement toward an ideal in which the state is the *only* legitimate wielder of force in society and effectively commands far greater instruments of force, both domestically and externally, than those illegitimate (mostly criminal) armed elements that remain. Even in the West, only during the nineteenth century did this development become effective enough to allow the separation of police from military functions, and in many new states this distinction still has shallow roots. This contrasts with the situation within feudal states and most forms of classical empires, where both the capability and the right to use force normally existed at more than one level of society (feudal barons, cities, and freelance mercenaries; governors and other local rulers in classical imperial systems) (Watson 1992; Buzan and Little 1996). Among the developed states, the United States has conspicuously deviated from the Westphalian ideal, constitutionally retaining the right of its citizens to bear arms and of its component states to retain their own militias as a defense against the hegemony of the federal government (Deudney 1995). Switzerland, Israel, and South Africa also retain strong elements of armed citizenry, the former linked to territorial defense and the latter two to individual security.

When securitization is focused on external threats, military security is primarily about the two-level interplay between the actual armed offensive and defensive capabilities of states on the one hand and their perceptions of each other's capabilities and intentions on the other. External threats range from fear of the complete obliteration of state, society, and people to gunboat diplomacy–style coercion and intimidation on particular issues of policy. Fear responses may also work on prospective future capabilities rather than on present ones, as in some contemporary perceptions of China (Dibb 1995). Crude forms of realist theory notwithstanding, there is no absolute correlation between the existence of external military capability and its securitization. The literature on democracy and peace, for example, builds on the idea that democratic states do not fear each other's military capabilities (Ember, Ember, and Russett 1992; Maoz and Russett 1993; Mintz and Geva 1993; Lake 1992; Owen 1994; Schweller 1992; Weart 1994). Desecuritization is possible even in the presence of separate military capabilities.

But separate military capabilities do create the potential for securitization. When elites and populations begin to treat the armed forces of other states as threatening, interstate relations generate the classic military security dilemma involving on the one hand the proliferation of military technologies, arms racing, and the interplay of national policies for defense and deterrence and on the other the array of policies aimed at muting the security dilemma, such as arms control, arms reduction, nonoffensive defense, and at times alliances (Jervis 1978; Buzan and Herring forthcoming 1998; Møller 1991). Once military relations become securitized, this agenda is heavily shaped by the instruments of force possessed by states and the impact of these instruments and changes in these instruments on the way in which states interact. The military agenda then has its own distinctive logic and technological imperative, but it does not operate in isolation. The entire interplay of military capabilities between states is deeply conditioned by political relations. At the interstate level, the military security agenda is primarily about the way in which states equip themselves to use force and how their behavior in this regard is interpreted and responded to by other states. Where states have failed and primal anarchy prevails among gangs and warlords, the logic of threat perception linked to the armed capabilities of other actors works more directly.

Referent Objects and Security Actors

Referent Objects

Much of traditional theory and practice in international relations is built around the idea that the state is the only legitimate referent object for military security. In the state-centric, Westphalian conception of international society that grew up in Europe and was transplanted to the rest of the world, the state was conceived to be, and in some places came close to being, the sole repository of both the right and the capability to use force. In this conception, the state evolved from dynastic absolutism, in which the prince lay at the center of sovereignty and security, to popular sovereignty, in which the nation and civil society, as well as the government, played those roles. Although both dynastic and national states claimed exclusivity as the legitimate referent object for military security, as sovereignty came to be located more broadly, the security content of the state expanded. If the national state was militarily threatened, so were its civic constituents, as well as its government.

In practice, however, many states are less than perfect manifestations of the national model, and even those that approach it do not fully incorporate all elements of their civil societies. In many places, tension still exists between the rulers and the ruled. This leaves a great deal of room for other units, especially tribes or nations, to be inserted as referent objects for military security within and between states—a process all too evident in the Balkans and the Caucasus, as well as in parts of Asia and much of Africa. But in the modern world, many of these nonstate units are seeking to acquire statehood, and if they succeed they have only transitional status as nonstate referent objects.

In the contemporary international system, some prestate referent objects are still active. The remnants of tribal barbarians still exist in parts of Central Asia and Africa. Some hint of how these tribes worked as referent objects for military security can be gleaned from contemporary civil wars in Afghanistan and Somalia. Kings and princes, empires, and cities have largely disappeared or have ceased to play a role as referent objects in the military sector, although royal families such as those in Kuwait and Saudi Arabia still preserve some autonomy as referent objects. Private armies also remain relevant, as was seen during the 1930s when the Chinese state had partially disintegrated, resulting in largely autonomous warlords ruling large swaths of territory.

Religion remains potentially available as a referent object for military securitization, but as the cases of the former Yugoslavia and the Middle East show, in the modern world religion is often entangled with state (Israel, Iran) or nation (Serbia, Croatia). In the contemporary world, religion has not yet transcended the state as a referent object for military security except on the small scale of extremist cults (Branch Davidians, Aum Shin Rykyo). Lying in the background, however, are Western fears of Islam, the rise of "Hindu nationalism," and theories about the "clash of civilizations" (Huntington 1993, 1996)—all of which suggest that the Westphalian state's claim to exclusivity as the referent object for military security is not beyond challenge from both larger and smaller entities.

The national state is also vulnerable to challenges from within. The most obvious candidates are secessionists, unionists, revolutionaries, and other would-be states. These groups are asserting a claim to statehood but do not yet have the power either to free themselves from or to overthrow government by others and do not yet enjoy widespread recognition of their claim by other states. Membership in this category is diverse. It includes secessionist and autonomist movements (Chechens, Tamils, Kurds, Karens, East Timorese, Quebecois, Basques, and the now successful Eritreans), unrequited nationalities spread across several states (Kurds, Palestinians, Serbs, and possibly Russians), and rebel movements (the Khmer Rouge and UNITA). In many cases, would-be states are in effect nations claiming status as actors at the unit level, as in the failed Ibo attempt to secede from Nigeria. Since nations can reproduce themselves and, up to a point, act, there is a case for accepting them as autonomous units (Wæver et al. 1993). The very nature of would-be states, and their position in the international system, means they are frequently objects of military interest and action and therefore of securitization. They can easily be cast as threats to state sovereignty and, by the kind of statelike activities they engage in, can motivate the existing state to use military force to secure its monopoly over legitimate violence.

In addition to would-be states, the state also has challengers that have no aspiration to replace it or to seek the status of states. These include so-called militias, like those that became prominent in the United States during the early 1990s as military self-defense groups against what they saw as the erosion of individual liberties by the state, and criminals organizing outside the state to pursue economic activities free from state regulation and taxation. Both militias and mafias can serve their members as referent objects for military security. And when the state fails—as in Afghanistan, Yugoslavia, several places in Africa, and, in a much milder sense, Italy—militias, mafias, clans, and gangs come to the fore. Some still speak in the name of the state, but others become self-seeking and self-referencing security entities (Kaplan 1994).

Here we find ourselves on the border between international and domestic security. Worth noting, although not normally an international security issue, is the way intrasocietal violence has recently risen on the agenda in the West. From Russia to the United States, a sense of pervasive societal violence is a platform national politicians can utilize in the classical securitizing move of law and order to the point at which human rights are threatened by countercrime policies and "strong man" logic begins to emerge. This situation does not normally involve the military; it is clearly a police affair, but it is placed on the security agenda for two interrelated reasons. In the West, the police are normally an institutionalized part of society that ensures continuous functioning. But the image in the United States and much of the post-Soviet world is rather that having police would be a good idea—that the situation is out of control and "something has to be done." Second, securitization takes place, and extraordinary measures are advocated. The securitization itself has society at large as its referent object (or its law-abiding part) and state agents or politicians as major actors. This deviates from standard security only by being directed inward.

A final issue at the substate level is not massive at present but is interesting to note. In some countries—notably the United States and Canada—gender and race are becoming securitized even in relation to violence. Domestic violence and race-biased patterns of violence and prosecution are far from new, but what *is* new is that these patterns are increasingly seen by active groups as a collective phenomenon. If a wife is beaten up at home, that situation is not easy to securitize. But if feminists can construct an image of collective violence being conducted by one group—men—against another—women—and, for instance, conceptualize rape as a security problem for all women because of the existence of men, new collectivities begin to emerge as referent objects on the violence agenda.

Although as a rule military securitization is focused strongly on states and would-be states, some possibilities exist for securitization of referent objects at the subsystem and system levels. Alliances such as the North Atlantic Treaty Organization (NATO) and, in a different way, the EU/Western European Union (WEU), with its aspiration to a common security policy, can achieve this status (see Chapter 8). In one sense, this simply entails adding together the claims of a set of states, but in another it overlaps with larger-scale referent objects such as civilizations. To invoke the security of the EU is little different from invoking the security of European civilization, and to invoke the security of NATO is little different from invoking that of the West. So far, the EU has not been significantly invoked in the military sector, but during the Cold War NATO was successfully invoked as representing the military security of the West.

More abstractly, principles such as the balance of power, international society, nonproliferation of some types of weapons (nuclear, biological, chemical, or blinding), and international law (nonaggression) can also be invoked as referent objects of military security. Again, there may be a direct link to state security, but the call for action is made in terms of some general principle, such as human rights, collective security, or international stability. Nuclear nonproliferation is particularly interesting here given that some states explicitly hinge their own security on possession of these weapons while at the same time arguing that the acquisition of these weapons by other states constitutes a security threat to the international system. Also interesting is the United Nations which in the context of its peacekeeping operations (PKOs) has begun to acquire the beginnings of referent object status (voiced in terms of concern about the future credibility and functional survival of the organization should it suffer too many PKO defeats or failures).

Securitizing Actors

As discussed in Chapter 2, when the referent object is the state, fairly clear rules usually exist about which state representatives can speak security on its behalf. For less institutionalized units such as nations, the rules are less clear, and the legitimacy of attempts to speak security is determined by the scale and depth of support they receive. State representatives will speak on behalf of their state, but as military security managers they are also the most likely to invoke more abstract principles (balance of power) or more collective ones (civilization, NATO, nuclear nonproliferation). Officials of intergovernmental organizations (IGOs), such as the Secretary-General of the United Nations or NATO, also have some authority to invoke more abstract and collective principles as referent objects of military security.

One cannot assume, however, that the state is always coherent. In democracies, many voices, including pressure groups and defense intellectuals, will engage in the discourse of securitization—sometimes effectively, as in the case of U.S. opposition to the Vietnam War. States can also lose control over their armed forces, as happened in Japan during the 1930s, when the army pursued an independent policy in Manchuria, and possibly in Russia starting in 1995, when the government seemed to lose control over military operations in Chechnya. Intelligence services may also come to think of themselves as the true guardians of national security, as possessing the full picture, and on this basis they may pursue their own security policies (although they seldom give voice to doing so).

Since many of the other units that serve as referent objects for military security are both aspirants to statehood and organized as political hierarchies, they often share with the state relatively clear rules about who can speak security on behalf of the organization. Mafias, gangs, clans, tribes, and rebel or secessionist movements are all likely to have clearly defined and authoritative leadership. Think, for example, of Chief Buthelezi's role as leader of the Zulu nation in South Africa or Pol Pot's role in Cambodia. Because military security generally requires a highly organized and well-equipped collective response, it is less prone to ambiguity about legitimate securitizing actors than other sectors and is more likely to reflect the structure of power relations. This logic remained broadly true in premodern times, when cities, empires, leagues, principalities, religions, tribal federations, and other referent objects for military security generally came equipped with hierarchical structures. In modern national states, however, the logic does not rule out significant roles for others in opposing or supporting specific processes of securitization.

Functional Actors

The military sector is rich in actors that influence the dynamics of the sector without being either referent objects or securitizing actors. Many of these actors are either the agencies of force, ranging from assassins and mercenary companies through defense bureaucracies to armies, or providers of the instruments of force, most notably the arms industry. Individuals can and do use force against each other, but this situation is not normally considered "military" and does not typically fall within the purview of international relations.

Subunits within the state are of interest in military security terms either because of an ability to shape the military or foreign policy of the state or because they have the capability to take autonomous action. Within a modern state, many subunits have the ability to influence the making of military and foreign policy; this is the familiar world of bureaucratic politics (Allison 1971). Governments (here narrowly defined as the present holders of military power) are the most obvious of such actors. Governments may have survival interests of their own (usually wanting to keep themselves in power) that can be distinguished from the national interest (generally defined in terms of threats to the sovereignty or survival of the state). Since the government is the authorized securitizing actor for the state, separating the two can be difficult. Some nondemocratic governments may be able to securitize their own survival directly without embarrassment. But most governments, especially democratic ones, resort to linking their own survival to that of the state.

Also prominent are the armed services, whose individual cultures exert strong pressures on military strategy and procurement. The preferences of navies for large surface ships and of air forces for manned aircraft, regardless of cost-effectiveness, are well-known examples. In addition, the typical division of armed services into distinct branches (army, air force, and navy) generates the much studied phenomenon of interservice rivalry in decisions about military procurement. Other subunits, such as the Defense, Finance, and Foreign Ministries, are also key players in making military policy.

Outside government, one has to take into account various private-sector players, most notably the firms that make up the arms industry. In the late nineteenth century, European arms companies were sufficiently independent to gain notoriety as the "merchants of death." Their salesmen were not above a little private diplomacy to stoke tensions and conflicts to improve the market for their wares. Since the 1930s, most arms manufacturers' activities have been regulated by government licensing, but even so they can pressure the state on issues such as employment, balance of payments, and the maintenance of industrial skills and production capacity necessary for mobilization.

The Logic of Threats and Vulnerabilities

As argued in Chapter 2, securitization is essentially an intersubjective process. The senses of threat, vulnerability, and (in)security are socially constructed rather than objectively present or absent. Nevertheless, it is easier to achieve securitization under some conditions than under others. Heavily armed neighbors with a history of aggression are more easily construed as threats than are lightly armed, pacifist ones. As illustrated in NATO by the diversity of the intensity of threat perceptions of the Soviet Union (e.g., the United States compared with Denmark), different societies will respond to the same "objective" security situation in different ways. Short of tanks coming across the border, there are very few objective threats. Paranoia (the securitization of nonexistent threats) and complacency (the nonsecuritization of apparent threats) are both possible. But other things being equal, historical and material facilitating conditions affect the processes of securitization and desecuritization in a fairly systematic way. Once military securitization has occurred, issues such as balance and technology development take on a more autonomous role.

Military threats and vulnerabilities have traditionally been accorded primacy in thinking about national security, for several good reasons. Unlike some other types of threat, military ones are frequently intentional and directed. When used, they represent a breakdown or abandonment of normal political relations and a willingness to have political, economic, and social issues decided by brute force. Restraints on behavior in such contests are few and fragile. Societies engaged in war put at risk not only the lives and welfare of their citizens but also their collective political, economic, and social achievements. Losing a war against a ruthless opponent can be a catastrophe. Think, for example, of the Nazi occupation in Poland and the Soviet Union or of the Japanese occupation of China. Think of Bosnia. Military threats threaten everything in a society, and they do so in a context in which most of the rules of civilized behavior either cease to function or move sharply into the background. They are the existential threat par excellence.

Other things being equal, in this sector the logic of threats and vulnerabilities between any two units in an international system is a function of the interplay between their respective military capabilities and their degree of amity and enmity, which are the outcomes of the (de)securitization process. Once the process of securitization has locked into enmity as the framework of relations, threats and vulnerabilities will be perceived primarily in terms of the military capabilities of possible aggressors. In making these calculations, both the absolute capabilities of opponents and their capabilities relative to one's own must be taken into account. The absolute capabilities of potential attackers determine the nature and extent of military threats. An opponent equipped with large numbers of nuclear weapons and suitable delivery systems can pose a threat of the rapid obliteration of a society that is not available to an opponent that does not possess weapons of mass destruction. Similarly, the size and equipment of armies shape the type of threat they pose. Large, heavy mobile forces of the type deployed by both NATO and the Warsaw Pact during the Cold War generate threats of invasion in a way smaller and less mobile armies do not. Japan, for example, has tried to avoid threatening its neighbors by denying itself both the long-range strike weapons and the sealift and airlift capability that would allow it to project force off its home islands.

The dialectic of relative military capabilities between established rivals can be elaborated almost endlessly according to variations in strength, technology, and strategy (Buzan 1987; Buzan and Herring forthcoming 1998). The dialectic spins into the larger matter of balance of power versus bandwagoning and whether military security is best sought by internal balancing (increasing one's own strength to reduce vulnerability), external balancing (finding allies who share one's perception of threat), or bandwagoning (appeasement of, or subordination to, the main source of threat). It also involves extensive debate about the nature of technology: high tech versus low tech, conventional versus nuclear, and the like. These matters are familiar ground and do not require elaboration here. The point to make is that the orthodox logics of military dialectics apply mainly *after* securitization has taken root. Military capabilities, whether absolute or relative, do not determine the process of securitization itself. If they did, Western European states would have worried as much about U.S. capabilities as about Soviet military capabilities after 1945 (as indeed some of their citizens did). A number of variables other than military capability can play a significant role in the establishment (or not) and maintenance of military securitization; the principal ones are geography, history, and politics.

Geography shapes the perception and operation of military threats and vulnerabilities in two ways: through distance and terrain. Distance works on the traditional principle that military threats are more difficult to mount and easier to defend against when they have to travel over longer distances than over shorter ones. Most states have the capability to make threats of attack or invasion against their immediate neighbors. Great powers can generally project military power beyond their immediate neighbors and into their regions. In modern times, only a handful of states have developed the capability to operate militarily worldwide. As modern military capability has diffused throughout the international system, mounting a global military posture has become increasingly more difficult than it was in the days when the Spanish conquistador Pizarro was able to overthrow the Inca Empire with 164 men, 62 horses, and two cannons. Arguably, only the United States now falls into the world military power class.

The effect of distance is what underlies the regional premise of security complex theory. Although world-class powers can engage and defeat significant opponents at great distances (Britain's takeover of India during the eighteenth century, the U.S. role in World Wars I and II and the Gulf War), the general rule of military relations is that states are worried more about their neighbors than about distant powers. With nontraditional military relations, the distance rule applies more unevenly. It remains largely true for local criminal and inner-city scenarios and failed-state anarchies, but terrorists and mafias may deliver threats with little concern for distance, and speculation about cyberwar points toward modes of conflict in which distance may not matter much (Der Derian 1992).

Terrain works similarly to distance in that it tends to amplify or reduce vulnerability to military threats. Countries such as Poland and the Ukraine occupy largely flat terrain that poses few obstacles to military movement. By contrast, Japan and Britain have benefited from the logistical obstacle to invasions by neighbors created by open water. It is hard to imagine that Taiwan would exist as a separate state were it not for the protection offered by the Taiwan Strait. Switzerland has benefited from its mountain barriers, Russia from its distances and climate. Israel and Kuwait, by contrast, have no strategic depth and few physical barriers to invasion.

History affects military threats largely in terms of the impact of past experience on present perception. The existence of historical enmity and repeated war will tend to amplify present perceptions of threat. After World War I, France feared Germany even when the latter was disarmed. Poland has long historical suspicions of Germany and Russia, Korea and China of Japan, Vietnam of China, Greece and Armenia of Turkey, and Iraq and Iran of each other. Such memories can be very long and deep (Vietnam and China, Iraq and Iran—especially if viewed as Arabs versus Persians), or they can be fairly recent (France and Germany). Some seem almost ineradicable (Greece and Turkey), whereas others have either faded from military significance or been replaced by more recent events (Britain and France, Denmark and Sweden). As was seen during the Cold War, history is not a necessary condition for strong feelings of military threat. Neither the United States nor the Soviet Union/Russia had any serious history of enmity before they plunged into the Cold War. But the existence of a bitter history and memories of previous wars facilitate the process of securitization. As Japan and Germany have learned, such memories can obstruct the process of desecuritization even when well-established present political and military realities seem to pose no objective grounds for threat perception.

Political factors affect military threats in two ways: through the degree of recognition that exists between the actors and through harmonies and disharmonies in their political ideologies. In the case of the Cold War, historical enmities were largely absent, but the United States and the Soviet Union were locked into a zero-sum ideological conflict that served just as well to stimulate the process of securitization. The confrontations among democratic, fascist, and Communist powers during the 1930s had a similar quality, and the same dynamics can be found when religious divisions interact with military threats, as between Israel and the Arabs, India and Pakistan, Armenia and Azerbaijan, and within Bosnia.

Ideological divisions can operate in international systems when the political units continue to recognize each other as legal equals. But one does not have to look far back in history (or perhaps far ahead into the future) to find it accepted as normal that both states and peoples should regard each other in hierarchical terms, as superior and subordinate. In historical terms, the decades since the end of World War II represent a sharp break with historical practice. Decolonization made it necessary, at least for a time, to accept all states as legal equals and all peoples as equally human. The establishment of human rights means the human side of this equation will probably endure, but there are real questions as to whether a number of postcolonial states will be able to govern themselves well enough to sustain their status as equal members of international society. Some—such as Haiti, Somalia, Liberia, Bangladesh, and Cambodia—might already be slipping into a kind of mandate status, not as colonies but as dependents on the international community.

Differences in status make a difference to military threats. When one political unit does not recognize another as of equal status or, even worse, does not recognize its political status at all, a variety of significant restraints on the resort to force are removed. The process of securitization is correspondingly facilitated, because behavior by the other—which one would have to live with if it were a recognized state—can more easily be castigated as an unacceptable threat to, say, one's supplies of necessary goods or the security of one's citizens abroad. Relations between Europe and much of Asia had this unequal quality during the nineteenth century, a story told excellently by Gerrit Gong (1984).

Elements of this "standard of civilization" approach recently reappeared in Europe, when some post–Cold War successor states were confronted with conditions regarding democracy, human rights, and economic law before being accorded recognition. When a political unit is not recognized by others, its sociopolitical institutions are not considered to embody legitimacy, and its territory is considered politically empty and available for occupation. If, in addition, the people are not recognized by others as fully human, they risk being treated either like domesticated animals and so enslaved or like vermin and so eradicated. Some parts of the European expansion into the Americas, Africa, and Australia approached this extreme, as did Nazi policy against Jews and Slavs during World War II. Between the exterminations in Tasmania and parts of Africa and the Americas and the unequal treaties between Europe and such Asian countries as Japan, China, Siam, and Turkey lay a whole range of degrees of unequal treatment. Political and social recognition do not begin to guarantee freedom from military threat, but their absence makes military threats much more open to securitization (Buzan 1996).

Regionalizing Dynamics?

In the military sector, the end of the Cold War has caused a marked shift away from global-level security concerns and toward regional and local-level ones. A case can be made that the international system is emerging from a long period in which the regional level of military security had been suppressed. Initially, this suppression took the form of European and, later, Japanese and U.S. imperialism. Especially when imperialism was formal (as opposed to when it was informal), it largely replaced regional security dynamics with a system-level pattern of great-power relationships.

The Cold War played a major role in breaking down the formal imperial framework and in doing so freed the former colonial countries of the Third World to begin to find their own local patterns of regional military security relations. Part of the decolonization process was the diffusion of modern weapons to new states throughout the international system. At the same time, however, the extreme bipolarity of the Cold War also imposed overlay on some regions and heavy levels of outside pressure on, and intervention in, many others. During the Cold War, most regional security dynamics could not avoid strong interactions with the superpower rivalry.

The end of the Cold War can thus be seen as greatly reinforcing the liberation of regional military security dynamics begun by the process of decolonization.

In principle, three types of development can undermine the natural dominance of the regional level in military security in favor of the global level. The first occurs if military threats cease to matter in international relations, in which case all of the military sector would fade into the background and emphasis would shift relatively to the other sectors, some of which (especially the economic sector) are more globalized. The second occurs if military technology becomes so advanced and cost-effective that distance and geography cease to matter in the transmission of military threats, in which case the distinctive logic of regional security complexes would disappear. The third occurs if the concentration of power in the international system becomes so great that the regional level either ceases to exist (because all states are globally operating great powers or integrated regions) or ceases to matter (because the great powers overlay regional security complexes).

In the post–Cold War world, a case can be made that military threats are ceasing to matter in relations among the advanced industrial democracies. A substantial part of the international system, including most of its major centers of power, now lives in a pluralistic security community in which the members neither expect nor prepare to use force in their relations with each other. Opinion varies as to whether this is evidence for the "democracy and peace" or the "interdependence and peace" hypothesis or simply a result of historical war weariness and nuclear deterrence. Whichever is right, it has become undeniably more difficult and perhaps impossible to securitize military relations among these states.

In some regions, notably Western and Central Europe and North America, this development means the logic of mutual military threats has virtually ceased to exist within the region, replaced by a shared commitment to political means of conflict resolution and a displacement of security and rivalry to other sectors. At best, as sometimes in Europe, past memory is invoked as a future possibility to sustain commitment to the desecuritized arrangements. Except for a number of quasi-global regimes restricting the spread of weapons of mass destruction and their delivery systems, there is little sign that this development is about to become systemwide. Its principal effect is more on relations among the great powers at the global level than on the regional level. Some analysts (Goldgeier and McFaul 1992; Singer and Wildavsky 1993) characterize this development in terms of two worlds, one within which the military factor has largely been expunged from relations between states and the other in which it continues to operate in classical realist form—albeit lightly constrained by arms control regimes.

A case can also be made that distance and geography matter less than they used to in relations between states. In the economic realm, transportation costs have dropped virtually to zero, enabling goods to be produced competitively almost anywhere on the planet for consumption almost anywhere else. It was only a few hundred years ago that civilizations were able to exist in virtual political, social, and military isolation from each other because of the barriers posed by distance and geography.

Yet the present situation has little affected military relations for most states. A few great powers can deliver huge amounts of military power anywhere on the planet within a short period of time, and the combination of nuclear weapons and long-range missiles means distance and geography matter less in relations between the great powers. The proliferation of technologies of mass destruction (nuclear, chemical, and biological) and the means to deliver them (missiles) might indicate a more general move toward global capability, but if so that move is very slow and very partial. Most existing and potential nuclear weapons states (Britain, France, China, South Korea, Japan, Taiwan, India, Pakistan, Israel, Iran, and Iraq) have means of delivery confined largely to their own regions, thus reinforcing the regional military security dynamics. For the bulk of states, such weapons play no role in present status or future plans. For them, the reality remains that conventional forces are very much constrained by distance and that the regional logic of military security relations remains prime.

In terms of the concentration of power, the direction of events seems to be firmly away from any globalizing trend and toward the diffusion of power and regionalization of interaction. The era of European imperialism and the Cold War both represent versions of power concentration that were able to override the regional logic. Both of these eras have passed, and in going both have encouraged an underlying diffusion of military power. Most of the major centers of power are now rather inward looking, concerned with their own problems, and disinclined to use military power abroad either for expansion or for more than minor peacemaking efforts in local conflicts. They will use substantial force when their interests are threatened, as in the war against Iraq, but in general the major powers are not driven to use force abroad either by rivalry with each other or by internal pressures. They have become resistant to the appeal of military securitization.

It might be argued that the United States retains a unipolar military-technological superiority and level of expenditure so overwhelming as to sustain a centralizing trend. But although it is true in a technical sense, this fact is offset by the deep U.S. unwillingness to bear the costs or take the risks of using this power for any but a few select contingencies. The United States enjoys a kind of technical-military unipolarity, but U.S. aversion to casualties and entanglements marginalizes its impact on the other factors pushing toward regionalization. As Somalia demonstrated, most states and even some nonstates now have the capability to resist effectively any attempt at military occupation. Many are able to mount serious attacks on their neighbors. Although one might see the process of diffusion of power as leading eventually to a multipolar world of great powers, that outcome is still a long way away. In the military sector, for the near and middle-term future, current developments point away from globalization and toward regionalization. Some regimes are restraining the spread of weapons of mass destruction, but these are not watertight; in general, regional security dynamics are much freer to operate than they have been for a long time.

The introversion of the great powers is complemented by the diffusion of power to the regional states, few of which are constrained about securitizing their relations with their neighbors. This development should extend the process begun by decolonization of increasing the importance of regional security dynamics relative to that of the great powers. As military power diffuses in the system, intervention by outside great powers into regional conflicts becomes more difficult and costly. The war against Iraq illustrates this fact well. That war demonstrated U.S. military superiority, but the situation was far removed from the days when all great powers needed to do to intervene was to send a gunboat and a few troops. This same lesson can be taken from the U.S. experience in Vietnam and the Soviet one in Afghanistan. Thus, to the extent that bipolar conflict has disappeared and the concentration of power in the center is weakening, the current outlook should favor less competitive military intervention by the great powers in regional security affairs. Whether a lower weight of intervention will mute or exacerbate regional conflicts very much depends upon the circumstances conditioning securitization within the various regions.

The Cold War fostered a habit of superpower intervention in Third World military conflicts, both domestic and regional. Local powers appealed to the superpowers for support by trying to locate their own security concerns within the context of superpower rivalry. In turn, the United States and the Soviet Union defined *their* security in global terms. The Cold War facilitated the process of military securitization all around. The superpowers saw many local conflicts as expressions or extensions of their own rivalry, notably in the Middle East and Southeast Asia, and they frequently viewed the outcomes of such conflicts as significant indicators of success or failure in their own wider struggle. This meant they were willing to supply arms and support to local conflicts, often to balance the fear or perception that the other side was already doing so. On this basis, the two superpowers pumped vast resources into Third World conflicts, thereby increasing the scale, intensity, and duration of armed confrontations in many places.

It would be difficult to prove that the Cold War actually generated many conflicts in the Third World except in a few instances, such as the division of Korea. But it is easy to show how the United States and the

Soviet Union were drawn into local conflicts, with the consequence of synergy between the global and local security dynamics. The United States poured arms into Pakistan, South Vietnam, Israel, and Iran, whereas the Soviet Union did the same for India, North Vietnam, Syria, Egypt (up to 1972), and Iraq. Both sides poured arms into Somalia, Angola, Nicaragua, and Afghanistan. In the post–Cold War world, global-level military securitization will be much harder to achieve; consequently, this kind of military and political support will be much less readily available. Arms will still be plentiful from an expanding array of producers, but they will have to be paid for. And given the absence of ideological or strategic motivation, the major powers are unlikely to be easily moved to intervene directly in Third World conflicts, as they were in Vietnam and Afghanistan. Of the other great powers potentially capable of projecting significant military influence, neither the EU nor Japan has either the will or the constitutional capability to do so. Both are introverted, absorbed in their own problems, and extremely hesitant to resort to military means.

For all of these reasons, the end of the Cold War seems likely to bring greater freedom for the operation of local military security dynamics. This effect is easiest to illustrate in Europe, where decades of heavy superpower overlay virtually extinguished the natural (and historically very vigorous) operation of the European security complex. With the end of the Cold War, the implosion of Soviet power, and the weakening of U.S. engagement, the European states are once again faced with the necessity of sorting out their relations. Institutions such as the EU and NATO, which bind potential rivals into strong patterns of military integration and political cooperation, and the Organization for Security and Cooperation in Europe (OSCE) and Partnership for Peace (PFP), which provide security regimes as a first line of defense against the process of securitization, obviously make a huge difference in comparison with pre-1945, when no such barriers to securitization existed.

In Eastern Europe, an entire set of new or newly independent states are groping toward a pattern of security relations for which no historical precedent exists. In some parts of this huge region (the Caucasus, the Balkans, around Hungary, between Russia and the Ukraine, Central Asia), conflict dynamics are either active or in the offing (Buzan et al. 1990; Wæver et al. 1993, chapter 1). As the dust of the Soviet collapse settles, we could be looking at the formation of several new security complexes. Crucial to this process will be how well or how badly the EU handles the tensions of its integrative-disintegrative dynamics. Also crucial will be whether Russia succeeds in reasserting itself as the hegemonic player within the Commonwealth of Independent States (CIS) and whether the EU and the CIS conduct their relationship so as to create one integrated security region or two separate ones (Wæver 1996a). It is still an open question whether the EU and Russia will succeed in maintaining the desecuritization of their relationship that ended the Cold War or whether a process of resecuritization will gather strength.

The end of the Cold War also seems likely to have a sharp effect on regional security in East Asia. With the removal of Soviet power and the reduction of the U.S. presence, the states of this region are—for the first time in their modern history—facing the need to sort out their relations with each other largely free from the foreign presence that has dominated the area since the mid-nineteenth century. One possibility is that East Asia will turn into a balance-of-power regional system (Buzan 1994b; Buzan and Segal 1994; Dibb 1995; Buzan 1997). In many ways, the region resembles nineteenth-century Europe; it is a cluster of substantial powers packed together. Many of these are industrializing, with the result that nationalism is high and the distribution of power unstable. One large, centrally located, rapidly growing power threatens most of the others in a context in which nearly all of the states in the region have territorial, status, and historical disputes with their neighbors. Habits of cooperation are weak; historical memories are long, active, and mostly negative; and apart from ASEAN, regional institutions are remarkably underdeveloped. Modernization of armaments has been proceeding apace, and many of the states in the region could quickly become nuclear powers if the need arose.

Military relations between the two Koreas and the two Chinas are already acutely securitized. Under these conditions, other relations could easily become securitized. All that stands against such a process are strong domestic resistance to it in Japan (which ironically could increase the threat others perceive from China), a few rather feeble-looking transregional institutions (the ASEAN Regional Forum and the Asia-Pacific Economic Cooperation), and a shared interest in maintaining the momentum of economic development. There is a curious duality to the security discourse in this region, with much rhetoric about cooperative security (i.e., desecuritization) on the one hand (and some real cooperative measures, as in ASEAN) combined with blunt and regular expressions of fear and hatred, as when Chinese and South Korean leaders jointly recall Japanese wartime atrocities in public.

Europe and East Asia stand out, because the overlay effects of the Cold War on their regional dynamics were extreme. The release of those effects has inevitably had strong local consequences. The effect of the end of the Cold War has generally been less dramatic in the Third World than in Europe and East Asia, but the principle is the same: A much weakened superpower presence leaves more room for local security dynamics to take their own shape and to operate more on the basis of local resources, issues, and perceptions. The consequences of this greater regional security autonomy are by no means uniform. In some areas, the superpower withdrawal seems to have facilitated desecuritization; in others, it seems to have unleashed higher levels of local securitization.

The main beneficiaries of this autonomy appear to be Southeast Asia, the Middle East, and Southern Africa. In all three of these regions, the end of the Cold War has coincided with substantial desecuritization and a move toward the settlement of the issues underlying conflict. In the Middle East, the loss or weakening of superpower sponsorship helped Israel and the Arabs come to the negotiating table. In Southern Africa and Southeast Asia, the collapse of ideological conflict at the center has undercut parallel confrontations at the periphery and has thus facilitated dialogue and conflict resolution at the local level. The anti-Communist stance of the South African government and the Communist affiliations of the African National Congress (ANC) lost much of their significance when the Soviet Union disintegrated. Settlements were facilitated in Namibia and Mozambique; although the settlement in Angola succumbed to local rivalries, that conflict is no longer supported by ideologically motivated external arms supplies and interventions. Similarly, in Southeast Asia, Vietnam's loss of Soviet ideological and military support encouraged it to move toward membership in ASEAN. ASEAN, for its part, sees the significance of its connection to the United States declining and is aware of the need to create a more coherent regional regime to deal with expanding Chinese power.

The main losers from the post–Cold War release of regional security dynamics are the Caucasus, the Balkans, and Central Asia. In all three of these regions, the collapse of Soviet power has unleashed intense processes of securitization and local conflicts over territory, population, and status. Active wars have occurred both between states (Croatia and Serbia, Armenia and Azerbaijan) and within them (Bosnia, Georgia, Tadjikistan, Russia). Even where wars have been avoided, the security dilemma is often strong, and military-political tensions exist that could easily lead to war. Numerous minority problems and many unresolved border disputes exist in all three regions. In Central Asia, strong potential exists for disputes over water resources in the river systems that focus on the Aral Sea. In the Balkans, the status of some new states—notably Bosnia and Macedonia—is still in question with their neighbors, as is the ultimate relationship between both the Albanian and Serbian and the Croatian and Serbian states and their respective nations. Between Eastern Europe and the Caucasus lies the simmering possibility of rivalry between Russia and the Ukraine. The resources for successful securitization are plentiful and the restraints against it far from overwhelming.

In other Third World regions, the effect of freer regional security dynamics is as yet difficult to call. In both South Asia and the Gulf, long-standing patterns of rival military securitization continue much as before. India and Pakistan have lost their superpower allies and supporters; unless

Pakistan can compensate by strengthening its Islamic or Chinese connections, over time this development should favor the naturally greater military weight of India. Should it do so, a shift to explicit postures of nuclear deterrence in the region will become more likely. In the Gulf, external intervention still plays a strong role in the wake of the war against Iraq. The interest of outside powers in oil resources is likely to make this area one in which continued great-power involvement can be guaranteed. Nevertheless, the basic regional security dynamics among Iraq, Iran, and Saudi Arabia look set to continue, and here, too, the threat of nuclearization exists, although probably not on as short a timescale as is possible in South Asia.

For the most part, interstate relations in Latin America were not heavily affected by the Cold War and, except for Cuba, are little affected by its demise. Serious wars among Latin American states have been rare, although military rivalries and tensions have been somewhat common, as has the use of force in domestic politics. To the extent that the current democratization in the region is a product of the end of the Cold War (because of the weakening of the anti-Communist justification for authoritarianism), Latin America is probably a beneficiary, enjoying a significant and sustained trend of desecuritization. In the longer run, however, the question is still open about what kind of international relations will develop in this region. On the one hand, there are firm signs of moves toward a regional security regime, as indicated, inter alia, by the regional nuclear weapons–free zone and the significant desecuritizing moves between Argentina and Brazil. On the other hand, Brazil still harbors a strong image of itself as a great power, and the region contains many territorial disputes and status rivalries that periodically generate the process of securitization. Either trend could dominate in an international environment that favors the operation of regional security dynamics.

In Africa, other than the southern subregion, the immediate military effect of the end of the Cold War is fairly small, and the longer-term effect is unclear. The new South Africa and its neighbors have undergone a process of desecuritization as profound as that in Europe and are well advanced in turning what was a zone of confrontation into a southern African regional security regime. But most other states in Africa are weak, and some seem to be disintegrating. Security problems are often more domestic than interstate, and spillovers from domestic conflicts are more significant than international wars. Except in the Horn of Africa, no strong patterns of regional military security interdependence have emerged. One can see possible beginnings in the Economic Community of West African States (ECOWAS) intervention in Liberia, the Tanzanian intervention in Uganda, and the interplay of internal instabilities in Rwanda, Burundi, Zaire, and Uganda; over time, these may evolve into regional security complexes. In most of Africa, as in Latin America, the main impact of the Cold War and of its end was on domestic rather than international politics.

Great-power engagement in Africa's conflicts was, with few exceptions, never large. Post–Cold War, it will probably be even more minimal, as the disengagement of the Soviet Union and, to a lesser extent, France from the region attests. Many domestic conflicts in Africa were largely ignored by the international community during the Cold War, and as the recent tragedies in Liberia, Sierra Leone, Rwanda, and Somalia suggest, this policy will probably continue. Interstate regional security dynamics in Africa are weak, because few states are capable of projecting much force beyond their own boundaries. Africa is potentially a morass of territorial and population disputes, like the former Yugoslavia on a huge scale. The nature of the issues and the limits of power available to local actors suggest the possibility of numerous microcomplexes rather than the larger regional patterns one finds in areas where stronger states and powers prevail.

Military security in Africa will very much depend upon what Africans make of the strange sociopolitical legacy the combination of their own cultural patterns and the colonial impositions of the Europeans has left them (Buzan 1994a). Only in the Balkans, the Caucasus, and perhaps Central Asia does one find conditions similar to those prevailing in much of Africa. The danger is not of external intervention but of the international community simply ignoring these places. The abortive humanitarian interventions in Somalia and Rwanda and perhaps Bosnia will act as a deterrent to intervention in subsequent collapses of domestic political order elsewhere.

In places such as these, where weak states totter toward collapse, there is a real possibility that the diffusion in military security away from the global level will not stop at the regional level but will unravel all the way down to the local one. This scenario, captured powerfully by Robert Kaplan (1994), is already visible in places such as Bosnia, Somalia, Liberia, Colombia, Afghanistan, Tadjikistan, Sudan, and Sierra Leone, where failed states are opening the way for gangs, clans, and mafias. For the peoples involved, such developments mean military (in)security becomes a paramount feature of daily life, which takes on many features of a Hobbesian anarchy. Such political failures are extremely difficult and costly to remedy from outside, and they can gain support from the internationally organized mafias that are the dark side of increasing economic liberalization and that can make good use of areas that lack effective state control.

This localizing dynamic can be seen as part of a much wider process in which increasing liberalization is weakening state structures everywhere and pushing individuals toward more "tribalist" forms of association (Horsman and Marshall 1995). Where states are strong and societies well developed and relatively cohesive, such weakening may be manageable. But where states are weak and societies poorly developed and fragmented, the real danger exists that the localizing of military security will corrode most of the foundations of political order. Substantial areas of Africa and the Middle East, as well as some parts of Asia and Latin America, have the potential to drift toward this fate, including some significant countries such as Nigeria and Zaire. Should such tendencies develop, they would result in the unstable microcomplexes of a primal anarchy.

Summary

States and would-be states have traditionally been, and largely remain, the primary referent objects for military security. Protecting the territorial integrity of the state is the traditional object of military security, and the two immediate environments for the state—regional and domestic—are again the main concerns in this sector. Most of the subsystems found in this sector are geographically coherent and thus constitute security complexes. Some alliances and regional organizations and some general principles of international society also have some status as referent objects in this sector. When states disintegrate, lesser units emerge as the primary carriers of military (in)security. As a rule, there is little ambiguity about securitizing actors in the military sector. Relative and absolute military capabilities do not determine securitization, although they can facilitate it. Geographical, historical, and political factors also shape the process of securitization. Once securitization has taken root, military security relations can fall into well-understood patterns of action and reaction.

After a long period in which the global level has dominated this sector, a clear shift is now underway toward primacy for regional military security dynamics. In some cases, this has muted regional conflicts; in other cases, it has exacerbated them. In a few regions, processes of desecuritization have largely eliminated the military security dilemma among local states. In regions dominated by weak or failed states, real prospects exist that the local level will become dominant, with securitization forming microregions. To the list of microregions we should perhaps add the Hobbesian anarchies in some inner cities of megalopolises. When political authority breaks down, inter alia, the distinction between police and military dissolves.

The main conclusion is that the military sector is still dominated by regional security dynamics but with an increased prospect for local dynamics in weak states—that is, regional security complexes and microcomplexes. Open to further research is the question of whether these microcomplexes will link up to form a major disruption of the international system as such—to create holes, as it were, in the fabric of international society (Kaplan 1994; de Wilde 1995). But in general, the logic of classical security complex theory remains substantially valid for this sector.

CHAPTER 4

The Environmental Sector

The Environmental Security Agenda

Some analysts describe environmental security as "ultimate security" (Myers 1993a), others as a pollution of security proper (Deudney 1990). Most others oscillate somewhere in between.[1] Some scholars filter environmental security through a political and military lens (Homer-Dixon 1991), others perceive it as a social welfare issue (as reflected, e.g., in Article 130R of the Treaty of the European Union). In the study of international relations, moreover, the environment seems to be a welcome garden for case studies in regime theory (Haas, Keohane, and Levy 1993). But attempts to securitize environmental values have a very short history compared to what can be seen with regard to the other four sectors we discuss. The discourses, power struggles, and securitizing moves in the other sectors are reflected by and have sedimented over time in concrete types of organizations—notably states (in terms of Tilly 1990, the product of sword and capital), nations (identity configurations), and the UN system. It is as yet undetermined what kinds of political structures environmental concerns will generate. So far, epistemic communities, social movements, governmental departments, and international organizations have emerged from the environmental discourse, but whether these groups represent just the beginning or the pinnacle of this development is hard to say—especially given the fluctuations in environmental threat perceptions.

This discourse has been manifest only since the United Nations Conference on the Human Environment in 1972. More than twenty years later, it has gained enough momentum to turn the environment into a lens through which to observe politics. There is even a new professional journal called *Environment and Security.* We are not arguing that the environment (or any of the other sectors) *should* be securitized; we merely observe that at least some actors are attempting to do so.

One of the most striking features of the environmental sector is the existence of two different agenda: a scientific agenda and a political agenda. Although they overlap and shape each other in part, the scientific agenda is typically embedded in the (mainly natural) sciences and nongovernmental activity. It is constructed outside the core of politics, mainly by scientists and research institutions, and offers a list of environmental problems that already or potentially hamper the evolution of present civilizations. The political agenda is essentially governmental and intergovernmental. It consists of the public decisionmaking process and public policies that address how to deal with environmental concerns. As such, the political agenda reflects the overall degree of politicization and securitization (as contrasted with private securitizing and desecuritizing moves). The two agenda overlap in the media and in public debates. Ultimately, the scientific agenda underpins securitizing moves, whereas the political agenda is about three areas: (1) state and public awareness of issues on the scientific agenda (how much of the scientific agenda is recognized by policymakers, their electorates, and their intermediaries—the press); (2) the acceptance of political responsibility for dealing with these issues; and (3) the political management questions that arise: problems of international cooperation and institutionalization—in particular regime formation, the effectiveness of unilateral national initiatives, distribution of costs and benefits, free-rider dilemmas, problems of enforcement, and so forth.

Obviously, the scientific agenda—like the political one—is a social construct, albeit a different one. The scientific agenda is about the authoritative assessment of threat for securitizing or desecuritizing moves, whereas the political agenda deals with the formation of concern in the public sphere about these moves and the allocation of collective means by which to deal with the issues raised.

A very practical argument favors this distinction. If a politician or a civilian is told by a specialist or a group of respected scientists that the oceans are overfished, the hole in the ozone layer will cause widespread skin cancer, and population growth is exceeding the carrying capacity of the earth, he or she has no reason to question this report (apart from general healthy skepticism). Two years later, if new investigations point to opposite conclusions, again the individual has no choice but to follow those conclusions (or to dismiss them for secondary reasons). The general public can do no more than trust or mistrust the professionals and make its political choices on that intuitive basis.

This is true for all of the sectors under consideration, but the extent to which scientific argument structures environmental security debates strikes us as exceptional. The particular difficulty in dealing with the cumulative global effects of local developments, as well as in many cases threat assessment within a time frame beyond present generations, causes this specific form of dependence upon scientific authority. According to James Rosenau, the demand for scientific proof is a broader emerging characteristic in the international system: "Questions of evidence and proof have become organising foci of global controversies" (1989: 36; see also Rosenau 1990: 425–429). Given the relatively recent emergence of the environment as a politicized set of values, one may expect this process to be comparatively strong in this sector. This view is consistent with the "epistemic communities approach," which is based on the assumption that state actors are not only pursuers of power and wealth but are also "uncertainty reducers" (Haas 1992). Faced with the complexity of an international system in which many processes are beyond the control of individual governments, the urgency to decrease uncertainty about the effectiveness of policy initiatives has risen. This situation has enhanced the prestige and power of epistemic communities, particularly because most of them are transnational in scope and hence are able to accumulate knowledge not easily available to government departments.

Despite an obvious overlap and interdependence, the two agenda follow different cycles. The scientific agenda must meet academic standards (again, however arbitrary these may be). The political agenda can be shaped by governmental, media, and public standards, which are influenced much more by short-term events. Critical for the political agenda is not whether specific threats to the environment are real or speculative but whether their *presumed urgency* is a political issue. Such securitizing moves will often be dominated by immediate threats to the environment—the Chernobyl-type lessons (de Wilde 1994). Additionally, the political agenda deals with more substantial parts of the scientific agenda, as was seen during the UN Conference on Environment and Development (UNCED), 1992. The impact of this agenda is often less visible, because environmental considerations have entered a variety of intergovernmental negotiations and national policymaking practices. In the early phases of regime development, for example, scientific actors tend to play a particularly important role in agenda setting. These actors are often involved in both science and politics: for example, scientists who are attentive to political logic—for instance, who are aware of the necessity to develop scientific consensus positions—but who are also obliged to avoid being stabbed in the back scientifically. Typically, these actors will link up with political actors who have specialized in relating to the field of science; thus, a chain forms from science to politics without the two having to meet in their pure forms (Skodvin 1994).

It should be emphasized that the political agenda does not only address the more sensational, emotional manifestations of environmental issues but has also become a part of ordinary politics. Political parties, departments, and many firms must formulate environmental policies as a part of their ordinary activities, regardless of whether they believe in them. This situation constitutes politicization rather than securitization. As long as environmental concerns fall outside established economic and political practices and routines, their advocates tend to—and probably must—overemphasize the overwhelming importance of those values and issues. Many securitizing moves can be found in the reports that bridge both agenda, ranging from the Club of Rome reports to the work of the Brundtland Commission. These reports present Silent Spring–type lessons (de Wilde 1994; Carson 1962): It is not the actual disasters but their prediction that leads to securitization. Concepts such as *resource scarcity* and *sustainability* have successfully mobilized public concern. When picked up by governments and firms, however, these concerns are often merely politicized; they constitute a sub-agenda within the larger political context. The environmental sector displays more clearly than any other the propensity for dramatic securitizing moves but with comparatively little successful securitization effects (i.e., those that lead to extraordinary measures). This finding points to the unsettled standing of the environmental discourse as such within public debate.

Priorities within the two agenda are not always clear. Disagreement exists over what type of concerns have to be politicized and what issues require immediate, extraordinary investments to turn the tides. Obviously, concrete disasters (such as Chernobyl and Bhopal) dictate action to make sure they will never happen again. In general, geographic location and level of welfare play decisive roles in determining the issue ranking on both agenda. Governments in poor countries tend to perceive industrial environmental policies as a luxury, an add-on dimension of regular economic policies, something they cannot afford (MacNeill, Winsemius, and Yakushiji 1991). People upstream on a river may perceive a new source of political power in the ability to control the quantity and quality of the water supply downstream, as with Turkey's potential clout over Iraq and Syria because it controls the headwaters of the Euphrates (Schulz 1995). Other states may discover and accept their interdependence of a common water resource, as did the members of the nineteenth-century Rhine and Danube River commissions. Similarly, within national societies the price of taking up the scientific agenda is distributed rather unevenly: For example, the scientific agenda on fishery management is less likely to convert traditional fishing communities throughout Europe than it is to convert white-collar workers in Brussels.

The environmental sector is made complicated by its great variety of issues. In the literature that draws up the scientific agenda, several partly overlapping key issues reappear (de Wilde 1994: 161; compare also the agenda presented in MacNeill, Winsemius, and Yakushiji 1991: 131, and Böge 1992). This is the widest formulation of the environmental agenda and therefore includes issues the present study deals with primarily in other sectors.

- *Disruption of ecosystems* includes climate change; ioss of biodiversity; deforestation, desertification, and other forms of erosion; depletion of the ozone layer; and various forms of pollution.
- *Energy problems* include the depletion of natural resources, such as fuel wood; various forms of pollution, including management disas-

ters (related in particular to nuclear energy, oil transportation, and chemical industries); and scarcities and uneven distribution.

- *Population problems* include: population growth and consumption beyond the earth's carrying capacity; epidemics and poor health conditions in general; declining literacy rates; and politically and socially uncontrollable migrations, including unmanageable urbanization.
- *Food problems* include poverty, famines, overconsumption, and diseases related to these extremes; loss of fertile soils and water resources; epidemics and poor health conditions in general; and scarcities and uneven distribution.
- *Economic problems* include the protection of unsustainable production modes, societal instability inherent in the growth imperative (which leads to cyclical and hegemonic breakdowns), and structural asymmetries and inequity.
- *Civil strife* includes war-related environmental damage on the one hand and violence related to environmental degradation on the other.

Obviously, not every publication on environmental security deals with all of these topics, and not all of them are permanently subject to securitization. It is also unclear that a consensus exists regarding this comprehensive list. "Disruption of ecosystems" is the most purely environmental issue area. The other items on this agenda overlap with the agenda of other sectors, but here they are viewed through an environmental lens. Western-oriented agenda put more emphasis on the role of population issues; Southern-oriented agenda put more emphasis on the role of economic issues. Gareth Porter and Janet Brown (1991) are probably right in arguing that both population growth and economic activity fall at the bottom of the entire agenda.

Security Actors and Referent Objects

On the face of it, the environment as such, or some strategic part of the environment, is the referent object of environmental security. This is the implicit view of many Greens, which is seen in the presentation of lists of urgent issues meant to enter the realm of high politics (Lodgaard 1992; Myers 1993a). Yet in much of the debate another concern can be detected: a concern for the preservation of existing levels of civilization. In this view, the ultimate referent object of environmental security is *the risk of losing achieved levels of civilization—a return to forms of societal barbarism— while apparently being able to prevent doing so.*

The environmental security debate has taken over from the anti–

nuclear weapon lobby this concern about the loss of civilization, a shift registered in the cinema by the move from postnuclear war (*Mad Max*) to postenvironmental apocalypse (*Waterworld*) barbarism. But the debate moves beyond this Northern middle-class Hollywood perspective. The referent object applies to every achieved level of civilization, whether northern elite, middle class, or Amazon Indian. The concern in all cases is whether the ecosystems that are crucial to preserve (or further develop) the achieved level of civilization are sustainable. Implicitly, this concern forms the deeper motive behind many, although not all, environmental debates. At stake is the maintenance of achieved levels of civilization, including a development perspective free of environmental disasters. In short, environmental security "concerns the maintenance of the local and the planetary biosphere as the essential support system on which all other human enterprises depend" (Buzan 1991: 19–20).

It is in relation to this ultimate referent object (human enterprise) that a paradox arises similar to that inherent in the classic security dilemma in an anarchic system: The only way to secure societies from environmental threats is to change them. In the twentieth century, civilization—simply perceived as a process of spiral progress from the Stone Age to the present—has reached potentially self-defeating forms. This is true for civilization writ large and particularly for various small, local communities in their immediate environment.

It is important to note that in this reading of it, environmental security is *not* about threats to nature or to "Mother Earth" as such. From a geological point of view, no problem even exists: The earth has been in its place for billions of years, and what has been happening on its crust since, say, the Industrial Revolution is rather unimportant. Also, for the crust itself a nuclear winter, global warming, a hole in the ozone layer, the disappearance of dinosaurs, and the future marginalization of human beings are relatively meaningless events.

Thus, in the environmental sector two different kinds of referent objects represent two wings within the environmental movement: the environment itself and the nexus of civilization and environment. So far, these wings have coexisted in coalition. It is worth noting, however, that by definition the coalition is not harmonious. Especially when it involves the protection of endangered species—like elephants, whales, and rhinos—those who have the environment as such in mind collide with those who put the security of human enterprise at the top.

Consensus does exist, however, about the underlying problem: Human enterprise is not merely determined by environmental conditions but is also conditioning the environment itself. Awareness of this fact is relatively recent. Instead of a one-way, linear causal relationship between structural environmental conditions and likely policy options (classical geopolitics), a dynamic, interdependent relationship exists between environment and politics: Civilization is held responsible for part of its own structural environmental conditions, which limit or enlarge its development options and influence incentives for cooperation and conflict.

A high degree of controversy surrounds environmental issues. In addition to securitizing actors are actors who oppose securitizing moves by either contesting or ignoring the attempt to prioritize a threat. Of course, this might also be said for the military sector, where peace movements sometimes try either to debunk state moves toward securitization (by denying the validity of the threat) or to turn the state against itself (by pointing to the securitization itself as the threat—e.g., in generating arms races or raising the risk of war). But in the environmental sector, the security status of issues has only recently been asserted and, lacking any depth of social sedimentation, is much more vulnerable to such countermoves. Porter and Brown (1991) have captured this concept using the idea of *lead actors, veto actors,* and *veto coalitions.* (Their exact term is veto *states,* but they also apply that term to firms and other functional actors.) These categories embody both political and security moves, but they do give useful insight into the security actors in this sector.

Lead actors have a strong commitment to effective international action on an environmental issue in specific cases. These actors may be states. Australia, for example, took the lead in regime formation for Antarctica. Sweden and Norway pushed international action on transboundary air pollution, especially acid rain. Related to the scientific agenda, however, the lead actor is not a state but a global, environmental epistemic community (Haas 1992) that investigates the urgency of a wide range of environmental subjects, constructs an agenda, and communicates that agenda to the press and political elites. It is worthwhile to consider this loose "community" as an independent political force in this sector, because its members have proved able to exert major political influence. For the political agenda, the distinctive lead actors are activist and lobbying nongovernmental organizations (NGOs), of which Greenpeace and the World Wildlife Fund are among the most outstanding examples. Securitizing the environment is their trade.

Porter and Brown (1991: 36–37) distinguish several strategies for lead actors, in particular the states among them. They might raise awareness of an issue by financing research and informing public opinion in target states (i.e., mobilizing the scientific agenda). For this purpose, they can make use of the environmental epistemic community to support their position abroad. These actors may take unilateral action (lead by example), or they may use diplomacy to put the issue on the agenda of international organizations or to isolate veto actors. In most cases, however, these initiatives cannot be called securitizing moves; they constitute politicization. This is characteristic of the entire practice of environmental regime formation in the international system.

Veto actors can also take the form of NGOs, such as industrial and agricultural lobbies (e.g., the U.S.-based Global Climate Coalition) that try to play down environmental issues, but the main actors are states and firms. Obviously, the veto power of states and firms is different, because the latter lack formal sovereignty rights. But they may have actual veto power because of monopolies or quasi-monopolies on technological knowledge and implementation or effective lobbying, winning states for their positions.

Lead or veto positions tend to be issue specific. Environmental politics are therefore not ruled by fixed hegemonic power structures or balance-of-power structures. The positions are strategic: Japan is a leading blocking state in the veto coalition in relation to whaling; "Brazil, India, and China could block an international agreement on climate change by refusing to curb the use of fossil fuels in their own development programs" (Porter and Brown 1991: 17). In the 1950s and 1960s, international shipping—organized as the International Chamber of Shipping and the International Marine Forum—and the Seven Sisters first blocked and then determined the content of environmental regimes on maritime (oil) pollution. During the 1970s and 1980s, international action on ozone protection was blocked by the 19 chlorofluorocarbon (CFC)-producing chemical companies, especially Du Pont (25 percent of world production), Allied Chemical, Imperial Chemical Industries (ICI), and Great Lakes Chemical (Porter and Brown 1991: 65–66; Benedick 1991). Similarly, veto actors can be identified in relation to biodiversity (e.g., states and companies involved in the exploitation of tropical forests), acid rain (industries with high emissions of sulphur dioxide and nitrogen oxide), river pollution (upstream states and companies), and even population growth, where the policies of specific states (China, Indonesia, and India in particular) may make a difference.

Geopolitically, one might expect veto actors to operate around the physical sources of environmental problems. They can be determined geographically and functionally, whether the home ports of fishing fleets, the location of unsafe nuclear reactors, or the workplace of firms logging tropical forests. Leading actors are generally found on or close to troubled areas—the areas affected by environmental degradation. Direct victims of degradation can be expected to be found in the front lines (for example, Sweden and Norway over acid rain)—provided they are not occupied with more imminent threats to their existence.

When victims lack the resources to lead (as is true for most developing countries), they are likely to be *support actors*. Leading actors, and support actors even more so, are not by definition located at the danger spots. Especially when the issue is global (such as ozone depletion), economic (as with the demand side of the tropical forest issue), or moral (such as whaling), these actors can be found anywhere—although this generally means in countries that can afford to put energy into remote problems and in which people are free to do so. Because of the issue-specific nature of these positions, they have (so far) not cumulated in overall power constellations. Nor have environmental values (yet) become a conscious ordering device for society as a whole in the way military, economic, and identity interests have done.

As with the military sector, the environmental one is rich in functional actors. One large category is economic actors (transnational corporations [TNCs]; state firms; agricultural, chemical, and nuclear industries; fishing; mining; and the like), whose activity is directly linked to the quality of the environment. These are functional actors whose behavior affects ecosystems but who generally do not intend to politicize, let alone securitize, this activity. Their common denominator is that they are large-scale economic actors, generally motivated by profit making. They exploit ecosystems to build or maintain the human habitat. Much of the environmental debate is concerned with how these actors operate. What are the acceptable types and limits of exploitation? Can one find sustainable forms, living from nature's interest (and if possible increasing that interest) rather than spending its capital? This places these actors in the spotlight of environmental security debates, often in a negative sense.

Another set of functional actors is composed of governments and their agencies and also some IGOs. Governments set the environmental rules for economic actors and determine how well (or how badly) these rules are enforced. They allow some institutionalization of environmental security concerns by forming (sub)departments of environmental affairs, creating IGOs such as the United Nations Environment Program (UNEP), developing international law, and adding new tasks to existing IGOs such as, for example, the FAO and the World Bank (White 1996, Chap. 10). But governments and their agencies also share some of the roles and responsibilities of economic actors. Also in relation to military functions, they are major exploiters of the environment in such activities as nuclear testing; military exercises; nuclear, chemical, and biological weapons production; dumping of surplus weapons and retired naval vessels; and the like.

The Logic of Threats and Vulnerabilities

In principle, three relationships of threat define the possible universe of environmental security.

1. Threats to human civilization from the natural environment that are not caused by human activity. Earthquake and volcanic events count (although even here there are debates about human agency), but the most incontrovertible examples are fears of large meteorite strikes and concerns about a natural swing back into a cycle of extensive glaciation.

2. Threats from human activity to the natural systems or structures of the planet when the changes made *do* seem to pose existential threats to (parts of) civilization. Obvious examples here are, at the global level, greenhouse gas emissions and the effects of CFCs and other industrial emissions on the ozone layer. At the regional and local levels, this relates to environmental exploitation (by extraction, dumping, or accidental destruction) beyond the carrying capacity of smaller ecosystems, which upsets the economic base and social fabric of the states involved.

3. Threats from human activity to the natural systems or structures of the planet when the changes made *do not* seem to pose existential threats to civilization. An example of this might be the depletion of various mineral resources, which may be inconvenient but which can almost certainly be handled by advances in technology (i.e., the shift from copper to silicon in the electronics industry and potentially a shift from metal to ceramics in some engineering applications).

The last of these relationships registers little in the discourse of environmental security, with the notable exception of concerns over the extinction of various animals (especially birds and large mammals). The first does register but only at the margins. It could grow if the scientific agenda provides more compelling reasons to worry about it or if those securitizing actors that have an interest in it (e.g., the space defense lobby) become more influential.

The second relationship is the main reason to talk about environmental security: It represents a circular relationship of threat between civilization and the environment in which the process of civilization involves a manipulation of the rest of nature that in several respects has achieved self-defeating proportions. From a global perspective, this circular relationship is mainly the result of two developments: the explosive growth of both the world population and economic activity in the second half of the twentieth century. During the last 2,000 years, world population increased from an estimated hundred million to about 6 billion. In the 10,000 years before that, world population grew from a mere 4 million to a hundred million (Ponting 1991: 90, 92, 241; Porter and Brown 1991: 4). Between 1960 and 1990, the estimated gross world product almost quadrupled, from about $6 trillion to almost $20 trillion (Porter and Brown 1991: 5). Ideas for integrating environmental concerns into economic accounting are fairly new (van Dieren 1987) but are being pushed by the rise in pollution statistics in the late twentieth century.

Crucial for understanding environmental security is the idea that it is within human power to turn the tide. The problem is one of humankind's struggle not with nature but with the dynamics of its own cultures—a civilizational issue that expresses itself mainly in economic and demographic dimensions and that potentially affects the degrees of order in the international system and its subsystems.

This basic principle of population concentration and the concentration of economic activity straining or exceeding the existing carrying capacity of ecosystems is foundational at all levels of analysis, not just the global level. Urbanization, for example, is typically related to local problems of overpopulation, pollution is typically related to local industrial problems, and soil erosion is typically related to combined small-scale economic and population pressures.

At first sight, there seems to be more room for natural hazards of the first type of threat: Nature threatens civilization, and this is securitized. Many societies are structurally exposed to recurring extreme natural events, such as earthquakes, volcanoes, cyclones, floods, droughts, and epidemics.[2] They are vulnerable to these events, and much of their history is about this continuous struggle with nature. The risks involved are often explicitly securitized and institutionalized. In the Netherlands, for example, protection against the sea and flooding rivers is a high-ranking national interest; the same goes for protection against earthquakes in Japan.

As soon as some form of securitization or politicization occurs, however—that is, when some measure of human responsibility replaces the role of fate or God—even this group of conflicts tends to develop a social character (the second type of threat). Following the river floods in the low countries in 1995, the debate in the Netherlands was about political responsibility for the dikes: Who was to blame, and what should be done? In Japan, following the Kobe earthquake in early 1995, designers of seismological early warning systems and of construction techniques, as well as governmental civil emergency plans, were under fire. Where the means to handle natural threats are thought to exist, the security logic works less against nature than against the failure of the human systems seen as responsible. Moreover, with links suspected between human activities and "natural" catastrophes, the distinction between natural and manmade hazards is becoming blurred. Therefore, except for cases in which people undergo natural hazards without any question, the logic that environmental security is about "threats without enemies" (Prins 1993) is often misleading.

The basic logic of environmental security is that in a global perspective, humankind is living beyond the carrying capacity of the earth. In local and regional circumstances, this condition is often even more manifest. The exact meaning of the concept *carrying capacity* is disputed, but for the present context it can be defined as the total patterns of consumption the earth's natural systems can support without undergoing degradation (cf. Ehrlich 1994). These patterns of consumption involve several variables, such as total population, production modes, and gross per capita consumption levels. In short, carrying capacity depends on numbers, technology, and lifestyle. Compare also the notorious E=PAT equation (Environmental degradation = Population x Affluence x type of Technology), which, despite criticism of its operational value, still captures the three main elements of the environmental security agenda. One billion Westerners is enough to tilt the system; around 4 billion people in low-income economies will do the same.[3] The limits-to-growth scenarios (Meadows, Meadows, and Randers 1992; Meadows et al. 1972) tried to reveal the critical breaking points for the earth's carrying capacity for each combination of trends in these variables.

The security debate addresses the reliability of such predictions (Meadows's work, for example, is widely contested), the prevention of breaking points, and measures to reduce vulnerabilities in case prevention fails. The ultimate question is whether there are civilized ways out of the problems created by civilization. How will people adapt to the new constraints of their environment? So far, two debates about threats and vulnerabilities have arisen in response. Both are substantially affected by a lack of knowledge of the actual levels and probabilities of threat and of what measures might reasonably be taken.

The first debate is about the economic-liberal case that questions whether we should do anything. *The Economist* (1–7 April 1995) argues for discounting the future to avoid huge, perhaps unnecessary economically disruptive expenditures in the present. The argument here is to let the future (with its presumably greater resources and more knowledge) take care of itself. Critics call this unlimited faith in the skills of future generations to deal with problems created here and now "the myth of the techno-fix" (Smith, Okoyo, de Wilde, and Deshingkar 1994).

The second debate takes the form of a powerful agenda for the periphery against the center (the West), and many studies treat it as such (e.g., WCED 1987; Adams 1990; MacNeill, Winsemius, and Yakushiji 1991; Myers 1993a, 1993b [1984]; Williams 1993; Smith, Okoyo, de Wilde, and Deshingkar 1994). The time seems ripe for a neo–New International Economic Order (NIEO) debate in North-South relations. The asymmetries and inequities in the economic, political, and military sectors—legitimized by the global dominance of Western values—mirror the structures of poverty and affluence that, for different reasons, cause progressive deterioration of the environment. The local variant of this debate is about the domestic balance of interests among elite, middle class, and poor and their respective burdening of the environment.

It should be noted that a major difference in these debates involves whether one discusses causes or effects. The essence of the environmental lobby is to deal with causes—attempts to change society by coordinated effort before nature changes it through disaster. Although this policy involves many securitizing moves, it primarily results in politicization only. In terms of politicizing causes, much is happening, but most of the threats are too distant to lead to securitization. Environmental issues often point to an unspecified, relatively remote future and therefore involve no panic politics. It is assumed that it hardly matters whether we act now or next year; therefore, "urgency" becomes reappropriated as a part of "normal politics." This, of course, is exactly what radical environmentalists question. They argue that taking action is literally an urgent matter, and their rhetoric is definitely one of securitization: It will soon be too late, we *have* to act even when we must take unpleasant steps that would normally be totally outside the acceptable spectrum, because the nature of the threat demands this.

Generally, however, "emergency measures" are still designed and developed in the realm of ordinary policy debates. Especially when we look at regime formation (at the global and regional levels) or at the work of departments of environmental affairs (at the local level), it is difficult to label this work as securitization. Obviously, environmental NGOs such as Greenpeace try to securitize causes as well as effects. Institutes like World Watch Institute do the same in a somewhat more sophisticated manner. Especially intergovernmental organizations such as the Alliance of Small Island States (AOSIS) have manifest reasons to view environmental issues in terms of existential threats, although overall they have achieved little more than politicization.

When crises force the debate to change from one about causes to one about effects, the focus of securitization tends to move into other sectors. Once the AOSIS states have actually been swallowed by a sea-level rise, it is no longer useful to try to securitize the environmental dimension of their problems: The issue becomes one of political and societal disintegration, of migration, of finding or conquering new land on which to live. These are not environmental security issues.

Effects come in two types, each of which involves different forms of securitization. The first type is that of acute disasters. Here, in the early stages securitization of effects is still occurring in the form of acute crisis or disaster management. The making of contingency plans beforehand is not necessarily a form of securitization, but the execution of those plans is. The preparation phase is like discussing the size and sources of a fire brigade, the police, or the army: It is an aspect of ordinary politics unless the allocation of resources is possible only with securitization. But once the fire, the riot, or the war breaks out, the contingency plan receives priority and replaces ordinary politics.

The second manifestation is that of creeping disasters: a slow but steady deterioration of living conditions. Here, most of the effects are open to securitization mainly along nonenvironmental lines. In many cases, the creeping types of environmental disaster cannot be compared with fires, riots, and wars but rather with slow decay: Soil erosion and overpopulation, for example, do not endanger living conditions overnight. It takes time to pass certain thresholds and points of no return, at which point it is simply too late for contingency plans. In cases where erosion or overuse has evidently contributed to conflicts, there has been no serious attempt to securitize these environmental problems (the wars in Sudan are just one example). In most cases, the securitization focuses on conflicts in other sectors: Environmental degradation may lead to interstate wars, ethnic conflict, political disintegration or civil strife, and economic deprivation (hunger and poverty). Hylke Tromp (1996) has argued that environmental conflicts will express themselves along the traditional fault lines in societies. This argument seems plausible when securitization moves occur in reaction to the slow effects of environmental problems, provided disaster management is impossible, too late, or not prepared for. Moreover, given the short history of manifest environmental concerns, as well as the issue-specific nature of most actor constellations, firmly rooted environmental enemy images are hard to find.

In other words, the environmental sector provides a lens that enables us to highlight root causes of existential threats that become manifest in other sectors. This finding is similar to that for the economic sector. This may sometimes point to misperception or scapegoat functions (e.g., blaming Jews for the economic depression in the 1930s) and sometimes to the overspill from one sector to another: For example, failing to distribute scarce water jeopardizes basic human needs and will stimulate "my family first" policies—that is, extremism. If we define environmental security in terms of sustaining ecosystems that are necessary for the preservation of achieved levels of civilization, it follows that when and where this security fails, the conflicts will be over threats to these levels of civilization—that is, threats to nonenvironmental existential values. The environment, modified by human interference, sets the conditions for sociopolitical-economic life. When these conditions are poor, life is poor.

Regionalizing Dynamics?

The contemporary environmental agenda was originally conceived as global. Its emergence is not the result of the globalization of local developments but, on the contrary, of the discovery of global consequences of seemingly harmless individual or local practices. This contrasts with the development of other security agenda, which evolved out of the gradual globalization of problems that originally had a local character—military security, for example, in which it took centuries for warfare to develop on a global scale. Hence, the rhetoric of the political agenda makes us believe we are dealing with an essentially globalized sector. The bulk of the literature is arguing that, to use the words of Andrew Hurrell and Benedict Kingsbury (1992: 2),

Humanity is now faced by a range of environmental problems that are global in the strong sense that they affect everyone and can only be effectively managed on the basis of cooperation between all, or at least a very high percentage, of the states of the world: controlling climate change and the emission of greenhouse gases, the protection of the ozone layer, safeguarding biodiversity, protecting special regions such as Antarctica or the Amazon, the management of the sea-bed, and the protection of the high seas are among the principal examples.

This sounds good, but it is not entirely true. The concern here is global, but most pollution-related problems require first and foremost joint action by the highly industrialized states only; in principle, the protection of Antarctica, except for the hole in the ozone layer, could be left to the seven states that have legal rights there. The Amazon region (and thus, to a large extent, biodiversity) would be protected best by leaving it alone, a decision that rests essentially with the Brazilian government and a few business enterprises. The global dimension is present but not as overwhelmingly as is often suggested.

Threats and vulnerabilities in the environmental sector are issue specific and seldom universal. Moreover, causes and effects may be located at different levels and in different regions. Global events seldom have the total character of a potential nuclear winter. Most global events, including climate change and massive migrations, can be compared to events such as the two world wars and the Great Depression: Every corner of the earth is affected but not to the same degree. World War I, for instance, caused more Australian than Dutch casualties, even though the Dutch lived a mere 200 kilometers from the main front. Most global environmental crises have similar uneven effects and involvements. For a proper assessment, it is therefore necessary in every case to establish a chain of cause-effect relationships and to position actors and regions along this chain in terms of the immediacy and the nature of their involvement.

A useful starting point for tracing security complexes in the environmental sector is disaster scenarios. What if the hole in the ozone layer widens, sea levels rise, massive migrations occur, or another Chernobyl-type accident occurs? Who is immediately affected? How permanent is the damage? What are the regional political consequences, and are there global consequences? In other words, what is the highest level on which the effects will occur?

The next question is, at what level are the causes located? What and who are causing the hole in the ozone layer, the sea level rise, and the like? These locations can sometimes be linked in coherent regions: For example, acid rain in the Nordic countries originates in Britain and Central Europe. Sometimes the complexes of causes and effects are less coherent: The hole in the ozone layer (effect) can be located regionally, whereas the causes are cumulative and dispersed worldwide.

Because cause and effect do not always match, a third sequence of questions is required—namely, about the actual securitizing moves that are made. What possibilities exist to turn the tide? What are the immediate costs? How can success be assessed? Who has to pay the costs? Who can be held responsible? The last two questions are especially important in light of the fact that causes and effects are not necessarily located at the same level and do not always involve the same actors. Prevention of a Chernobyl-type accident, for example, requires proper management of the nuclear power plant in question—a local issue. The scale of the damage caused by mismanagement, however, turns the issue into an international one that involves all of Europe: A regional regime for the proper management of nuclear power plants seems to be required. In other words, it makes a difference whether the causes are securitized (e.g., local safety prescriptions) or the effects are (e.g., regional international regimes).

The third sequence of questions is decisive, because it is here that a political constellation of mutual security concerns is formed. Who feels threatened? Who must those parties cooperate with if action is to be effective? Effects and causes are significant conditions in disposing who will become involved with whom and how, but they do not fully determine outcomes. Securitization always involves political choice; thus, actors might choose to ignore major causes for political or pragmatic reasons and therefore may form a security constellation that is different from what one would expect based on one's knowledge of effects and causes.

Occasionally, pragmatism may prescribe global action, but even then it is necessary to subdivide global issues according to the context of their causes and effects. Dealing with the causes of, for instance, global warming requires a global context. The fossil CO_2 emissions that contribute to the greenhouse effect occur worldwide and are therefore a global problem, even though important regional differences should be realized.[4] Meeting the causes of global warming points to the urgency of a global regime, which was recognized at UNCED where the climate treaty that became effective in March 1994 was signed. It is telling, however, that at the follow-up conference in Berlin (28 March–7 April 1995), saving the intentions declared at UNCED was the optimum goal. Further decisionmaking and regime formation were postponed to the third Climate Summit, to be held in Tokyo in 1997. This postponement is in part a result of the fact that those who have to pay the price for prevention are different from those who pay the price of failure.

The effects of global warming are perhaps a global problem in moral terms and in secondary effects, but they are much more localized in immediate existential effects. Some coastal areas are vulnerable to a sea-level rise of even a few tens of centimeters. In case of a sea-level rise of one meter, many of these areas will disappear or become uninhabitable because of tidal waves and storm surges. At the same time, global warming may be a benefit for Russia and Canada because of the thawing of huge permafrost areas. This discrepancy of localized effects, of course, has a major impact on building successful international regimes. Arriving at a consensus is difficult, and it is hardly surprising that 35 of the most potentially vulnerable states joined forces in AOSIS.

This issue-specific set of questions intended to link (potential) disaster with cause and securitization is not an entirely novel approach. The line of thinking is typical for international relations (IR) theories in the functionalist tradition.[5] It also reflects the praxis of many regional regime formations around environmental values. Illustrative are, for example, the 13 regional arrangements for cooperation in combating maritime pollution. The mere fact that very similar arrangements are required for almost all seas allows us to conclude that we are dealing with a common set of problems. But is this therefore a global problem? Yes and no. No because effective management on the regional level is possible. Cleaning up the Baltic Sea is not conditional on cleaning up the Mediterranean or vice versa. Incentives to negotiate a comprehensive scheme that includes both seas are therefore absent: The seas are separate, sector-specific regional security complexes. On the other hand, both require similar knowledge, research and development (R&D), investments, political cooperation, legal schemes, and the like. In other words, on the scientific agenda one can expect maritime pollution to be presented as a global challenge, whereas it will boil down to its specific regional contexts on the political agenda.

Certainly, not all regional and global action on the environment deserves the label *security policy*. In 1980s, for instance, when the Convention on the Conservation of Antarctic Marine Living Resources (CCAMLR) was signed, followed by the 1991 Madrid Protocol for the Protection of the Antarctic Environment, these events pointed at politicization but not securitization. It may even be better to perceive such events as acts to prevent the need for securitization. With timely management of potential problems, panic politics can be avoided. The Madrid Protocol banned mining activities for 50 years, for example, and the CCAMLR is trying to set up rules for the extraction of krill (a main link in the food chain).

The popular motto "think globally, act locally" fits the environmental sector very well. All disaster scenarios and the ways to prevent them involve local features, which consist of several aspects. First, much of the debate ultimately does focus on specific groups (certain professions and industries) that have to change their behavior more than other groups. Not everyone in every society is expected to pay the same price, and enforcement of specific measures is clearly needed. This may explain why environmentalists count few captains of industry among their members (retired ones excluded, of course). It also explains why Galician fishermen fail to see the necessity to stop fishing halibut off the shores of Newfoundland: The potential loss of 7,000 jobs is involved.[6]

This is the first way in which localizing dynamics are present in this sector: When specific interest groups are forced out of business for the general good, opposition can be expected. Most of this opposition will come from local groups or firms. The question then is whether the measures for the general good of the public sphere can be properly implemented despite local opposition against them. This will often be a question of cross-sectoral conflicts: Local opposition to environmental security policies may cause or aggravate tensions in the other security sectors, in particular leading to political tensions (the legitimacy of the political regime is at stake), economic tensions (the well-being of specific groups is at stake), and societal tensions (if the affected groups have an ethnic or a cultural identity).

Whether this type of localizing dynamics will flourish is not decided by environmental criteria alone. A more important factor seems to be the resilience of the states involved: The stronger the state (in Buzanian terms), the less likely it is that environmental problems will create political insecurities at the local (substate) level. Another modifying factor in avoiding local conflicts caused by environmental problems is the work of NGOs and IGOs. In regions characterized by weak states (e.g., sub-Saharan Africa), these global and subsystem actors are especially important: They fill a vacuum at the unit level.

The reference to the general good is important; it implies that local conflicts are the result of considerations about wider contexts. Dealing with the causes leads to preemptive, low-intensity conflicts to avoid high-intensity disaster. In the face of such environmental security policies, the local scale may be the main level of implementation and conflict, but it is not the level at which security in this sector crystallizes. The fear of cumulative negative effects on regional and global scales motivates the policies.

Obviously, small-scale environmental problems require action, too; in pragmatic terms of enduring environmental disasters or, the opposite, contributing to sustainability, however, the local level is largely negligible in physical terms. It does not dominate the logic of the scientific agenda and, except for a few particular cases, seldom dominates the political one. Only when cameras are present can the local drama perform important symbolic or mythic functions. If, additionally, similar situations exist worldwide (think, for example, of pollution problems in urbanized areas), negative and positive experiences can become chapters in social learning. The precondition, however, is the presence of a reporter (the press, a researcher, or a foreign diplomat) and an audience on a wider scale. Hence, in terms of the political agenda, regional and global communication networks determine the context of most local environmental disasters. In their absence, very few local experiences (and then only negative ones) will have physical regional or global repercussions. Who outside of Kuwait remembers the more than 300 oil lakes and excessive fires in the desert during the Gulf War?

There is one important exception to this general argument: the risk that local events will cumulate or escalate into larger-scale problems (e.g., many small fires compose a big one or one small fire can expand). Urbanization problems provide an important example: How will the world deal with urbanization problems when up to 50 percent of the world population lives in cities in the year 2000?[7] The destruction of the Aral and Caspian Sea regions is another example, with many different water extraction projects cumulating in the drying up of the two inland seas. Also, local accidents related to nuclear waste, such as the nuclear submarines at the bottom of the Barents Sea, should be mentioned. In such cases, ocean currents may spread the pollution, turning it into a regional risk.

To better trace the essence of such localizing, regionalizing, and globalizing dynamics, empirical research is needed issue area by issue area. For a concrete assessment of security dynamics in the environmental sector, the following sequence of questions should be answered:

1. (a) What does the disaster scenario look like? How does it manifest itself in time and space? This involves mainly the scientific agenda and provides structural (physical) characteristics of the issue area. (b) Is the disaster scenario (expected to be) politicized and securitized? In other words, at what point are we talking about environmental security in this issue area? This involves the political agenda.

2. (a) Who are the veto and other functional actors in this issue area? In other words, who is causing the problem? This provides structural characteristics. (b) Who are the actual or potential lead and support actors? This provides political characteristics of the issue area. The resulting actor typology provides a strong indication of the localizing, regionalizing, and globalizing dynamics of the political agenda. If actors become interconnected in a political constellation over these security issues, they represent a security complex.

3. How independent an issue area are we dealing with? (a) Is there structural issue linkage? For example, in poverty-related forms of desertification, the issue of erosion is linked to those of population growth and domestic and North-South economic asymmetries. This again mainly involves the scientific agenda. (b) Is there political issue linkage? Structurally unrelated issues may become interlinked by veto and lead actors, as, for example, when biodiversity in rain forests is linked to debt negotiations. This type of linkage will show from the political agenda.

We expect that on this basis, maps can be drawn presenting crucial regions with concentrated environmental problems, often securitized ones.

One such map has already been mentioned: potential victims of a sea-level rise. Clearly, these areas form a nonregional subset of the international system. Other examples can be given in regard to hydropolitics. In the mid-1990s, there are many unresolved international water issues. The most quoted examples are located in the Middle East: Iraq, Syria, and Turkey form a water security complex because of their disputes over sharing the Euphrates and Tigris Rivers. Their security interdependence involves the issues of dams, reduced water flow, salinization, and hydroelectricity. The Jordan, Yarmuk, Litani, and West Bank aquifer links Israel, Jordan, Syria, Lebanon, and West Bank Palestinians in another hydro security complex, with conflicts occurring over the allotment of water (Ohlsson 1995). It is typical that some charts of the Jordan aquifer are qualified as top secret by the Israeli army (Warner 1996). Other examples of emergent water security complexes include Egypt, Ethiopia, and Sudan (over the Nile); India and Pakistan (over the Indus, Jhelum, Chenab, Ravi, Beas, and Sutlej Rivers); Burma and China (over the Salween); Kampuchea, Laos, Thailand, and Vietnam (over flooding, irrigation, and hydroelectricity in the Mekong); and various others (Ohlsson 1995: 21).

Similar maps can be made for virtually all aspects of environmental degradation. A map of soil erosion and desertification shows 14 "erosion hot spots" (Myers 1993b) yielding regional subsystems ranging from the Himalayan foothills and the Sahel to parts of the United States. Regional regimes are probably the most effective for dealing with each of these hot spots. In the Himalayas the problem is deforestation, in the Sahel the problem is wind erosion, and in the United States it is unsustainable pressure on soils in the grain lands. But the incentive for building such regimes is clearly global because of the long-term effects of the cumulative loss. Another way of drawing maps of regional environmental security complexes is by linking the issues. This has been done for the former Soviet Union (Feshbach and Friendly 1992).

Central Asia is confronted with "the greatest single, manmade ecological catastrophe in history" (Feshbach and Friendly 1992: 88). The dehydration of the Aral Sea will trigger an "eco-domino effect," ultimately creating a "united front of ecological degradation from Scandinavia to the Black Sea" (Wolfson and Spetter 1991, quoted in Does and Gerrits 1994: 409). René Does and André Gerrits (1994) identify three types of environment-related conflicts in this region: (1) interstate conflicts over the distribution of water and land in Central Asia, over pollution and economic exploitation of the Caspian Sea and the Black Sea, over the nuclear power stations in Armenia, and over Semipalatinsk;[8] (2) interregional conflicts among the CIS member states (especially in the Krim, Kalmykia, Dagestan, and Karakalpakstan); and (3) "ethnocide" of the Karakalpaks and the small ethnic groups in the north.

The earlier research questions and the geophysical maps of hot spots allow us to pin down the regional security complexes of the environment more concretely. In many cases, there will be an interplay of global motive (steered by the politicization of remote effects) and local, relatively independent troubled areas or disturbing practices; in many other cases there will be strong securitization of local drama for its own sake; in still other cases there will be regions of cumulative environmental problems—states caught up in intense security interdependence in the face of preserving their country in the most literal terms.

Summary

The system level seems dominant in this sector, because most securitizing moves take place at that level as a result of the existence of an international environmental epistemic community that drafts and securitizes the environmental agenda. The political power of that community, however, is limited, which results in the need to distinguish two agenda: the scientific agenda of the environmental epistemic community and a political one of how this agenda is accepted as high politics by public spheres and transnational corporations. This turns the unit level, and hence localizing dynamics, into the second dominant level in this sector. Crucial for environmental security is whether states, major economic actors, and local communities embrace the scientific agenda. In other words, even when the concern is global, its political relevance is decided at the local level.

Securitizing moves at the global level have resulted in considerable politicization, but successful securitization has been limited. Successful securitization has occurred mainly at the local level, where the actual disasters take place and thresholds of sustainability are passed. But even so, it is not necessarily the environment that is securitized: Environmental conflict often travels under the guise of political turmoil or ethnic strife.

Because of the strong localizing dynamics, regional environmental regimes are only in part a spin-off of global structures. The concern and knowledge that feed the emergence of these regions are global—the cognitive dimension is global—but the size of security complexes is determined bottom-up. These complexes cover the smallest areas within which specific environmental issues can be addressed—that is, they are the largest expression of local security interdependence. There are, for example, more than 10 regional arrangements for cooperation in combating maritime pollution, not because of global competition or the inability to create one comprehensive global arrangement but because a regional approach proved more effective.

A *tour de globe* of regional subsystems is difficult, not because the regions are not there but because they are based on so many different issue areas. World maps exist of regions related to water issues, land issues, pollution, deforestation, population pressure, and so forth.

Another difficulty in analyzing environmental security in terms of regions is that causes and effects of environmental issues frequently involve different regions and different actors—the actors who cause environmental damage are distinct from those who suffer from it. There may be one set of actors in one region whose security interdependence is high if one wants to deal with the causes of a specific ecoproblem (e.g., agricultural policies in semiarid regions), whereas another set of actors in another region may be involved in case of failure caused by the spillover of negative developments (e.g., environmental refugees fleeing hunger after crop failure). This leads to larger and more complex patterns of security linkage.

What kinds of security complexes are created? Global warming has worldwide causes, but its likely negative effects are not global. Conversely, strictly local or regional problems, as in many cases the protection of endangered species, are securitized in the global debate about biodiversity. The same is true for local dramas, such as the Exxon *Valdez* accident, Chernobyl, or French nuclear testing on Muroroa. NGO activities combined with wide media coverage turn these local problems into global issues. This global village image of the environmental sector is a strong nonregional feature. Yet, many of the manifest existential threats involved are expressing themselves locally, which means people usually do not have to wait for a global-level solution to tackle these local problems.

In sum, securitizing moves are attempted at almost all levels but mostly at the global level. Most successful securitization, however, is local. Some subsystemic formations do emerge, regional as well as nonterritorial.

Notes

1. Over the past ten years, there has been an impressive output of articles and books on environmental security, some at a descriptive level and others more theoretically. A comprehensive list cannot be offered here, but see, in addition to the various direct references in this chapter, for example, Brock 1991; the various "State of the World" reports of the Worldwatch Institute (e.g., Brown et al. 1993); Brown 1989; Carroll 1988; Käkönen 1992, 1994; Levy 1995a, 1995b; Lodgaard 1992; Lodgaard and Ornäs 1992; Matthew 1995; Matthews 1989; Sjöstedt 1993; Thomas 1992; Westing 1988, 1990.

2. Be aware, however, of potential myths about the impact of natural disasters on humanity as such. In the branch of research on disasters and natural hazards, scholars calculated the ratio of reported deaths from disasters during the twentieth century (1900–1990): 48.6 percent died as a consequence of civil strife, 39.1 percent of famine, and the remaining 12.3 percent from earthquakes (4.7%), volcanic outbursts (2.1%), cyclones (1.75%), epidemics (1.65%), floods (1.6%), and other hazards (0.5%). (Source: *Disaster History,* "Significant Data on Major Disasters

Worldwide." Washington, D.C.: Office of Foreign Disaster Assistance, 1990; quoted in Blaikie et al. 1994: 4.) If one considers that most of the war-related deaths occurred during the two world wars, famines stand out even more profoundly as the dominant potential threat to human life.

3. Population figures (in millions): low-income economies, 3,127 in 1991 (3,686 in 2000); middle-income economies, 1,401 in 1991 (1,561 in 2000); high-income economies, 822 in 1991 (864 in 2000) (World Bank 1993: 288–289).

4. In 1991, the Organization for Economic Cooperation and Development (OECD) countries accounted for 49.5 percent of the emissions, the former Soviet Union and Eastern Europe 21.1 percent, China 11 percent, and the other developing countries around 18.4 percent (percentages are derived from figures in Thomas 1992: 171); in terms of per capita contributions, the share of the OECD multiplies significantly, since it hosts less than 20 percent of the world population. None lived up to the intention expressed at the Framework Convention on Climate Change to reduce emissions to 1990 levels. Meanwhile, the developing countries' share will rise to about 50 percent in 2025 as a result of industrialization and population growth. Emissions in China, the worst example, had risen 80 percent since 1980, making it the world's second-largest emitter by 1994. Emissions in Brazil rose 8 percent between 1990 and 1993; India's rose 13 percent and Turkey's rose 16 percent during the same period (Flavin and Tunali 1995: 13).

5. The functionalist tradition of IR started in the 1920s and 1930s with people like David Mitrany and Francis Delaisi (de Wilde 1991); the tradition flourished during the late 1940s and 1950s, developed into neo-functionalist integration theory (Haas) and social communication theory (Deutsch), but was discredited in the 1960s because of the sclerosis in European integration. In the 1970s, it returned in themes like transnationalism and interdependence theory (Keohane, Nye, Rosenau) and developed into regime theory (Ruggie, Krasner, Keohane; see Hansenclever, Mayer, and Rittberger 1996). Keohane's institutionalist approach is the latest step in the process.

6. In May 1995, a confrontation occurred between these fishermen and Canadian authorities in which the latter used environmental arguments to legitimize extraordinary measures, whereas the former legitimized their protest in terms of sovereignty and international law—a typical cross-sectoral clash of interests.

7. In 1900, a mere 14 percent of the world population lived in urban centers (Myers 1993a: 197).

8. Semipalatinsk-21 was the name of the secret nuclear city Kurtshatov in Kazakhstan. It was the biggest test site in Kazakhstan but not the only one. According to Does and Gerrits (1994: 423), 20 million hectares of the total Kazakh territory of 270 million hectares was reserved for testing. From 1949 to 1962, 113 aboveground nuclear tests occurred; since the Partial Test Ban Treaty, another 343 underground tests have been conducted. In 1989, the antinuclear movement Nevada-Semipalatinsk was created and has since become a political force of some importance.

CHAPTER 5

The Economic Sector

The Economic Security Agenda

The whole idea of economic security is exceedingly controversial and politicized. In a capitalist system, the very concept is fraught with contradictions and complications, not the least being that actors in a market are *supposed* to feel insecure; if they do not, the market will not produce its efficiencies (Buzan 1991, chapter 6; Cable 1995; Luciani 1989). This chapter sketches the main sources and positions in the debate about economic security. Using the definitions from Chapter 2, it tries to distinguish what can genuinely be thought of as economic security from both that which is merely politicized economics and that which reflects security spillover from the economic sector to other sectors.

The idea of economic security is located squarely in the unresolved and highly political debates about international political economy concerning the nature of the relationship between the political structure of anarchy and the economic structure of the market (Buzan 1991: 230). The main contending positions reflect different views about whether states and societies or markets should have priority and whether private economic actors have security claims of their own that must be weighed against the verdict of the market. Baldly stated, the positions are as follow.

Mercantilists and neomercantilists put politics first, seeing the state as both embodying the social and political purposes for which wealth is generated and providing the security necessary for the operation of firms and markets. From this perspective, economic security is simply part of a wider priority given to state or "national" security, and economic success tends to be seen as zero sum.

Liberals put economics first, arguing that the economy should be at the root of the social fabric and that the market should be left to operate as freely as possible without interference by the state. The state is necessary to provide law and politico-military security and to support the social fabric in areas in which the market fails to do so. From this perspective, the main object of economic security is to develop rules that create factor mobility among national economies, although it can also be argued that liberalism is about protecting the position of the capitalist elite. Liberals value economic efficiency and take a positive-sum, joint gains view of economic relations.

Socialists fall awkwardly in between the two, arguing that economics is at the root of the entire social fabric and that to the extent that states can escape this logic, their task is to tame economics toward social and political goals of justice and equity. The security focus of socialists is toward the economically weak and against the strong.

In a very broad sense, both socialists and mercantilists can be seen as species of economic nationalism, wanting to privilege the state over the economy, albeit for different purposes. Most states claiming to be socialist have pursued economic nationalist policies, especially those under Communist governments where strict economic control is necessary for their project of social transformation. These perspectives represent incompatible ideological positions and generate different logics and priorities of economic security (McKinlay and Little 1986). There is no denying the existence of a substantial securitizing discourse in the economic sector, albeit one that pulls in several different directions. Sometimes individuals are the object of securitization, sometimes the state, and sometimes the international economy.

The crushing victory of the West in the Cold War marginalized the socialist element of the ideological debate and weakened, but by no means eliminated, the economic nationalist element. In rhetorical terms, that victory pushed much of the ideological debate (probably temporarily) into the background, leaving an economic security discourse shaped largely by liberal concerns and by the effect of an international political economy attempting to operate under liberal rules. Moreover, the type of liberalism now in fashion is particularly pure. It has much less attachment to the national economy than did its nineteenth-century predecessor, and it has pushed aside much of the "embedded liberalism" (Ruggie 1982) enshrined in the post-1945 Bretton Woods system. In its more virulent forms, this liberalism seeks to recreate Karl Polanyi's (1957 [1944]) nightmare of the total subordination of social values to market values.

In practice, much economic nationalism remains, finding its political space in the ambiguity that exists within the liberal position over how large the role of the state should be and the extent to which the market should be allowed to override national and individual security. Trade continues to evoke fierce opposition between liberal and protectionist forces, but production and, even more so, finance have developed an increasingly unrestricted global transnational character. The liberal ideal is ultimately to dissolve national economies, with their exclusive currencies and restrictions on factor movement, into a global economy with relatively few restraints on the movement of goods, capital, services, and (more hesitantly) people. The problems are how to maintain economic and political stability and how to handle the widening gap between the very rich and the very poor that unrestricted markets tend to generate while simultaneously removing many powers and functions from states. This explains the concern within the field of international political economy (IPE) about how to maintain order and stability in a liberal international political economy, with the focus first on hegemons (Kindleberger 1973, 1981; Gilpin 1987) and then on regimes and institutions (Keohane 1980, 1984).

These developments mean the discourse on economic security is now shaped largely by the dominance of the liberal agenda and by the consequences of attempts to implement that agenda in the areas of trade, production, and finance. The particular characteristics of the liberal ascendance mean the contemporary discourse on economic security centers on concerns about instability and inequality. Concern about instability raises questions about the relative economic decline of the United States as hegemon and about the domestic and international management problems arising from the increasing integration and liberalization of the world economy. Concern about inequality raises questions domestically about the role of the state and internationally about the disadvantaged economic position of most Third World states.

The relative U.S. decline was an inevitable result of the exaggerated position of global dominance it held in 1944. This position was challenged by both Europe and Japan as they recovered from World War II and by some newly decolonized countries that were finding effective paths to modernization. By the 1970s, some in the United States were already beginning to feel threatened by dependence on imported oil, trade deficits, and pressure on the dollar. The inclination to securitize this process arose in part from sheer U.S. unfamiliarity with the pains of economic interdependence but mostly from concerns about hegemonic decline and the effect of a weaker United States on the global order.

Alongside U.S. decline was the growing integration and liberalization of the global economy, first in trade and, beginning in the 1970s, also in finance. This condition had two effects. First, it meant national economies became progressively more exposed to competition from other producers in a global market and to ever more powerful transnational corporations and financial markets. The effects of the global economy in promoting unemployment and deindustrialization came to be seen as a threat to both welfare and sovereignty by those who were not doing well within it. Some also saw the global economy as a threat to the state itself or at least to much of the traditional conception of what the state was supposed to do (Cerny 1995). Second, this condition meant all national economies that had become adapted to an open global trading and financial system were dependent upon its continued stability and smooth functioning. All of these economies were therefore threatened by the possibility of systemic crises that might disrupt the worldwide flows of goods and capital.

The particular plight of Third World countries arose from the dependent economic position as suppliers of primary goods many had inherited from their colonial period. These countries found themselves locked into disadvantageous terms of trade that some argued prevented their economic and sociopolitical development. Viewed from another perspective, these countries found themselves politically independent but heavily penetrated by outside market and political interests and burdened with societies and leaderships whose traditions, skills, resources, and internal divisions often provided poor foundations for the development of a modern political economy (Galtung 1971).

Out of these general conditions grew a varied agenda of specific issues cast in terms of economic security:

1. The ability of states to maintain independent capability for military production in a global market or, more broadly, the relationship of the economy to the capability for state military mobilization
2. The possibility that economic dependencies within the global market (particularly oil) will be exploited for political ends or, more broadly, questions of the security of supply when states abandoned the inefficient security of self-reliance for the efficient insecurity of dependence on outside sources of supply
3. Fears that the global market would generate more losers than winners and would heighten existing inequalities (manifested internationally at the top of the range by U.S. fears of hegemonic decline, at the bottom by developing country fears of exploitation, debt crises, and marginalization, and domestically by fears of permanent unemployment and growing social polarization)
4. Fears of (a) the dark side of capitalism and the open trading order in terms of illegal trade—especially in drugs, which empowers criminal fraternities, and light weapons; (b) the trade in certain kinds of militarily significant technology (particularly technology concerned with making and delivering weapons of mass destruction); and (c) the pressure on the global environment created by spreading industrialization and mass consumption (see Chapter 4)
5. Fears that the international economy itself would fall into crisis from some combination of weakening political leadership, increasing protectionist reactions, and structural instability in the global financial system

One peculiar characteristic of economic security under liberalism is that it is about the creation of stable conditions in which actors can compete mercilessly. In this sense, economic security has parallels with military security in Europe during the ancien régime and the nineteenth century. The monarchs of the ancien régime recognized the need for rules about warfare to keep wars within limits but not to avoid wars. Similarly, the Concert of

Europe was meant to avoid only certain wars (great-power wars on the continent). But warfare as a legitimate instrument of diplomacy, if not the fulfillment of successful diplomacy, was banned in Europe only after the "European Civil War" of 1914–1945.

This ancien régime character of economic liberalism shapes the essence of the discourse about economic security, much of which is driven by the tension between vulnerability and efficiency (Buzan 1991: 236–237). As long as the world economy lacks a global welfare system (i.e., global social security)—and we can assume this will remain a structural feature for a long time—states and individuals will favor efficiency only when they expect to be efficient enough to profit from it. This is one of the reasons hegemonic powers tend to advocate free trade.

Related to hegemonic power or power positions in general, states are faced with an economic security dilemma: Relative economic growth plays a major role in determining the power of states in the system (Kennedy 1989; Gilpin 1987). In contrast to military power, however, relative wealth is not normally of a zero-sum character; for example, the rise of Japan has not made the rest of the OECD poorer. If the Japanese economy were to collapse tomorrow, the resultant loss of capital and markets would drag the rest of the OECD economies down with it. In other words, economic interdependence is much less black or white when it comes to enmity and amity than military interdependence; consequently, economic security is a much more blurred concept than military security. In a liberal system, as illustrated by the tensions in U.S.-Japanese trade relations, the preservation of joint gains vies with that of individual ones.

It is often difficult to separate attempts to securitize economic issues from the more general political contest between liberal and nationalist approaches to economic policy. During the Cold War, the superpower rivalry muted protectionist voices because of the overriding common military and political security concern all of the capitalist powers shared against the Soviet Union. As long as the Soviet threat existed, the capitalist states worried more about it than about the commercial rivalry among themselves. But after 1989, with the ideological confrontation consigned to history, the common interest that had kept the capitalist economies together despite their rivalry was significantly weakened.

One of the central questions in this chapter is, how much of what is talked about as economic security actually qualifies for that label? The focus will be on how to answer this question in terms of the prevailing mode of pure liberalism. The argument will be that because of the essentially competitive nature of market relations, much of it does not properly rise above the merely politicized. Much of that which does rise above the politicized does so because of its effects in other sectors. Under extreme forms of liberalism, little can be counted as purely economic security.

Security Actors and Referent Objects

In the economic sector, it is important to remember that although each sector generates its own distinctive units, once established these units can show up as key players in other sectors. The state is remarkable for showing up in all sectors; even though its roots are in the political and military sectors, it is one of the major units in the economic one.

The economic sector is rich in referent objects, ranging from individuals through classes and states to the abstract and complex system of the global market itself. These objects often overlap. Concern about the global economy might be securitized in its own terms, but it might also be securitized in terms of a national economy or of groups of individuals within a national economy (such as displaced workers). The most immediate peculiarity of the sector is that under liberal logic its most distinctive unit, the firm, has a relatively weak claim to status as a security referent object because of the contradiction between the inherently instrumental, ephemeral nature of the firm and the logic of existential threats that underlies security. In the liberal perspective, firms are fundamentally organizations of convenience. They may grow very large and may last a long time, but even the oldest and largest are subject to the market, and when they cease to be efficient or to produce desired goods and services, they are dissolved and replaced by new firms. Firms struggle to survive; when industry-dominating names such as Pan Am, Austin, or Triumph disappear, however, there may be shock and regret, but few consider the event unnatural or wrong. Apple and IBM may be replaced by newer computer makers with little disturbance.

Only two sorts of securitizing logic can usually attempt to elevate firms to the status of referent objects. The first is local and concerns the immediate effect on individuals and towns when a firm goes under. Individuals, trade unions, city governments, and the local political representative of the national government may all attempt to save the company by casting its demise in security terms. The second type of securitizing logic is national and involves the government's attitude toward the place of a firm in the state's industrial base. For example, if the government is committed to a high degree of self-reliance for military mobilization, this argument may extend very widely—covering firms as diverse as boot makers, shipyards, and electronics. Here, the securitizing actor may be the firm itself (pleading for subsidies or government orders) or a trade union or local elected government official (concerned about jobs), or it may be the state acting preemptively in pursuit of its own sense of military security. Economic nationalist governments embrace such arguments, whereas liberal ones resist them. Perhaps the major exceptions even for liberal governments are very large manufacturing firms and especially banks, whose collapse would threaten the stability of the entire economy and, in the case of banks, possibly the stability of the international financial system.

There is some difficult ground here in which the rhetoric of security may be misused in pursuit of merely political objectives, such as employment, regional development, or pork barrel politics (misused in the sense that this is not really an attempt to securitize because the full sequence, from existential threats to extraordinary countermeasures is not present; it is rather a loose use of the *word* security). In a liberal economy, the local argument usually fails unless it is linked to the national one. The national argument remains strong as long as states think they might have to fight a serious war—especially if they might have to do so alone. But where states are embedded in liberal security communities—as we see now in Europe and the West—the imperative for military self-reliance declines, and the willingness to depend on external sources for supplies of weapons and other military materiel rises. Even traditionally self-reliant European powers are increasingly dependent on each other and on the United States for weapons and military supplies. Thus, only in special circumstances, when firms are seen as crucial to the stability of the market system itself, can firms be successfully securitized in a liberal system.

The Marxist logic of class "war" could be read as elevating classes to the status of referent object, with the class depending upon whose side one is on. Although politically effective for several generations, this rhetoric failed to attract a wide following in international security terms, as illustrated most famously by the failure of both workers and intellectuals to rally to the socialist international in 1914 and the willingness of most of them to respond to the security symbolism of state and nation. If the explicit attempt to securitize the working class failed, a case might be made that much liberal rhetoric about economic efficiency and stability masks an implicit attempt to securitize the interests of a transnational capitalist class. Such an argument would appeal to most types of economic nationalists but would be rejected by liberals on the grounds that market efficiency serves the wider community, not just the elite. Classes cannot be ruled out as potential referent objects of economic security, but so far the attempt to securitize class has had only patchy and short-lived success. It is worth noting that nonmonetary economies (especially subsistence farming) have the family or even the extended family as their unit. Although entire regions (especially sub-Saharan Africa) are based on this principle, there is no politicization or securitization of these economic activities except for some community-based development literature.

At the unit level, states far outshine firms and classes as the principal referent objects of economic security, even for liberals. When security arguments are used to legitimize, for instance, a violation of General Agreement on Tariffs and Trade (GATT) rules, the basis is a security logic related to state interests rather than a firm. The principal reasons for this situation may lie outside the economic sector, either in concerns about military capability (especially for great powers) or in concerns about threats to political status (declining hegemons, marginalized developing countries) or threats of political leverage (exploitation by suppliers of import dependencies—for example, oil, food, or weapons). Whether the national economy itself can meet the criteria for securitization is an interesting question that is taken up in the next section.

Much the same question arises in relation to subsystem- and system-level referent objects in the economic sector. These referent objects may be relatively concrete, in the form of IGOs—understood here as everything from regimes (most-favored-nation [MFN] agreements) through treaties (GATT, NAFTA) to permanent organizations (the World Trade Organization [WTO], the World Bank, or the EU)—or relatively abstract, principally the liberal international economic order (LIEO)—meaning the entire nexus of rules and norms about open trading and financial arrangements. These higher-level referent objects are typically securitized by officials of the IGOs or by representatives of states, industry, or capital with interests in their maintenance.

But does the securitizing call come primarily for economic reasons or for reasons in other sectors? Again, the linkage to military-political concerns is strong. The example of the 1930s is still used frequently to warn against measures of national economic closure that may threaten the LIEO. In part, this comparison is about levels of prosperity and fears of repeating the Great Depression, but it also reflects the concern raised in Cordell Hull's famous dictum that "if goods can't cross borders, soldiers will" (Buzan 1984). It is not clear whether the key worry is about economic chaos itself or about the impact economic closure will have on politico-military relations.

The strongest attempts to securitize the economy are those that make clear that although doing so is a question of economic loss and thus part of the ordinary business of life, it is a matter not of degree but of a possible collapse of welfare. This argument can be used in relation to the LIEO or with a specific state or group of individuals as referent: If, for example, we are left out of the next round of information technology, we will be on a steady downward curve relative to the global economy and will therefore be unable to uphold levels of welfare; ultimately, this situation can lead to social instability, breakdown of order, even revolution. This attempt can either be defined out of the sector as a political threat, or it could be kept in the economic sector as a class securitization: Such arguments are often thinly veiled claims about a potential economic-political threat to *our* position.

Similar arguments can be made about regional institutions, most notably the EU. Part of the founding logic of formal European integration was to link the basic industries (iron, steel, coal, and nuclear) of Europe together in a way that would reduce states' capability for independent military mobilization. This linkage between economic structure and military-political security goes back to arguments between liberals and mercantilists about the nature of the international political economy. The liberals have largely held the high ground in linking the neomercantilist policies of the 1930s to the slide toward world war, successfully sidetracking the case that the failure of an unstable liberal system was what started the ball rolling (Polanyi 1957 [1944]).

To sum up, in the economic sector one finds a range of referent objects at the unit, subsystem, and system levels of which the most important seem to be the state and the LIEO. Securitizing actors can be found at all levels, although the representatives of states and IGOs and sometimes, more quietly, firms are generally the most effective. Abstract entities such as the LIEO are incapable of having voice and can only appear as referent objects. Under liberalism, the unit most distinctive to the sector—the firm—appears mainly in the role of a functional security actor that affects the security dynamics within the sector, most notably as the demon or savior of less-developed national economies. The state also plays this role, as do IGOs. The state's gatekeeper function regarding how permeable it allows its borders to be to economic transactions sets the basic conditions for the IGOs and the international political economy as a whole. The question of whether the motive for securitization lies primarily in the economic sector or in other sectors is as yet unanswered, and it is to that question that we now turn.

The Logic of Threats and Vulnerabilities

How do threats and vulnerabilities in the economic sector measure up to the securitization criteria, especially existential threat? As we saw in the previous section, there are clear links from economic issues to other security sectors (and it is worth noting that these operate in reverse, with wars—both hot and cold—and environmental crises capable of inflicting serious damage on local, national, and world economies). But within the difficult and contradiction-ridden terrain of the economic sector itself, where is the boundary between politicization and securitization? Given that insecurity is a basic feature of life in a market economy, how do economic issues move up the scale from simply technical problems to politicized problems to securitized ones?

What constitutes an existential economic threat depends upon the referent object. For individuals, economic security can be understood most clearly in terms of basic human needs. Individuals live or die (or, in the case of malnutrition in children, have their development as human beings compromised) according to the provision of the basic necessities for sustaining human life: adequate food, water, clothing, shelter, and education. So-called food security, and calls to eradicate mass starvation are clearly within the realm of basic human needs, as is disaster relief. But beyond these basics, it is not clear that the individual can legitimately be securitized in the economic sector. Issues of relative levels of welfare, of differential access to more exotic resources, and even of unemployment may be enormously important to individuals and indeed to societies, but in economic terms they are not about survival. Lacking an existential quality, they remain economic or political (or possibly societal or environmental) issues and not security ones.

In the liberal perspective, firms, as discussed earlier, generally lack the existential qualities needed for economic securitization unless, as with major banks, their demise threatens the economy itself. The word *security* is often used in economic relations, most notably in relation to investment. Investment has both economic and political risks. The latter are now related less to the ideological color of states than to potential civil strife—the weak-strong state criterion (Buzan 1991: 96–107). Another political risk remains that of collective boycotts: Investors in Libya and Iraq have lost money as a result of international economic boycott. At present, no clear trend seems to exist in the international excommunication of states. Moreover, it is unlikely that such a trend would be allowed to take on proportions that threaten the world economy as such. Regional subsystems, however, might be put at risk; in the past, the UN member states have not shied away from that risk in Southern Africa. Investment "security" is not, however, of the same quality as international security.

Unlike firms, states do have the qualities necessary for securitization. They are expected to be (although they are not always) permanently rooted structures. The fact that states are seen as indissoluble causes problems for their role as actors in the global economy. Whereas firms are expected to disappear as economic actors if they play the economic game unsuccessfully and become bankrupt, states cannot disappear. States can technically go bankrupt (as was the case with Mexico during the debt crisis and almost again in 1995), but they cannot be dissolved, and the inhabitants cannot be fired—although many may try to migrate. Takeovers are rare and difficult, and as Iraq discovered with Kuwait, hostile takeovers are now generally treated as illegal. The end of the German Democratic Republic (GDR) is an isolated recent case of a successful takeover of one state by another. Attempts by TNCs to control local politics and military security run up against the same adverse logic of costs that inspired decolonization. For firms, the costs of taking on governmental responsibilities are higher than the risk of unwanted nationalizations of property abroad. There is, after all, a powerful logic in that most central of liberal arguments, the division of labor between states and firms: Neither can do the other's job efficiently.

States are thus peculiarly immune to some existential threats that bear on other actors in the economic sector. The bankruptcy of a state may threaten its political security (by having the International Monetary Fund [IMF] and the World Bank infringe upon its sovereignty) or its military security (by raising threats of forceful debt collection, as in the gunboat diplomacy of the colonial era—which is no longer acceptable), but it rarely affects a state's economic security.

The logic of economic security for states is similar to that for individuals except that in principle (although rarely in practice) states can form entirely self-contained economic systems. There is, in effect, a state equivalent of basic human needs. Unless a state is self-reliant in the resources required to feed its population and industry, it needs access to outside supplies. If that need is threatened, the national economy can be clearly and legitimately securitized.

Beyond this basic level, however, it is difficult to see how economic security can be legitimately invoked by liberals. Whereas economic nationalists have no problem invoking economic security in state terms, liberals are (or should be) constrained from doing so by their commitment to efficiency and thus to openness and competition. In principle, this commitment should exclude from securitization a great range of things that might count as serious economic or political issues: how well or how badly states do in the race for industrialization and development, how well they do in competition for market share, how fair or unfair the terms of trade and access to credit and investment are perceived to be, whether the presence of direct and indirect foreign investment is economically beneficial, whether global competition is good for development, whether absolute economic gains are more important than relative ones, and the like.

Perhaps the only thing liberals can try to treat as an economic security issue is the need to sustain the reform programs that keep the national economy in line with the international economy. Without such reforms, states risk the marginalization or even devastation of their economies because of debt default, loss of investment, or currency instability. But this situation scarcely reaches existential proportions and rarely comes in a form abrupt or dramatic enough to lift it out of normal politics. Like the issues listed earlier, it is much more likely to be about how well or how badly the state does in absolute and relative terms than it is to be about the existence of the state or the national economy. To the extent that clear existential threats arise from such economic issues, they do so because of their impact in other sectors rather than their impact within the economic sector itself. When economic securitization is attempted, the actor will often use the element of security logic, which is a dramatic break point: Yes, this is about levels of welfare but not in a gradual or incremental sense; if we take a downward course, it points toward a situation that does contain existential threats.

What is merely economic or political within the economic sector may have security implications in other sectors. Can society, with its wider set of values, survive the impact of international marketization? Will breakdowns in the international economy lead to war? Does the spread of mass consumption market economies threaten to overwhelm the planetary ecosystem? The logical difficulties within liberalism caused by the acceptance of economic insecurity as the price of efficiency work against attempts to securitize issues in the economic sector. They do not prevent such attempts, although it is easier for economic nationalists than for liberals to make those attempts. It is difficult for liberals to speak of economic security without becoming intellectually incoherent.

One interesting feature of the economic sector is that system-level structures (the market, the trading system, the financial system) and the institutions associated with them are routinely invoked as objects of security. This contrasts with the discourse in the political sector, where, although various regimes and institutions and even international society itself can become referent objects, the anarchic structure as such is almost never invoked in this way (even though the obsession with sovereignty implies support for an anarchic structure). When economic systems—whether abstract markets or concrete IGOs—are constructed as referent objects of security, the question of what constitutes an existential threat can be answered only in terms of the principles by which such systems are organized. The LIEO is existentially challenged by anything that threatens to unravel commitments to remove border constraints on the international movement of goods, services, and finance. More subtly, it is also threatened by the development of monopolies, which undercut the rationales of competition and efficiency that underpin the system. The LIEO thus lives in permanent tension with impulses toward both protectionism and monopoly. To the extent that these other impulses gain ground, the LIEO is diminished and eventually extinguished. The same logic applies to IGOs. In the economic sector, something like the EU can be existentially threatened by whatever might unglue the rules and agreements that constitute its single market (cf. Chapter 8).

Although clear in principle, this criterion for securitization is not so simple in practice. At least two questions arise: When does the scale of a threat become sufficient to count as a legitimate security issue, and how does one deal with systemic crises and their effects on the units within the system?

The problem with scale is endemic to all kinds of security logic. In principle, any armed force in the hands of a neighboring state can be constructed as a threat to military security, but in practice, only when such forces become capable of invading or massively damaging others and are accompanied by perceptions of hostility can they easily be made to take on the full character of credible security threats. With liberal economic systems, any moves toward monopoly or protectionism can be taken as security issues, but to do so, as in the case of small military forces, risks paranoia. Considerable ebb and flow will always occur around basic organizing principles within the huge complexities of international market systems. Some states may need temporary protectionist measures to ease adjustments within the larger framework. This need can be accepted and institutionalized within an overall liberal framework and so need not trigger securitizing reactions. The postwar regimes of "embedded liberalism" contained escape clauses to make such adjustment possible without threatening the ordering principles (Ruggie 1982).

The Cold War period, moreover, demonstrated that a "world" economy can flourish even without the participation of large parts of the world (the Communist bloc). Like humans, firms, and states, systems can lose an arm or a leg without being existentially threatened. Security threats to such systems occur when leading actors or large numbers of members begin either to question the constitutive principles of the system or to break or fail to support the rules and practices that uphold the system.

Securitization is sometimes attempted on less significant threats. Such attempts usually fail, but sometimes they function to legitimize action against dissenters from the global liberal economic order. One can see this in elements of U.S. policy toward Cuba and in the emerging tougher international stand toward the Swiss banking policy.

Systemic crises may result from such disaffected behavior, but they may also result from malfunctions or cyclical patterns within the system. Are disruptions that affect the structure of (large parts of) the system to be considered security issues, and if so, what or who can be presented as existentially threatened? In this view, individual actors, such as TNCs, or specific trade relations may not be important, but the key issue is stability in the global traffic of goods, money, services, and people. "Stability" means changes occur only within known limits—that is, that the misfortune of individual actors or relations does not trigger damaging chain reactions that threaten the system. "Known limits" can be interpreted as socially accepted risks of economic enterprise or as calculated risk. The Great Depression is the classic example of a chain reaction shredding the entire fabric beyond calculated risk. Black Monday (October 1987) shows, however, that similar crises can now be handled—although not without costs. The international debt crisis (in the early 1980s) is another example of disaster traveling fast through the international economic system and testing its resilience.

When such chain reaction disasters bring down the system, as occurred in the 1930s, they clearly fit within the logic of security in terms of existential threats to the system. This possibility underlies and justifies much of the economic nationalist position (focusing on the dangers of exposure under liberalism) and also of the liberal attempt to securitize protectionism (as the supposed cause of systemic crises). Such views may well justify securitizing responses to events that are less than threatening to the entire system but that may trigger chain reactions.

But here, some of the inherent contradictions of liberal economic security arise to obscure the picture. How does liberal security logic deal with systems whose organizing principles are themselves defective in the sense that they create a significant probability of systemic crises (Polanyi 1957 [1944])? What does it mean to protect the stability of a system if the system is a threat to itself? This question takes us back to the basic ideological disputes at the heart of IPE. It can be argued, for example, that the LIEO contains such faults. The relentless pursuit of free trade may eventually create such pressures of adjustment and loss on states, as well as the polarization of societies, that it triggers reactions against the basic principles of the system. Or financial deregulation may give certain kinds of economic actors (futures "securities" traders are ironically the currently favored candidate) sufficient freedom to pursue their own interests that they overreach the carrying capacity of the system and bring it down. The typical case here would be a chain reaction collapse of credit that might result from the huge resources now being gambled on futures and derivatives. It is difficult to know in what sense, if any, one can think of such prospects as threats to the system, although one way into the problem may be to think in terms of threats to the joint gains fostered by the LIEO.

The other obvious way to think about threats in security terms is to shift to thinking of systemic crises as threats to the units (states, firms, IGOs) within the system. Here, it might be argued that what matter are the speed and scale of fundamental change—its shock value. If Japan dropped out of the world economy tomorrow (e.g., as a result of a hypothetical natural disaster of the Atlantis class), the entire system would be disrupted. But if an economic power like Japan diminishes slowly and gradually— say, over a period of one or two generations, as Britain has done (albeit not without two world wars)—the system can adapt to the process.

Sudden and massive structural change thus might count as an economic security issue as it does at other levels. Losing a job on the spot creates huge insecurities, as does finding one's house burned down, whereas receiving notice a year ahead allows for timely adjustments. Many mechanisms exist for providing security against the effects of unexpected systemic disruption on units within the system. Insurance companies are a classic example, although they typically exclude damage from many disasters that would cause widespread claims, such as earthquakes, hurricanes, and wars. Social security systems cushion the blow of unemployment and are also important in preventing a spillover of economic conflicts into political ones. Banks may play a similar role for firms. But these examples all concern measures to help individual units that get into trouble. Most either cease to function or are swept away if the system itself collapses.

The increasing internationalization of the world economy and the fear of another 1920s-style collapse have led to the increasing institutionaliza-tion of system-level security guarantors in the LIEO. The IMF and the World Bank provide support for states that get into economic trouble, and the GATT-WTO contributes to resilience against crises by providing rules and settling disputes. Central banks operate more and more independent of national governments, and their representatives meet regularly to discuss and coordinate policy in forums such as the Bank for International Settlements and the International Organization of Securities Commissions (Underhill 1995). The major OECD banks are also connected by hot lines to enable immediate communication and coordination in case of a crisis. Such measures suggest a serious and sustained response to threats against economic security at the system level. One astute observer even compared the personnel involved in these arrangements to the "mafia of nuclear strategists" who once inhabited the military security world (Healey 1989: 413).

The securitization of systemic crises runs up against the arguments made earlier that within the economic sector, existential threats constitute a fairly narrow range of conditions. But given the particular nature and vul-nerability of the LIEO as a referent object for economic security, the sys-tem level would seem to be the strongest legitimate candidate for securiti-zation in this sector (as well as having impacts in other sectors). Although some other aspects of the economic sector can be securitized, they are rela-tively few and reflect extreme cases. Because of the basic nature of a liber-al economy, much of what might be seen as economic security issues is in fact either normal or politicized economic relations. One feature of security in this sector is that although genuine economic security issues are relative-ly rare, normal and politicized economic activity frequently spills over into other sectors, with security consequences. Another feature is that although frequent attempts at securitization are made, covering many types of refer-ent objects, few attract wide support. These discourses of securitization are part of the ideological disputes about policy for the political economy. When pure liberalism is in the ascendant, few economic security claims will be able to surmount the hurdle that insecurity is the price to be paid for participating in the global market economy. Under this logic, losers are part of the game, and their attempts to securitize their plight are dismissed as attempts to change the rules of the game.

Regionalizing Dynamics?

Are the main trends in the security dynamics of the economic sector local, regional, or global? One of the problems in answering this question is the intrinsic difficulty of applying security logic to competitive economic rela-tions. Another, as shown earlier, is that whereas the strictly economic logic of security is rather narrow, economic dynamics have many security effects in other sectors. These linkages are what underpins IPE as a cross-sectoral enterprise. Keeping the economic security agenda distinct from other sectors is not easy or generally a good idea.

Globalizing Trends

On the face of it, one would expect the dynamics of contemporary economic security to be dominated by the strong globalizing tendencies that mark the LIEO as a whole. Unlike military and political relations, economic ones are currently little affected by geography and distance. The costs of worldwide shipping and communications today are very low, and in the LIEO many large firms are globally mobile. Many markets (particularly financial ones) now operate globally, and it is no longer an exaggeration to speak of a global economic system. Indeed, some writers (e.g., Cerny 1995) see the development of a global-scale division of labor as sufficiently advanced to be marginalizing the state.

The emergence and intensification of a global market economy is one of the major developments of our time, and the security question arising is about the stability of this complex network of competitive and collaborative relations. There has long been a debate about the coming destabilization of the liberal international economic order consequent upon the decline (or, in some versions, corruption) of the United States as a hegemonic leader (Hirsch and Doyle 1977; Keohane 1980, 1984; Strange 1984; Gilpin 1987; Kindleberger 1981). With the end of the Cold War, this debate has taken on an ironic Leninist twist with the possibility that the removal of their shared fear of communism and Soviet power will cause the main centers of capitalist power to fall into a gathering crisis of competition among themselves. The fashionable talk about competition for market shares (Strange 1994) cuts just close enough to Lenin's ideas of imperialism and to the struggle to redivide a saturated global market to generate a deep sense of unease. It also tends to undermine the main hope of political economy institutionalists, already understood as a fragile option, that shared understandings and ideologies plus a collection of international regimes and institutions (the Group of Seven [G7], the World Bank, the WTO, the IMF) might be able to sustain the liberal international economic order on the basis of collective hegemony (Keohane 1984).

What looms on the horizon, therefore, is the possibility of a major crisis in the global political economy involving a substantial collapse of the liberalizing regime developed during the Cold War. Two sets of pressures seem to be converging simultaneously on the weakening Cold War economic order. One is the intensification of trade competition that is consequent upon the increasing number of suppliers in almost every area of production (Paye 1994). The successful industrialization of areas outside the

West has increased the size of markets. But even more, it has generated surplus capacity in many industries. Surplus capacity intensifies competition and results in deindustrialization when older producers have become uncompetitive.

This globalizing of economic efficiency is good for consumers, but it places tremendous pressures of adaptation on states and societies, which have continually to reconfigure the way in which they earn a living. As liberal economists seem too easily to forget, to be a consumer one has to produce something to trade or sell. In older developed areas such as Europe, intensified trade competition confronts states and societies with major questions about social and political values. What, for example, do they do with the increasing segment of the population for whom no jobs seem likely to be available as a result of automation and the exodus of low-skilled agricultural and industrial jobs to cheaper labor countries abroad? The long, drawn-out saga of the GATT Uruguay Round was the bellwether of this gathering crisis in which the pursuit of economic efficiency creates societal and political costs that are increasingly difficult to sustain in a democratic political context. The barely successful conclusion of the round in December 1993 reflected a desperate hope that further liberalization would stimulate sufficient overall growth to stave off the accumulating social and political problems. Left unaddressed is the underlying tension between the economic realm on the one hand and the political and societal realms on the other and the intensifying pressures for protectionism these tensions feed.

The second set of pressures concerns the financial liberalization that has been underway since the 1970s. The progressive removal of states' financial controls has undermined the original postwar design for the global political economy set out at Bretton Woods. The Bretton Woods idea was to consolidate the welfare state by protecting it from the instabilities of deregulated finance that had precipitated the great crash in the late 1920s. Trade would be deregulated, but finance would not, and a system of stable exchange rates would facilitate trade.

Financial deregulation has both undermined the welfare state (in some places, such as the UK, intentionally so) and blown away any hope for exchange rate stability. Powerful financial markets organized on a global scale can now attack national currencies at will and wreck projects such as Europe's exchange rate mechanism (ERM) that, if successful, would greatly reduce the profits to be made from currency exchange and speculation. Deregulation has also reduced the financial management tools available to states, leaving them with only interest rates and fiscal policy—both of which are notoriously difficult to use in this way, because they have immediate and severe impacts on the domestic economy and are difficult to coordinate given the different rhythms of national economic cycles (Cox 1994; Helleiner 1994a; Webb 1994; and Stubbs and Underhill 1994). This development exacerbates the trade crisis in two ways: It weakens the ability of

the welfare state to deal with the domestic consequences of intense competition, and it complicates trade and industrial policy by deranging exchange
rates. The development also opens up the possibility of a major financial
crisis resulting from overextensions of credit, like the one that triggered the
Great Depression.

The combination of these three factors—weakened U.S. leadership,
surplus productive capacity, and financial instability—explains the seemingly peculiar combination of pervasive economic angst on the one hand
and liberal euphoria over the end of history and the defeat of communism
on the other. Some writers are predicting a severe "time of troubles" ahead
(Wallerstein 1993; Huntington 1993, 1996; Spence 1994: 4; Kaplan 1994).
This crisis may or may not come to pass, but the prospect of it and awareness of its possibility provide the basis for securitization of system-level
regimes, consultative mechanisms, and organizations that sustain the LIEO.
A major economic breakdown would have repercussions not only in the
economic sector but also in terms of political and military security.
Attempting to prevent such a breakdown and to retain the known productive efficiencies of the LIEO is the main globalizing dynamic for economic
security.

Regional Dynamics

Interestingly, a strong connection seems to exist between global concerns
about the security of the LIEO and securitizing dynamics at the regional
level. Economic regionalism (Helleiner 1994b; Anderson and Blackhurst
1993; Fawcett and Hurrell 1995) has come back into fashion as a result of
the widening and deepening of integration in the EU since the late 1980s
and the construction of NAFTA. The most ambitious of these projects, the
EU, trundles onward despite all of its difficulties and has unquestionably
become the central focus of security in Europe (Buzan et al. 1990; Wæver
et al. 1993). These two regional projects at the core of the global political
economy have spawned imitators (the ASEAN Free Trade Area [AFTA] in
Southeast Asia, Asia-Pacific Economic Cooperation [APEC] linking
Australasia and North America, the Southern Cone Common Market
[MERCOSUR] covering the Southern Cone of South America), as well as
much discussion about other regional economic zones (ECOWAS in West
Africa, the South Asian Association for Regional Cooperation [SAARC] in
South Asia, The South African Development Community [SADC] in
Southern Africa, the CIS covering the former Soviet Union). East Asia is a
puzzling case, with some interpreting it as lacking formal economic region-
alism (and therefore vulnerable) and others seeing it as developing a distinctive informal, transnational model of regional integration.

Regionalization comes in many different forms of integration, with
many different degrees of identity, depth, and institutionalization. Perhaps
the main difference is that between formal, rule-bound, institutionalized

versions (e.g., the EU) and informal versions led by "undirected processes of social and economic interaction," as in East Asia (Hurrell 1995: 333–338). As with the global level, the regional one can be securitized in itself or can overlap with securitizations at the state and individual levels. The debates about the European Monetary Union have this overlapping quality.

The low cost of transportation and communication makes the undeniable enthusiasm for economic regionalism look at first peculiar. Given the intrinsic mobility of so many economic factors, in purely economic terms it would make as much sense for Britain to be linked with North America or Japan as to be part of the EU.

Why do we find economic regionalism at a time when globalizing economic forces are so strong? The most obvious answer is that economic regionalism is a response to globalization. It can help states to cope not only with the success or failure of the LIEO but also with its day-to-day operation. To the extent that states fear a breakdown of the LIEO, it is prudent to construct regional blocs as a fallback position. There are dangers in this strategy, most notably that the insurance measure could take on an economic nationalist hue and could itself become the cause of the feared breakdown. But few want to see a breakdown of the LIEO all the way down to the state level, and regions are an obvious stopping point.

If no crisis occurs and the LIEO performs successfully, regional groupings offer the additional benefit of providing a stronger platform for operating and negotiating in the global economy (although again this can tend toward mercantilism). They can, as Andrew Hurrell (1995: 346, 356) argues, provide both a more achievable institutional scale for handling the problems of collective management posed by global liberalization and a way of preserving particular forms of political economy (such as the EU's Keynesian welfare statism). Regional groupings also offer potentially congenial ways of arranging economic relations between dominant local economic powers (e.g., Germany, the United States, India, South Africa, Japan) and their neighbors. Additionally, technical arguments explain some regionalizing trends in spite of powerful globalizing forces. In some places, local knowledge and sociocultural compatibility may favor regional patterns of trade and investment. In others, transportation costs may matter, as in Southeast Asia's so-called growth triangles, which seek to integrate production across compatible adjacent sources of capital, labor, and materials (Ariff 1996: 4).

The economic logic of regionalism can thus be seen mainly as a response to top-down threats from the dominant framework of globalization, although, as with the EU, significant bottom-up logics also support it. As long as economic regionalism remains liberal in its outlook, the two developments are compatible. Unlike the situation in the 1930s, most contemporary regional blocs have fairly liberal internal trading structures and in many ways are open to world markets. Their purposes are to reduce the pressures of an open global economy without sacrificing all economies of scale and to try to reduce the overstretched management demands of an open global economy by moving many of those demands to a more intimate regional scale. Economically, the trading structures are attempts to build stronger operating platforms from which to engage in the ever more intense trade and financial competition in the global market. And they are fallback bastions in case the global liberal economy succumbs to the effects of weak management, financial turbulence, or intensifying trade competition. Part of this function is about genuine economic security; the rest is about seeking an advantage in the politico-economic logic of competition within a global market.

Regionalization could become the dominant trend, but that would require a shift from liberal to economic nationalist views of the political economy and a consequent redefinition of what constitutes economic security. For the time being, regionalization is more derivative from than threatening to the LIEO. Nevertheless, the geographic element of economic regionalism is worrying to liberals because it seems to run counter to the efficiencies of a global market; it is worrying to strategists because it has echoes of the neomercantilist blocs of the 1930s that were forerunners of World War II. This parallel with the 1930s seems misplaced. The contemporary economic blocs differ in crucial ways from those of the interwar period, as do the incentives affecting imperialism and war (Buzan 1991: 258–261).

Although they do not point toward preparation for war, as was true in the 1930s, the contemporary economic blocs do have security roles in other sectors. They are, for example, politico-cultural defense mechanisms against the powerful homogenizing effects of open markets. Liberals like to think of the global market as, ideally, a place of uniform rules and universal logics of behavior. But one aspect of economic regionalism may be culturally based. As Eric Helleiner (1994b) points out, the three main economic groupings all have distinctive characters. Europe is heavily institutionalized and is driven by social democratic values. North America is lightly institutionalized and reflects liberal values. East Asia relies mostly on transnational links and reflects national development values.

It could be that part of contemporary economic regionalism is based in the desire to preserve societal security. In this perspective, Islamic economies might eventually qualify as a separate type that has regionalizing tendencies, although this would depend upon the outcome of the integrating versus fragmenting dynamics discussed in Chapters 3, 6, and 7. At least in the banking sphere, Islamic norms and principles are sometimes different from capitalist ones (in Islamic economies, for example, it is forbidden to calculate interest on loans). When Islamic and capitalist economies do relate to one another, the situation might be like that with IBM and Macintosh computer systems: The two are compatible rather than hostile, but there are permanent translation costs. The difference might contribute to regionalization (higher economic interdependence among the users of the same system).

In more conventional military-political terms, some realists have viewed regionalization as an attempt to construct superpowers. The EU is commonly seen this way both by its more extreme federalist advocates and by possible rivals in the United States and Russia. This argument was more convincing during the Cold War, when big was beautiful, and it has faded somewhat with the disintegration of the USSR and resistance to deeper integration within Europe.

Localizing Dynamics

Given the overwhelming force of globalization and the regionalizing responses to it, little room is left for serious security dynamics at the local level. Even the state, which not long ago would have factored very strongly at this level, has largely surrendered to the imperatives of liberalization, with domestic debates now dominated by system-level arguments. There are, however, economic security consequences to liberalization that clearly manifest themselves at the local level. Here, one would need to look at factors ranging from collapses in the provision of basic human needs (e.g., famine) through the local consequences of deindustrialization or financial crises (e.g., Mexico, Russia) to the antidevelopment of some national economies in which gross national product (GNP) per capita is in decline (e.g., Africa). In terms of security logic, these situations can clearly be constructed as security issues when they threaten the provision of basic human needs or the survival of the state. Also, there may increasingly be political room for actors at local levels as the state becomes weakened by the deregulating global economic order.

Summary

Because of the nature of economic relations under liberalism, economic security is a peculiarly difficult subject. This difficulty has to do in part with the instrumental quality of economic units and the inherent insecurity of market relations and in part with the pervasive and substantial consequences of economic activity in other sectors. Except at a very basic level, the logic of survival is difficult to argue within the economic sector itself. Attempts to securitize economic issues are essentially a part of the political-ideological policy debate within IPE. In this context, the language of securitization is a way of taking economic nationalist positions in economic policy debates without having to abandon superficial commitments to the liberal consensus. Perhaps the main exception to this condition is seen in the system-level referent objects—the institutions and organizations of the LIEO. Here, a clear logic of survival exists that entails obvious and drastic consequences. Liberal orders can collapse. As with political regimes and institutions (see Chapter 4, "The Logic of Threats and Vulnerabilities"), they are vulnerable to nonacceptance, violations, and challenges and also to the logic of the domino theory. Nobody knows whether any given violation, defection, collapse, or crisis of confidence will be the one that begins the slide toward a comprehensive unraveling of the system. Within that context, regionalism also takes on some security qualities.

Although little of a strictly economic security agenda exists within liberalism, economic activity fairly easily triggers survival issues in all of the other sectors—sometimes on the basis of economic failures (e.g., famine, negative development) and sometimes on the basis of economic successes (cultural homogenization, loss of autonomy in military production, pollution, the gutting of state functions). This overspill quality means that much of what is talked about as "economic security" has in fact to do with logics of survival in other sectors and not the economic one. If one reconsiders the list of issues said to constitute the current agenda of economic security (see "The Economic Security Agenda") this overspill effect is rather clear.

1. The ability of states to maintain an independent capability for mobilization is affected by the globalization of production, which gives states the choice of having lower-quality, more expensive domestically produced weapons or higher-quality, cheaper ones that are wholly or in part produced abroad. In the LIEO, security of supply is underpinned not by indigenous control of production but by the existence of surplus production capacity and a buyer's market.

2. Much the same logic applies to concerns about security of supply. The possibility of economic dependencies within the global market (particularly oil) being exploited for political ends is offset by the existence of surplus capacity in nearly all commodities as well as a buyer's market.

3. Fears that the global market will generate more losers than winners and will heighten inequalities are not survival issues unless they undermine the provision of basic human needs. They are instead the political consequence of an economic system that requires winners and losers.

4. Fears of trade in drugs and weapons of mass destruction are sociopolitical and military security issues rather than economic ones, and fears of pollution are environmental security issues rather than economic ones.

5. Only fears that the international economy will fall into crisis are clearly economic security issues.

To say that economic security is difficult and blurry may be true, but this description is not very helpful. At most, it sends a warning and invites care in the use and reception of securitization attempts in this sector. But given the desire of liberals to separate the economic sector from politics, the fact that most of the security consequences of economic liberalism turn up in other sectors is of more than passing interest. Liberal economics can only maintain its apparent pristine quality by making such separations; it is only when they are placed into a wider context that most of its security consequences come clearly into view. This conclusion points toward Chapter 9, where we expand the idea of security spillovers from the economic sector as a way of understanding the imperatives behind the entire phenomenon of the wider security agenda.

CHAPTER 6

The Societal Sector

The Societal Security Agenda

National security has been the established key concept for the entire area of security affairs, but, paradoxically, there has been little reflection on the nation as a security unit. The focus has been on the political, institutional unit—the state—and accordingly on the political and military sectors. If one zooms in on the nation, another sector enters the picture—the societal one. Societal security is closely related to, but nonetheless distinct from, political security, which is about the organizational stability of states, systems of government, and the ideologies that give governments and states their legitimacy.

Only rarely are state and societal boundaries coterminous. This provides a first motive for taking societal security seriously (for example, in thinking about the security of the Kurds), but second, even the state and society "of the same people" are two different things (and, when they are referent objects for security, they generate two different logics). State is based on fixed territory and formal membership, whereas societal integration is a much more varied phenomenon—possibly occurring at both smaller and larger scales and sometimes even transcending the spatial dimension altogether. For international security analysis, the key to society is those ideas and practices that identify individuals as members of a social group. Society is about identity, the self-conception of communities and of individuals identifying themselves as members of a community. These identities are distinct from, although often entangled with, the explicitly political organizations concerned with government.

The organizing concept in the societal sector is identity. Societal insecurity exists when communities of whatever kind define a development or potentiality as a threat to their survival as a community. Despite the impression one might get from the present and, especially, previous presentations, the *definition* is not in terms of nations. Definitionally, societal security is about large, self-sustaining identity groups; what these are empirically varies in both time and place. In contemporary Europe (for which the concept was originally elaborated; see Wæver et al. 1993), these groups are

119

mainly national, but in other regions religious or racial groups have more relevance. The concept could also be understood as "identity security."

Two misunderstandings about the term *societal* should be avoided. First, societal security is not the same as social security. Social security is about individuals and is largely economic. Societal security is about collectives and their identity. Empirical links will often exist when the social conditions for individual life influence processes of collective identification (cf. Wæver et al. 1993, chapter 2). The concept of *societal security,* however, refers not to this individual level and to mainly economic phenomena but to the level of collective identities and action taken to defend such "we identities." (The extent to which and how individual security can enter our study is discussed in Chapters 2, 5, and 7.)

Second, a problem with *societal* is that the related term *society* is often used to designate the wider, more vague *state population,* which may refer to a group that does not always carry an identity. In this terminology, Sudanese society, for example, is that population contained by the Sudanese state but which is composed of many societal units (e.g., Arab and black African). This is not our use of societal; we use societal for communities with which one identifies.[1]

The word *nation* contains the same ambiguity, since actual nations operate differently: Some self-define their nation in terms of the people living in and loyal to the same state; others define theirs as an ethnic, organic community of language, blood, and culture. In the former case, emotional attachment is to something nonorganic and more political, whereas in other cases—and sometimes among competing groups in the same case—the ethnic community of "the real X people" is contrasted with the more amorphous group of all those who happen to live on the territory.

These terminological complexities are ultimately derived from the nature of identity-based communities; they are self-constructed "imagined communities" (Anderson 1983). Nationhood is not a question of some abstract, analytical category applied to various cases in which it fits more or less nicely. Objective factors such as language or location might be involved in the idea of national identity, but it nevertheless remains a political and personal choice to identify with some community by emphasizing some trait in contrast to other available historical or contemporary ties. Threats to identity are thus always a question of the *construction* of something as threatening some "we"—and often thereby actually contributing to the construction or reproduction of "us." Any we identity can be constructed in many different ways, and often the main issue that decides whether security conflicts will emerge is whether one or another self-definition wins out in a society. If Russia is defined by Slavophiles or Euro-Asianists, several issues will constitute security problems that would not be considered such if Russia defined itself in a Western way. To engage in self-redefinition will in many cases be an important security strategy, whereas in other cases the identity is so stable that the best security strategy is for others to take this security concern into account (cf. Buzan and Wæver 1997).

The societal security agenda has been set by different actors in different eras and regions. The most common issues that have been viewed as threats to societal security are outlined here:

1. *Migration*—X people are being overrun or diluted by influxes of Y people; the X community will not be what it used to be, because others will make up the population; X identity is being changed by a shift in the composition of the population (e.g., Chinese migration into Tibet, Russian migration into Estonia).
2. *Horizontal competition*—although it is still X people living here, they will change their ways because of the overriding cultural and linguistic influence from neighboring culture Y (e.g., Quebecois fears of anglophone Canada and, more generally, Canadian fears of Americanization).
3. *Vertical competition*—people will stop seeing themselves as X, because there is either an integrating project (e.g., Yugoslavia, the EU) or a secessionist-"regionalist" project (e.g., Quebec, Catalonia, Kurdistan) that pulls them toward either wider or narrower identities. Whereas one of these projects is centripetal and the other centrifugal, they are both instances of vertical competition in the sense that the struggle is over how wide the circles should be drawn or rather—since there are always numerous concentric circles of identity—to which to give the main emphasis.

A possible fourth issue could be depopulation, whether by plague, war, famine, natural catastrophe, or policies of extermination. Depopulation threatens identity by threatening its carriers, but it is not specifically a part of the societal sector's logic of identity, except perhaps in cases where extermination policies are motivated by the desire to eliminate an identity and in extreme cases—such as AIDS in Uganda—where quantity turns into quality. As with unemployment and crime, these are threats primarily to individuals (threats *in* society); only if they threaten the breakdown of society do they become societal security issues.

Although analytically distinct, in practice these three types of threats to identity can easily be combined. They can also be placed on a spectrum running from intentional, programmatic, and political at one end to unintended and structural at the other. Migration, for example, is an old human story. People may make individual decisions to move for reasons varying from economic opportunity to environmental pressure to religious freedom. But they may also move as part of a political program to homogenize the population of the state, as in the Sinification of Tibet and the Russification of Central Asia and the Baltic states. Horizontal competition may simply reflect the unintended effects of interplay between large, dynamic cultures on the one hand and small, anachronistic ones on the other. But it can also become intentional, as in the remaking of occupied enemies (e.g., the Americanization of Japan and Germany) and in the cultural aspects of contemporary trade policy. Vertical competition is more likely to be found at the intentional end of the spectrum.

Integration projects, whether democratic or imperial, that seek to shape a common culture to match the state may attempt to control some or all of the machineries of cultural reproduction (e.g., schools, churches, language rights). In more repressive instances, minorities may lose the ability to reproduce their cultures because the majority uses the state to structure educational, media, and other systems to favor the majority culture. Thus, some types of societal security issues are fought in the hearts and minds of individuals, whereas others are about more tangible matters that influence identity. In the first case, the threat is about conversion—people start to think of themselves as something else. In the second, political decisions will influence identity, such as using migration or political structures to compromise the reproduction of a culture that lacks control of the institutions required for cultural reproduction. Societal security issues are always ultimately about identity; in some cases, the medium in which they are fought is also identity (horizontal and vertical competition), whereas in others it is not (migration, infrastructure of reproduction).

Society can react to such threats in two ways: through activities carried out by the community itself or by trying to move the issue to the political (and potentially the military) sector by having the threat placed on the state agenda. At the state level, the threat of immigration, for example, can be addressed through legislation and border controls. State-oriented responses are fairly common, which makes the societal sector difficult to analyze because it often merges gradually with the political sector.

In some cases, however, societies choose to handle what they perceive as identity threats through nonstate means. One example might be that of minorities that do not try to secede into their own state but still have a strategy for how to survive as a distinct culture. Generally, minorities strive for one of three basic options: to dominate the existing government (e.g., Tutsis, whites under apartheid), to form their own government (Slovenes, Zionists), or to be left alone (traditionally, Jews in Europe). The Chinese, when forming minorities abroad, typically do not use the institutions of the host society but prefer to try to run their own system of law, order, and social security.

The choice of whether to see societal threats as a task for society itself, as one for an existing state, or as an argument for gaining or regaining statehood can have a decisive impact on regional dynamics. In our terminology, that choice can be seen as a question of what actor to turn to and whether to forge close ties between the societal and political sectors. We have shown in a previous analysis of Europe how a strong link between these two sectors and thus remobilization of the state on identity issues would constitute a major threat to European integration, whereas a more separate securitization in terms of societal security could be more compatible with further integration—which, in turn, stimulates this increasing differentiation of society from state (Wæver et al. 1993, chapter 4).

Security Actors and Referent Objects

The referent objects in the societal sector are whatever larger groups carry the loyalties and devotion of subjects in a form and to a degree that can create a socially powerful argument that this "we" is threatened. Since we are talking about the societal sector, this "we" has to be threatened *as to its identity*. Historically, such referent objects have been rather narrow. For most people, they have been local or family based: the village, a clan, a region (in the local rather than international sense), or a city-state. In some eras, these objects were closely tied to political structures (city-states, clans, and the like). In others, political loyalties operated distinct from societal forms, as in classical empires in which political loyalties were to kings or emperors and people's "we" loyalties were mainly tied to families and religion. Communists tried to mobilize according to class but largely failed.

In the present world system, the most important referent objects in the societal sector are tribes, clans, nations (and nationlike ethnic units, which others call minorities),[2] civilizations, religions, and race. The operations of these different societal referent objects are spelled out in more detail in the following sections, in which the different regions are visited and their distinctive patterns of conflict in the societal sector outlined.

Nations sometimes closely correspond to a state, and in such cases references to the nation and its identity are often made by persons in positions of state power. In some instances, state leaders use references to state and sovereignty; in others, to nation and identity. This difference is in itself interesting and worth investigating. There might be a pattern in which oppositional political forces—that is, actors of traditional political form who are bidding for state power but do not possess it—use references to *nation* more than to *state*. The defense of state and sovereignty will tend to strengthen those in power. It is possible but complicated to argue that those in power imperil the security of the state; the logic of state security will tend to privilege the power holders as the natural interpreters of what should be done to secure the state. It is easier to argue that the nation is endangered; because the present leaders are not paying sufficient attention to this situation, we should be brought into power—a typical rhetorical strategy of nationalist politicians. The nation, with its mixture of connection to and separation from the state, is ideal for such oppositional political maneuvers.

Whereas these instances used references to the nation to get to the state, one can also make appeals about threats to the nation without wanting state power. This is the case with various social movements—nationalist, cultural, anti-EU, or anti-immigrant. In instances where state and nation do not line up, the minority nation will be the point of reference for actors ranging from a counterelite trying to achieve secession or independence (and thereby becoming the new state elite) to groups defending the cultural identity of the minority.

In all of these cases, the media is an important actor that contributes significantly to the definition of situations. Who are the parties to conflicts; what are the conflicts about? With its attraction to simple stories, the media will often tell the news in terms of "us" and "them" or, in the case of foreign news, of "Serbs" and "Muslims." When ethnic or religious categories are established as the interpretative instruments for understanding a situation, the media has often played a role in this.

Religious identification usually corresponds to some official or semiofficial—often contested—leaders who claim to be able to speak on behalf of the religious community. In many cases, however, there is not one generally recognized, tight hierarchy; therefore, various local groups—for example, fundamentalists in Egypt—can make their own appeals in the name of all Muslims and mobilize security action against the West and its local lackeys. The major religions vary as to their degree of formalized and generally recognized lines of authority. Tribes vary even more, and less can be said in a general sense about securitizing actors in their case.

The Logic of Threats and Vulnerabilities

Different societies have different vulnerabilities depending upon how their identity is constructed. If one's identity is based on separateness, on being remote and alone, even a very small admixture of foreigners will be seen as problematic (e.g., Finland). Nations that control a state but only with a small numeric margin (e.g., Latvia) or only through repression of a majority (e.g., Serbs in Kosovo) will be vulnerable to an influx or superior fertility rate of the competing population (e.g., Russians, Albanians). If national identity is tied to specific cultural habits, a homogenizing "global" culture, such as the U.S.-Western Coca-Cola (or, more recently, McDonalds) imperialism, will be threatening (e.g., Bhutan, Iran, Saudi Arabia). If language is central to national identity, the contemporary global victory of English combined with an increasing interpenetration of societies will be problematic (e.g., France). If a nation is built on the integration of a number of ethnic groups with mobilizable histories of distinct national lives, a general spread of nationalism and ideas of self-determination can be fatal (e.g., the Soviet Union, Yugoslavia, Czechoslovakia, the United Kingdom, India, Nigeria, South Africa); if a nation is built on a melting-pot ideology of different groups blending into one new group, the existing national identity will be vulnerable to a reassertion of racial and cultural distinctiveness and incommensurability (e.g., multiculturalism in the United States). If the nation is tied closely to the state, it will be more vulnerable to a process of political integration (e.g., Denmark, France) than will be the case if the nation has a tradition of operating independent of the state and of having multiple political layers simultaneously (e.g., Germany).

The variation in vulnerability has to be kept in mind during the following discussion in which the different kinds of societal threats are compared. In generalizations, it will be argued that one type of threat is generally more intense at some specific distance than another, but a particular unit may be more concerned about the distant threat than about the closer one, because it is more vulnerable to that kind of threat.

Keeping this caveat in mind, it is possible to compare the regionalizing and globalizing dynamics of different kinds of threats, following the earlier distinction among three kinds of societal threats—migration, vertical competition, and horizontal competition—arranged along a spectrum from intentional to structural threats. Migration operates most intensely as intraregional and neighboring region dynamics, as in the flow of Hispanics into the United States and concerns in Western Europe about immigrants from North Africa and the former Soviet empire. But long-distance migration also exists and might be growing. Some echoes former colonial overlay, such as patterns of intercontinental migration into erstwhile metropoles (e.g., South Asia and the Caribbean to Britain, North Africa to France, Indonesia to the Netherlands). But much long-distance migration simply responds to patterns of economic incentive, as in South and Southeast Asian migrations to the Gulf and Latin American and Chinese migration to the United States, to which is added the increasing flow of political refugees.

Vertical competition is the most intense when there are either political integration projects (e.g., the EU, the former Soviet Union and now within many of its successor states, Sudan, in some ways India and Pakistan) or fragmenting, secessionist ones (e.g., the former Yugoslavia, Belgium, Sri Lanka). Fragmentation and integration may occur together, as with the stimulation of substate identity projects in Western Europe within the context of the EU (e.g., Catalans, Scots, Corsicans, northern Italy).

Horizontal competition occurs at every level. Minorities within states (e.g., Welsh, Quebecois) worry about the influence of the dominant culture (English, Canadian). Smaller neighbors (e.g., Canada, Malaysia) worry about the influence of larger ones (the United States, China). At the global level, the "clash of civilizations" (Huntington 1993, 1996) comes into play, with Islamic and some East Asian worries about the influence of Americanization-Westernization. Concerns about intended—particularly coercive—threats tend to focus on tensions between integrating state projects and minorities, but they also surface in international trade negotiations when cultural issues become constructed as protectionism (e.g., the United States versus France and Japan).

Regionalizing Dynamics?

Just as military threats—other things being equal—travel more easily over short than over long distances, there is also a spatial dimension to the societal sector. It is easier to migrate over a short distance than over a long one and for cultural impulses to travel to neighbors than to faraway places. Competing ideas of who "we" are will usually be regional in the sense that the same person can be seen as Hindu, Indian, or South Asian or as European, British, and Scottish but only with some difficulty as Swede, Australian, and Muslim and not likely as Russian, Latin American, and Buddhist. But the spatial factor is not necessarily region producing in the same sense as exists in the military sector; even if it does produce regions, they are not necessarily the same regions. This was the foundational puzzle for the present book. When we wrote a book about societal security (Wæver et al. 1993), we did not want to invent a separate societal security complex; nor could we be sure there was one cross-sectoral complex in which to study societal security. So we took the easy route of generating the security complex mainly in the political and military sectors (where we knew it worked) and then adding societal security problems and dynamics into a complex thus established (Wæver et al. 1993, chapters 1, 10). But if the military and political sectors are no longer necessarily dominant and the other sectors are nonregional or differently regional, the security complexes might lose coherence, or we might have to contemplate studying sector-specific complexes.

Thus, the guiding question in the present section is whether societal security issues produce regionalizing dynamics and, if so, in what patterns and what regions—the same as those in other sectors, or different ones?

Africa

In Africa, the main societal referent objects are a mix of premodern—the extended family, village, clan, and tribe—and modern, the "state-nation."[3] Most attempts at constructing political authority take the form of state building, usually with ensuing attempts at nation building. Some social strata—especially the higher ones and the military—have some loyalty to these larger units from which they derive their income and prestige. Other strata are more prone to attaching loyalty to ethnic identities that cut across state boundaries or at least cut up state units.

As argued in Chapter 3, little of Africa (except Southern Africa, the Horn of Africa, and possibly the Maghreb) has the typical security complex type of threats in which one state threatens another. Military threats occur more often within states (over competition for state power) than between them (where capability for military power projection is low). As argued elsewhere (Chapter 8 in the present book; Wæver 1995c, chapter 11), an economic or societal issue is more likely to develop into economic or societal insecurity if the sender and receiver already perceive each other in security terms as a result of conflicts in other sectors (e.g., the military one). Thus, in the societal sector, the African states are usually less concerned about threats from other states than about threats from vertically competing loyalties (tribes and the like). The competition might take the form of an ethnification of state politics (political parties de facto being ethnic parties) or, more directly, of a struggle between the state center and other loci of authority (e.g., decentralization or disintegration of state control, secession).

Seen from the other referent object—the tribe—the cause of societal insecurity can be either other tribes or the state (state-nation building). The concrete form of threat among tribes can be migrational (e.g., South Africa) or about the control of political power (thus merging into the political sector; e.g., Nigeria) or territory (Ghana). Threats from the state are typically vertical; the state often tries to construct a competing loyalty, making people less oriented toward the old identity and thinking more in terms of a new one (cultural means), and the state can use the coercive means at its disposal to break up the tribal community (political and military means, as in Sudan).

As argued by Robert Kaplan (1994), units other than states have created new lines of division that operate differently from those on our maps. The booming megacities in the Third World, with their enormous slum suburbs, produce large populations that identify neither with their clans or tribes nor with states or nations. In some cases, these populations are the backbone of religious mobilization (as in Iran, Algeria, Egypt, and Turkey), but in many cases their identification reference is still largely open. Large groups of people who focus on immediate material survival needs become nonidentity factors and might enter the sociopolitical realm as the joker at some later point when they suddenly do acquire or generate an identity.

Another effect of Kaplanesque anarchy, especially the disease-crime-population-migration circles in Africa, is the unofficial erection of Atlantic and Mediterranean walls by which North Americans and Europeans define a category of Africa and Africans as the major zone of anarchy, danger, and disease to be shut off from "our world." So far, this has mainly been an identity category operating from the outside (thereby constituting a partial identification of "us rich Northerners" up against the dangerous premodern Third World). But to the extent that this wall is experienced the way it is intended to be—that is, by Africans running up against it—it could contribute to the formation of a similar mega-identity on the other side.

Except for these global-level clashes of civilization-type patterns, the patterns generated by these societal threats are similar to those of the military sector. They generally produce very small security complexes—not an African complex or even an Africa of, say, four or five complexes but microcomplexes focused within a state or, where identities cross state borders, on a small group of states.

Latin America

Latin America is also an odd continent in this sector. As in Africa but for different reasons, military security dynamics are relatively weak; in some ways, they are close to forming a traditional security complex but are still not clearly profiled. Being weak, they do not amplify insecurities in other sectors.

In the societal sector, there are two important perceived threats: Some segments within the dominant societies see an interregional threat from U.S. cultural and other imperialism; and some nondominant, nonstate societies—Indians—are threatened by the state-building, modernizing projects of the dominant societies (in very direct and brutal forms, with attacks on their land, lives, and resources, and in indirect forms, with increasing difficulties for the reproduction of cultural forms). Most of the other societal threats are absent. Migration is primarily an intranational problem—people are migrating to the major cities. There is little international or interregional migration, except for Central America—that is, through Mexico into the United States (few Latinos in the United States are South American; most are Mexican and Central American).

No significant vertical identity threats exist—no projects for Latin American identity or major cases of secessionism and other forms of microregionalism. There is a long history of economic projects for regional cooperation, and the old integration literature exhibited optimism that Latin America would follow Europe as the second region to integrate. This did not happen. There was no grand project; nor was it clear what a "we" Latin America would be about. The Catholic Church offers some glue, but generally the cultural area is divided because of the language factor and the big problem of Brazil thinking either in hegemonic terms or out of the region as a world-scale power that is too big for Latin America. When regional economic integration begins to operate again, one of the forms it takes is, revealingly, of NAFTA gradually admitting new members—from Mexico to Chile to . . . ? The other form is a concentric circle, a bit like Europe with MERCOSUR forming an inner elite core as the motor for the next layer of regional cooperation (Peña 1995). It is too early to say whether this integration will take on a regional identity quality and, if so, whether that identity will be Latin American, Southern Cone, or hemispherical. Regionalism is thus fairly unclear in the case of Latin America. Local (interethnic) and interregional (cultural, crime and drugs) threats are at play, but not much at the middle level.

North America

North America is an interesting and intriguing case in the societal sector and is often ignored in regional security analysis. Since the region is unipolarized, normal mechanisms, such as the security dilemma and balance of power, are largely suspended. Military security and even political security are rather insignificant in North America, where the main agenda is constituted by the global role(s) of the United States. In the societal sector, however, dynamics can be found on national and regional scales.

What are the referent objects for societal security; who are the "we" in North America? There is loyalty to Canada and the United States but also to Quebec and Texas. Increasingly, there is ethno-racial, multicultural attachment to the idea that African Americans, Hispanic Americans, Asian Americans, Native Americans ("first nations"), and other ethno-racial groups have a demand on the independent definition of their own culture, needs, and rules of social interaction against a general U.S.-societal set of norms and "universal" rules suspected of being a cover for a dominant Euro-white particularism (cf. Taylor 1992). To these should be added the older conception of regional differences, most importantly the South in the United States. State identity is rarely outspoken (it is mostly a negative, mobilized as a defense against federal authority when that authority is resisted for other reasons), but in cases such as California, Massachusetts, New York, and Texas, a certain state patriotism exists. Thus, the U.S. political universe is increasingly constituted as a complex constellation of overlapping and crosscutting identity groups in which the securitizing actors will typically be relatively small activist groups but the referent objects are fairly large collectivities such as African Americans and Hispanics, which make up 12.4 percent and 9.5 percent of the population, respectively (Bureau of the Census 1996).

All of these issues are more than security issues. They are general questions on the political and cultural agenda, but they often take on a security dimension because they are argued in terms of the survival of specific cultures (Native American, African American, and, on the other side, a white male U.S. culture that feels threatened by the new particularism). Mainstream liberals end up discussing whether the state should guarantee the survival of the distinct cultures within it (Taylor 1992). Most would argue—in a striking parallel to the logic of the economic sector—that "constitutional democracies respect a broad range of cultural identities, but they guarantee survival to none" (Gutmann 1994: x).

Whereas the classical divisions in the United States—the separate states—could be politicized and depoliticized in waves but could not really be securitized in recent times, the cultural and racial categories have a clear potential for escalating beyond politicization into securitization. As the Oklahoma City bombing and the growth of the militias have shown, fairly violent action can be deduced from an argument that defends the "true America" against what is seen as a coalition of all kinds of decadent racial and sexual minorities and liberal state lovers who curb the autonomy of straight, white Americans to live a "real" American life. The remobilization of the militias might be seen as an indication of the importance of the states (the Montana militia, the Michigan militia), but, with the exception of Texas, the often dramatic actions are taken not in the name of the state and its sovereignty but in the name of a people and a lifestyle—the real Americans and their idea of freedom—which are projected as a kind of national identity sanctioned by the Constitution and the Declaration of Independence but violated by various misinterpretations.

It is thus a peculiar kind of defense against a state (the United States) that is seen not as illegitimate as such but as illegitimate only when it operates beyond some very minimal tasks; thus, it is a defense not in the name of protosecessionist local units but an all-American defense of something like a nation, which is defined in its identity by having very little state and thus is threatened by what should be its own state (Wills 1995). This lifestyle-freedom-national identity is then intermingled with more classical reactionary rhetoric (Hirschman 1991) and articulated as a defense against perverted minorities and un-American racial and social groups. Here, the radical white categorizations often line up with the attempts of the avowed progressives of the movements of minorities, multiculturalism, and political correctness to produce a general U.S. trend toward a redefinition of cultural and societal categories in terms of distinct racial and gender groups. The one side wants these groups recognized to ensure affirmative action in favor of the disfavored; the other side wants to use these categories to picture minorities as the threat to them and thereby to the whole because as a particular group they simultaneously represent the universal American identity.

This entire redefinition of the structuration of cultural space in North America interacts with the second main factor on the societal agenda: migration. Migration was already once the key factor in a total reconstitution of North American society when immigrants, mainly from Europe, outnumbered and eventually overpowered the original population. Today, this dominant group faces a gradual shift in the population with an increase especially in the percentage of Spanish-speaking and Asian peoples, suggesting that the percentage of non-Hispanic whites will drop from 75.2 in 1991 to 60.5 in 2030 (Bureau of the Census 1996). At present, migration is securitized mainly at the state level for those areas—especially California—in which the population balance has already shifted the most significantly because of immediate adjacency to the mainland of origin for immigrants—Mexico. The two issues (changing self-definition and the physical change in the composition of the population) interact in several ways but perhaps most importantly in the reactions of white European Americans, who see immigration as a threat—not so much because the United States could become Spanish speaking (whites could become a minority) but rather because the increasing self-assuredness of different minorities threatens to produce a less unified, more multicultural, and thereby less universalistic United States.

The North American case has been given extra treatment here because it raises some interesting and unusual questions. One might ask, are novel phenomena such as multiculturalism really about societal security; do they not constitute social security instead? Since these phenomena are about various groups in society and are obviously "domestic," should they be included here? Yes, because they are about collective identities—"we blacks," "we real Americans"—and even identities that many people increasingly see as their main frame of reference. Thus, these phenomena clearly qualify as societal security. The sense of unease about including them in that category probably stems from two unconscious assumptions about units in international security studies, and the case can therefore help us to clarify important conceptual questions.

First, it is well-known that the major difference between Europe and the United States is that in Europe "nations" are largely territorial, whereas in the United States identity groups and political-territorial groups produce two crosscutting systems. The North American equivalents of Europe's nations—what today is often called race—live mixed among each other but still function similar to nations in many ways, even occasionally using the term *nation,* as in "the nation of Islam" and "first nations" (cf. also Hacker 1992; Rex 1995: 253).[4] There should be no presumption of territoriality in our concept of units in societal security; thus, the North American case fully qualifies in this respect. As registered by the use of terms like *tribalization* on European as well as North American developments (Horsman and Marshall 1995), we might see an increasing need for a conceptual apparatus able to discern ethnic and other identificational groups that operate separately from the state map both in Africa and in areas traditionally conceived of in state terms.

The second source of unease is probably related to the fact that these dynamics are obviously "domestic," should this not be a book about *international* security? In this book, we take the core meaning of security—its basic speech-act function—as it has emerged in the international field and study how this operation is increasingly performed in other contexts. Explicitly (see Chapter 2), we do not limit our study to states, but we do want to avoid the individualization of security; thus, for us security is an interunit phenomenon, and the units in this sector-chapter are identity groups regardless of whether they operate across state borders.

Europe

In Europe, societal security is mainly about nations and nationlike ethnic groups—minorities, regions, and Europe sometimes conceived in nation-building terms. We covered this topic extensively in our 1993 book (Wæver et al. 1993) and will not repeat the arguments at length here. In summary, Europe has strong regionalizing dynamics in the societal sector. The issue of minorities, nation, and Europe has produced a complex constellation of multilayered identities. And it can be argued that the fate of European integration and thereby of security is determined largely by the fate of this constellation—do the different identities evolve in a pattern of complementarity, or will some be seen by others as so threatening that they trigger panic reactions: the implementation of societal security policy and the use of extraordinary measures that block European integration (Wæver et al. 1993, chapters 1, 4, and 10; Wæver forthcoming-a).

More immediately, many local conflicts are related to vertical competition between nations-states and minorities-nations, and even those that are seemingly horizontal nation-state against nation-state usually have some of the minority, secession-irredentism element as the trigger or object of contest. Although in principle these various societal regionalizing dynamics could lead to regions rather different from those of the political and military sectors, in the case of Europe the intersectoral interplay tends to produce relatively convergent regions. Those threats in one sector that line up with urgent fears in another sector will tend to be feared more; thus, the different sectors leave a sufficient imprint on each other to create a relatively clear region in at least the military, political, and societal senses.

Among interregional and globalizing dynamics, the most important is the relationship to the Middle East, which is colored by migrants as well as historically conditioned religious suspicion. Migrants from Africa are also likely to be a continual concern.

Middle East

In the case of the Middle East, societal security has some of the same features it has in Europe. There is a constellation of states in which nations do not always fit into state boundaries. There are stateless minorities (e.g., Kurds, Palestinians). And there are overarching identities (Islamic and Arabic) that play several, sometimes contradictory roles: They can be seen as threatening to, and as threatened by, attempts to construct specific national identities and as useful in mobilizing on the international level. The various types of vertical identity conflicts presented in the European context can therefore also be found in the Middle East, with religion (the Shi'ia-Sunni divide) playing a stronger role than it does in modern Europe (but perhaps a similar role to that in post-Reformation, pre-Westphalian Europe).

There are two main differences between vertical identity conflicts in the Middle East and those in Europe (which should be expected to counter each other). First, despite the dominant rhetorics, the unifying Arabism and Islamism, the region is actually less integrated, more conflictual, and more a balance-of-power system than Europe. Second, the region has a stronger perception of external threat—of Western-orchestrated conspiracies, threats of divide and rule, cultural and economic imperialism, exterminism against Muslims in the Gulf and in Bosnia, and the like. Of course, the two are perfectly compatible if Western divide and rule is seen as a major reality, because the first feature—divisions—is then explained. Here, the picture is a complicated mixture of, on the one hand, a post-Ottoman, Western-imposed territorial fragmentation that only sometimes (e.g., Morocco, Egypt, Iran) reflected historical state traditions and, on the other hand, a wealth of local antagonisms arising over territory, ideology (conservative versus radical), kinship groups, religion, and attitudes toward the West. Evidence suggests that the state system is steadily deepening its roots, weakening the overarching Arab and Islamic identities, and taking on the characteristics of a classical security complex (Barnett 1995).

Migration in the Middle East is mainly intraregional (Palestinians, Egyptians, Yemenis, and others seeking work in the Gulf states) but with some inward (temporary) economic migration from Europe and South and Southeast Asia, also mostly to the Gulf. In some Gulf states, migrants compose a substantial proportion of the population, which poses problems of cultural difference and political exclusion.

The Middle East is in many ways the ideal type case of a regional security complex today, with deep divisions and recurring conflicts. Also, societal security concerns are largely focused within the region. There is, however, also a high degree of identification with a mostly religiously, pan-Islamic but in part pan-Arabic (thus metanationalist)-defined defense against Western dominance, cultural imperialism, and the imposition of Western standards of international society.

South Asia

South Asia's main security concerns have occurred in the political-military sector organized by the struggle between India and Pakistan. This conflict had some societal elements in that one root cause was the incompatible principles on which politics and identity were linked in the two countries (Buzan et al. 1986). India is multiethnic and to some extent multiconfessional, thereby posing to Pakistan a vision of including all of the subcontinent (including Pakistan). Pakistan, on the other hand, is religiously based and through this particularist logic questions the secular federal basis of India.

This dominant single-conflict dynamic, which integrated many dimensions in one conflict formation, is potentially giving way to a much more general, complicated, and confusing security scene in which societal conflicts within the states have become more prominent. Pakistan has tensions among its Punjabi, Pathan, Baluch, and Sindhi peoples, and its main port—

Karachi—is plagued by ethnically based political and criminal violence. India has a variety of ethnoreligious secessionist movements, most conspicuously the Sikhs and Kashmiris. Tension between its Hindu majority and Muslim minority continues to generate regular outbursts of communal violence, and the rise of Hindu nationalism as a political force could threaten the founding basis of the Indian state. Sri Lanka is still engaged in a long ethnoreligious civil war between Tamils (linked to a large community in southern India) and Sinhalese (Buddhists).

All of these situations create vertical identity conflicts between the states and the societal entities within them, and in many of these cases both sides have resorted to coercive strategies and military means. The resulting dynamics of insecurity pit defenders of the state and of its identity project (e.g., India, Pakistan) against a variety of ethnoreligious entities willing to challenge the state on the grounds of being unable to maintain their identity within it. To some extent, these internal insecurity dynamics are part of the old India-Pakistan conflict formation. Each government regularly accuses the other of aiding and arming its internal dissidents, but the societal dynamics also have a dynamic of their own.

Southeast Asia

Southeast Asia shows clear regionalizing trends institutionalized in ASEAN. The societal security agenda has two main elements—one global, one local-transnational. No strong elements of interlocking societal fears are found at the scale of the region. The global issue has to do with the conflict between a Western-dominated international agenda and "Asian values," in which Singapore and Malaysia have taken an ideological lead in articulating the counterposition to the West. The more successful (and authoritarian) of the East and Southeast Asian states are the most likely challengers to the West, because they have the credibility of an alternative development model that works.

In terms of the ethnic map of Southeast Asia, various minorities are in conflict with the central powers, but the most interesting and generalizable factor is the issue of the Chinese versus the locals, which has some similarities to the tensions between Jews and their host societies in Europe. Southeast Asia is one of the places in the world where "Greater China" as an ethnic empire is felt clearly for better (as an economically promising connection) and for worse (fear of Chinese economic dominance and political influence, especially in Malaysia, Vietnam, and Indonesia). This is one factor that reinforces the case made in the military chapter for analytically merging Southeast Asia into East Asia.

East Asia

In East Asia, which is likely to become more of a region in the military and political sectors (with general rivalry and power balancing among China,

Japan, Korea, and others), trends in the societal sector are mainly subregional (nationalizing) and interregional-global—that is, this is a case of sectors out of joint in which the regions produced by the different sectoral maps do not correspond. One of the jokers in East Asia is the coherence versus the regionalization of China (Segal 1994). Even if China does not follow the Soviet Union into decomposition, it could still be increasingly shaped by struggles between "layers," by vertical struggles rather than the horizontal interstate politics foreseen in the military and political sectors. On the other hand, if China grows as much as is expected, it might become powerful enough to be both more decentralized and still very powerful regionally; thus, the regional and intra-Chinese power games will be locked in one power constellation. It is difficult to judge to what extent Chinese regionalism should be seen as societal—that is, driven by identity diversity—or whether instead it is driven by a mixture of politics (control over the state apparatus) and the economy (different strategies and positioning) and is thus more a replay of warlords than a European-like pattern of nations.

Obviously, the region also has cases of the repression of minorities and thereby of well-known societal security dynamics, especially in the case of Tibet. This situation may feed into the more general and elsewhere less radical issue of region versus center.

In the case of Japan, the most relevant societal security issues are (despite a beginning interest in its own minorities and regions, most importantly Ainus and Okinawans) those related to globalizing–U.S. culture and national identity. Whereas this chapter has often run into the political-societal–sector boundary, Japan might be a case of economic-cultural connections. Japanese distinctiveness and difference is used as an argument in trade disputes, especially with the United States (but also with Europe), whereas some U.S. arguments about how one must organize to produce truly fair trade come very close to a demand for a U.S. socioeconomic and cultural model. After a defensive period during which the United States used arguments about the Japanese primarily to defend its own protectionism, recent years have witnessed a more offensive line in which Americans have tried (again) to structure a global regime according to their visions. This time, however, the United States has gone much further in saying other societies have to become multicultural, radical-pluralist, and the like.

There is a strong logic to this argument. When tariffs are reduced, nontariff barriers to trade become more important. When nontariff barriers are decimated, one will discover that trade does not distribute randomly. For example, Germans will keep preferring German beer even though they lost the case for using the *Reinheitsgebot* as legitimization for banning other beers. They will still drink more German beer simply because their taste and national prejudices cause them to prefer it. Likewise, the Japanese—despite their cultural addiction to things American—strongly believe in both the superiority of their own products and the collective rationality (i.e., economic-patriotic interest) of buying Japanese. Thus, built-in protection will continue, especially for those nations that are the most homogeneous, the most Gemeinschaft-like, and that operate the most on implicit, unspoken social rules—with Japan the prime case. Japan and the United States are therefore destined to continue to conflict at the interface of culture and economy.

Thus, East Asia is a complicated mixture of increasing security complex–like intraregional rivalries in the other sectors, possible societal disintegration in the case of China (which in terms of pure size could easily constitute a region itself; cf. de Wilde 1995), and societal conflict at the global level.

Former Soviet Union

The former Soviet region is probably still the most complex case for regional analysis. It is unclear into which regions this territory should be divided: Where does Europe end, where does Asia end? Is there a Russia-centered sphere that includes most of the post-Soviet countries (the CIS), and is there a Central Asian security complex?

Here again, societal, political, and military security are closely linked. Several of the new states are fragile projects. Their nature (ethnocratic or multiethnic) remains unsettled, and their degree of autonomy in relation to Russia is equally uncertain. Thus, we have problems of minorities—both narrowly geographical, in the sense of questionable borders (because concentrations of Russians are found right on the other side of the border in, for example, Estonia, the Ukraine, and Kazakhstan), and more generally as a certain percentage of the population in most of the new states. These Russian minorities are one of the main sources of incongruence among different components of nation-building projects in cases such as the Ukraine and the Baltics, where an inclusive, state-defined identity seems necessary for stability but an ethnically defined identity is an almost unavoidable component of nation and state building (Wæver et al. 1993, chapter 6; Poulsen-Hansen and Wæver 1996). This situation can be conceptualized as one of competing programs for the same state or as vertical competition between different circles of identity (e.g., ethno-Ukrainian, state-Ukrainian, neoimperial Russian).

In the former Soviet region, there are also cases of seemingly more classical interstate—that is, horizontal—conflict between two states or nations (most importantly Armenia-Azerbaijan). But again, as in the case of Europe, the trigger is a vertical problem—handling the status of a subunit, Nagorno-Karabach. The dominant type of security problem in the area is the combined societal-political issue of what units should exist and how they should be defined: Should there be several sovereign, equal states or one new Russian empire (plus possibly some smaller remnants such as West Ukraine and Southern Kazakhstan)?

It is still too early to say what kinds of security regions will emerge from the political-societal-military conflicts in Central Asia and the Caucasus. Central Asia is again a meeting point of many regions. China, Iran, Turkey, and Russia all compete for influence there, but it seems unlikely that all these powers will be drawn into one region; they all have primary or at least equal concerns elsewhere. Minority problems, water disputes, and awkward boundaries offer ample scope for the new states to drift into the classical form of a local complex. There is also a strong regionalizing dynamic in the sense that the problem of and for Russia is probably going to be the decisive issue that structures the entire region and ties a large number of security problems together into one complex.

Past migration from Russia into the other republics is the origin of the most important minority problems, and the remigration of these people returning to Russia is exacerbating social problems there. Interregional migration exists—both into and out of the region—but is secondary to internal migration.

The interregional, horizontal concern about other identities intruding is mainly a problem for Russia, which is worried about both the potential Islamification or Turkification of Central Asia and, more globally, a "world order" of concentric circles, with Russia somewhere in the second circle. The West/United States as a global factor plays an important role for Russia, both at the societal level in terms of a problematic privatization and marketization—which leads to a critique of the Western-imposed strategy—and at the diplomatic level in terms of a search for a dignified role for Russia.

All in all, strong regionalizing forces are pulling in the direction of some kind of complex that will be not purely societal but a mix of societal, political, and probably military; that will be organized by problems for and with Russia; and that will link—something like the CIS—most of the former Soviet Union, probably excepting the Baltic states. The outer boundary of this region and the nature of its relationship to neighboring regions remain uncertain, especially in the South but also toward the West and East. Global-level dynamics are present, but they also tie into the organizing controversy that is focused on Russia: What kind of Russia should exist, with what kind of regional order and what kind of global role?

Finally, one might ask if we have overlooked some forms of identification by proceeding by region. The major religions were registered where they were active and thus were not overlooked. One potential factor, however, could be the emerging cosmopolitan-postnational elite. As argued, for example, by Reich (1991, 1992 [1991]) and UNRISD (1995), the globalizing economy of the information age produces a winning class of symbolic analysts who do not think of themselves as tied to a national economy and do not necessarily see why they should feel any solidarity with unemployed people who happen to live in the same country. The industrial workers have decreasing importance, and the solidarity and loyalty of the nation-state are therefore of less value. For this elite, lifestyles and patterns of movement clearly transcend the nation-state as well. (Remembering how Benedict Anderson [1983] singled out career routes as decisive in the formation of nationalism and nation-states, the emergence of global patterns of career options might be crucial signs of a new era.)

What can be argued here is, first, that the emotional attachment to the nation-state is weakened for this crucial group. It is less clear whether these elites build up some other point of identification. In some cases, a loyalty to the multinational corporation for which one is working might substitute; in most cases, however, nothing but pure individualism prevails. In numerous instances—from the overall orientation of the United States after the Cold War to attitudes toward the EU in the northern part of Western Europe—the conflict runs between a cosmopolitan, liberal, internationalized part of society and a more locally tied, communitarian resistance. Much of societal security in the richest part of the world is related to this possibly overarching conflict—that is, the opposition is more between universalizing and particularizing cultures than between different particularizing cultures (Hassner 1996). In less privileged parts of the world the patterns are different, either because wider segments expect to gain from internationalization (e.g., EU support in southern Europe) or because much of the elite takes part in nationalist operations (the former Yugoslav area).

Summary

Proceeding region by region might produce a bias toward noticing regional dynamics, but even in this procedure some globalizing trends and factors were found. Interregional migrants played a role, especially in Europe; interregional cultural, religious, and civilizational factors were at play, especially in the Middle East and East Asia but also in Europe.

The main forces in the societal sector that push toward globalization are probably (1) the cycle of poverty in the South, migration, poverty-related diseases transmitted through migration, and migration-related organized or unorganized crime; and (2) the clash of civilizations, especially the dialectics of Westernization—a trend toward cultural homogenization and reactions against it. At least for the short to medium term, the second factor—the international political economy of culture—is probably the more important. Some claim the first factor will show its singular importance in the long run.

These two types of societal security problems are likely to take on increasing power in the future. But so will some of the more regional problems presented in the previous section, notably the multiculturalist fragmentation of the United States, the potential regionalization or fragmentation of India and China, the tribal-state conflicts in Africa, the new decentered identity constellations of Europe-nation-minority in Europe, and the problems of state and nation building in the former Soviet area. Thus, instead of concluding that globalizing dynamics will be strengthened relative to regional dynamics, it seems more appropriate to suggest that societal insecurity per se will be of increasing importance relative to other sectors, and that this will be the case at least as much in a regionalizing fashion as in a globalizing fashion.

In several cases, the regions generated by societal dynamics are essentially the same as, and are heavily intermingled with, those in the military and political sectors (Europe, South Asia, Southeast Asia, the former Soviet Union, Middle East, and, in its general confusion, Africa). In at least two cases (Latin America and East Asia), regional societal dynamics are weaker than the regional dynamics in other sectors, and in one case (North America) societal security dynamics are found when the two classical security sectors find little as regional and mostly act globally; it is not yet clear, however, whether the societal dynamics in North America are regional or more local.

Notes

1. Although our criterion for "society" does not demand that something take a romantic, organic form, it must entail more than the technical functioning together of the thinnest "society." To put this in terms of the familiar Gemeinschaft-Gesellschaft distinction (Tönnies 1926 [1887]), society can be merely a rational, contractual arrangement among individuals (Gesellschaft), or it can contain an emotional attachment and some sense of organic connectedness (Gemeinschaft). Since Gemeinschaft is traditionally translated as *community* in English, one could argue that our concept is really *community security,* but that will not do because in some cases it is possible to be loyal to a Gesellschaft ("association" in the translation of Tönnies's book) without this loyalty taking the form of organic connectedness (e.g., the United States). If we followed the widespread tendency to use society to refer to the population of any state, this would produce units that are not societies for themselves but that are societies only according to the state. That situation would remove independent judgment from the societal sector and make it derivative of state classifications.

2. *Nation* here can refer to the ethnoracial-type nation (Germanic) or to more state-related, civic nations, which some prefer to call societies; for example, some Dutch thinking in terms of the loyalty among all citizens of the Netherlands across ethnonational identification. In our terminology, this contrast is not between nation and society, but between two kinds of nations. We use the concept of society as the generic name for referent objects in the societal sector (cf. Wæver et al. 1993, chapter 2).

3. The term *state-nation* is used differently by different authors, but it is commonly taken to refer to nations being constructed by the states—cases in which state comes "before" nation—in contrast to at least the self-understanding of the classical nation-states, in which nation was assumed to come first (Buzan 1991, 73–74).

4. "In the United States we deal with what Herder would have recognized as national differences (differences, in Charles Taylor's formulation, between one society and another within the American nation) through concepts of ethnicity." And "the major collective identities that demand recognition in North America currently are religion, gender, ethnicity, 'race,' and sexuality" (Appiah 1994: 151).

CHAPTER 7

The Political Sector

The Political Security Agenda

Political security is about the organizational stability of social order(s). The heart of the political sector is made up of threats to state sovereignty. Since threats can also be leveled through military means and the military sector has its own chapter, the political sector will take care of nonmilitary threats to sovereignty.

From this core, political security concerns spread out in two directions. First, they include the equivalent nonmilitary threats to political units other than states. Second, beyond the units as such, we can also think of political security in defense of system-level referents, such as international society or international law. Among the principles that can be securitized are human rights and other demands relating directly to the condition of individuals; thus, this sector is probably the primary locus at which (seemingly) individual-level security appears on the security agenda.

A case can be made that each sector is the most difficult. When we wrote a book specifically on societal security (Wæver et al. 1993), it was because we thought that sector was the most understudied. Economic security is inherently problematic, and the environment raises unique problems. But perhaps now that the societal sector has been defined, the political sector will turn out to be the one that is the most perplexing. It easily gets squeezed between the military and societal sectors (for instance, in several articles Buzan has condensed arguments by combining sectors into either military-political or political-societal sectors) (Buzan 1994a, 1994b, 1996).

The problem with the political sector is that, paradoxically, it is the widest sector and is therefore also a residual category: In some sense, all security is political (Jahn, Lemaitre, and Wæver 1987; Ayoob 1995). All threats and defenses are constituted and defined politically. Politicization is political by definition, and, by extension, to securitize is also a political act. Thus, in a sense societal, economic, environmental, and military security really mean "political-societal security," "political-economic security," and so forth. When a political threat to the organizational stability of a state is made as a threat to its society (identity), this is cataloged as societal security; if military means are used, it is military security (although it is political too), and so forth. Thus, the political sector constitutes that subgroup of political threats that do not use massive military, identificational, economic, or environmental means. Therefore, there is a risk that the category will become less coherent than most of the others. From one point of view, as a sector it is produced by subtracting all of the other sectors. And the characteristics of political security will usually be general characteristics of security, because all security is political. Still, a sector exists that is made up of those cases in which the threats themselves are predominantly political in form, which does after all give the sector a certain coherence.

From another perspective, there is definitely an organizing problematic for this sector: What is necessary for stable organization? What is political security? According to Buzan (1991: 118ff.):

> Political threats are aimed at the organizational stability of the state. Their purpose may range from pressuring the government on a particular policy, through overthrowing the government, to fomenting secessionism, and disrupting the political fabric of the state so as to weaken it prior to military attack. The idea of the state, particularly its national identity and organizing ideology, and the institutions which express it are the normal target of political threats. Since the state is an essentially political entity, political threats may be as much feared as military ones. This is particularly so if the target is a weak state.

This quote shows how it is possible to define political security but also how difficult it is to circumscribe it, especially in relation to societal and military security—societal as indicated by the mention of national identity, and military as obvious throughout.

Typically, political threats are about giving or denying recognition, support, or legitimacy (which explains why it is possible to have purely political threats, that is, threats that do not use military, economic, or other means from other sectors—words matter in relation to recognition and related political demands). But what is politics? Much academic blood has been spilled over this question. A short definition that covers most of what people have tried to incorporate into the concept is Buzan's, in which politics is "the shaping of human behaviour for the purpose of governing large groups of people" (Buzan, Jones, and Little 1993: 35). As was the case when we defined "society" in our book on societal security (Wæver et al. 1993, chapter 2), our aim is not to be original or controversial; on the contrary, we need to establish a middle ground or a consensual view corresponding to what is generally taken to be the meaning of the term.

Therefore, we can attach our definition to neither extreme in what we might label two of the three dimensions of debates on the meaning of politics. These three dimensions can roughly be summarized as Arendt versus Easton, Schmitt versus Habermas, and Weber versus Laclau. In terms of

Arendt versus Easton, politics is not purely expressive; it is not about the individual doing great deeds and thereby striving for immortality (Arendt, Nietzsche). Nor is it purely functional, in which a sector of society performs specific tasks necessary for the whole (Easton, Parsons). In terms of Schmitt versus Habermas, politics cannot be reduced to the friend-enemy distinction (Schmitt); nor can it be seen as community and consensus (Habermas, Rawls). On both dimensions, both extremes are too narrow for our purpose; we want to steer a middle course as indicated by the Buzan definition.

On the third dimension, Weber versus Laclau, we must be more elaborate. This line of controversy is about identifying politics with stabilization or destabilization. On one side of this debate, "political" is used to cover the institutionalization of rule and the stabilization of authority. When rule is given relative permanence, the unit and the relationship that results are political (e.g., Max Weber). In contrast, writers like Ernesto Laclau define political as that which upsets stabilized patterns—politicization questions the taken-for-grantedness of social relations.[1] This Weber-Laclau duality might explain the puzzle noticed earlier about all sectors being political in some key sense. We use something like the Laclau sense when we talk of "politicization" in the sequence politicization-securitization (and in the contrast between the two, when politicization opens up and securitization closes down), but what is particular to the political sector is politics as something closer to Weber's meaning of the term: the relatively stable institutionalization of authority.[2]

Implied in this definition of politics is an image of specifically political types of units. Charles Tilly offers one way into this subject with his definition of states (we prefer political units) as coercion-wielding organizations that are "distinct from households and kinship groups and exercise clear priority in some respects over all other organizations within substantial territories. The term therefore includes city-states, empires, theocracies, and many other forms of government, but excludes tribes, lineages, firms, and churches as such" (1990: 1–2). This definition could be relaxed to include time-space locales that are not necessarily territorial in the classical sense, such as a church that takes on a political capacity (which Tilly opens up to with the phrase "as such"). A political unit is a collectivity that has gained a separate existence distinct from its subjects. It can be a firm or a church, not in their basic capacities as economic or religious units but only to the extent that they act according to the political logic of governing large groups of people.

Over time, these units have been of many different kinds. In some periods one type of political unit dominated, at others different kinds coexisted (Buzan and Little 1994, 1996). For a time (the seventeenth to twentieth centuries), politics converged on the sovereign "national state" as the form, and security became focused on this unit. But it is not necessary to prescribe a permanent continuity of the state as the dominant political form—

not even, despite the allegations of some critics, for realists (Carr 1939; Herz 1959; Morgenthau 1966) and neorealists (Ruggie 1983; Buzan, Jones, and Little 1993; Wæver forthcoming-b). Other units have in the past, and presumably will in the future, attain political primacy.

Beyond political units, politics can also be focused on political structures, processes, and (interunit) institutions. This opens up in the next section to a discussion of security that is focused not only on political units as referent objects but also on system-level referent objects.

Political security as distinct from politics in general is about threats to the legitimacy or recognition either of political units or of the essential patterns (structures, processes or institutions) among them. This follows naturally from the earlier argument about politics—and "political"—as characterized by attempts to establish order(s), to stabilize some political arrangement, some frame for the continued struggle. In the classical tradition that contains Machiavelli as well as Arendt, politics is a continuous struggle to establish the quasi-permanence of an ordered public realm within a sea of change. Then, the critical variables are obviously the recognition of such an arrangement from within and without that lends it legitimacy and thereby the stability needed for political activities to be framed by it rather than to be about it. As argued by English school theorists (Manning, Wight, Bull, and others), as well as contemporary constructivists (Wendt 1992, 1994), the identity of an international unit is not something it has for and with itself; it is very much a question of generally established categories of international subjectivity, of statehood and other forms of international being, to which the individual unit has to relate.

Political threats are thus made to (1) the internal legitimacy of the political unit, which relates primarily to ideologies and other constitutive ideas and issues defining the state; and (2) the external recognition of the state, its external legitimacy. Threats from outside are not necessarily directed at sovereignty but can very well aim at its ideological legitimacy—that is, its domestic pillar. It is possible for legitimacy to be contested from outside. In the India-Pakistan case and also during the Cold War, legitimacy was questioned externally (in the mutual exclusiveness of political forms) without this aiming to be a questioning of recognition. There is, however, good reason to focus specifically on external legitimacy, the recognition of the state as a state. A typical sequence of accusations and counteraccusations arises when political threats cross borders; see the section "The Logic of Threats and Vulnerabilities" in this chapter.

Only the modern, territorial, sovereign state has a clear, standardized form of recognition that constitutes an entire international system of equal and "like" units. But all units that interact need to achieve some kind of recognition in a general sociological sense. They need to be accepted as parties to be dealt with in their own right—if possible as equals, if necessary as vassals, but definitely not through their component parts (which means the external power has ignored and undercut the existence of the unit). Even in relationships of inequality, one wants to be recognized as vassal or as lord; if one wants to be recognized as lord or equal and achieves recognition only as vassal, this is a serious security threat, a threat to the political identity assumed by oneself.

In the modern state system, issues of political recognition are normally "either/or" matters: Basically, states do or do not recognize each other as equals. (The few cases of almost states that are almost recognized, such as the Palestine Liberation Organization, are so notorious exactly because they are exceptions to an otherwise rather rigid system.) In the postdecolonization world, international relations of formal political inequality are rare. In most of history before 1945, unequal political relations were the norm (empires and protectorates, mandates, colonies; suzerains and vassals). In the Middle Ages, for example, kings would sign treaties with equals, as well as with superiors (emperors, the pope) and inferiors—their own or other's subjects (local lords and other potentates, cities and monasteries) (Mattingly 1955; Holzgrefe 1989). In a study of medieval security, the greater variety of political actors and status would make the political sector more complicated, but in our late modern system, where states still dominate, political recognition has more clarity. Threats will typically be made to either the external pillar of stability—recognition—or the internal pillar of stability—legitimacy. In the latter, all kinds of ideological concerns can enter, as can factors relating to the role of the state as socioeconomic provider; thus, its legitimacy is tied to economic and social success.

Security Actors and Referent Objects

The predominant form of political organization in the contemporary international system is the territorial state, which is obviously the main referent object of the political sector. Other statelike or state-paralleling political organizations (i.e., other unit-level referent objects) that can sometimes serve as referent objects at the unit level are (1) emerging quasi-superstates, such as the EU; (2) some of the self-organized, stateless societal groups dealt with in the societal chapter—tribes, minorities, and clans—which have strong political institutions although not of the formal type international society recognizes (only those that take on very strong coercion-wielding and institutionalized forms enter this chapter; otherwise they are dealt with as societal); and (3) transnational movements that are able to mobilize supreme allegiance from adherents. Some world religions occasionally qualify here (the Catholic Church in earlier times, Muslims at times following such appeals but lacking one generally recognized authority), and more clearly but less significantly, some smaller sects clearly operate this way. Ideological movements also take this transnational form, but this phenomenon is often blurred by the fact that a movement strong enough to operate with power in international relations has a base in one or more states in which it is in power (e.g., communism in the Soviet Union). Gradually, the state-centered *raison d'état* of this homeland of the revolution comes to override the transnational logic of the movement as such (Herz 1950; Wight 1978; Der Derian 1987, chapter 7; Armstrong 1993).

By commanding supreme allegiance and wielding coercive power over subjects, all of these units will also be able to perform the security act. If the authoritative voice claims the survival of the unit is at stake, this will be a very powerful invocation.

The securitizing actors who can make appeals about the survival of these referent objects are—in contrast to some of the other sectors—relatively well defined. States by definition have authoritative leaders, the EU has a formal (though terribly complex) institutional structure, strong societal-political units also usually have clear leaders, and transnational movements normally have some persons in official locations. In the case of the latter, however, there can often be competing "leaders," such as the Chinese and Soviet Communist Parties during the Cold War and different Muslim leaders today.

In the case of a state, the government will usually be the securitizing actor. A government will often be tempted to use security arguments (in relation to the state) when its concern is actually that the government itself is threatened. This can be the case in relation to external threats as well as internal threats. Internal threats will be typical of weak states (Buzan 1991: 99–103), which are marked by a lack of firmly established stateness (Ayoob 1995: 4). In a weak state, the authority of the government as such is contested to a much greater degree than in strong states, where the framework and thus some basic legitimacy of the government are usually accepted. In weak states, basic institutions as well as ideologies are often challenged, and political violence is extensive; therefore, when the power holders try to make appeals in the name of the state, their authority to do so will be contested more systematically. Many will view the government's action as taken on behalf of its own interests rather than on those of the state (e.g., Zaire, Burma/Myanmar, Nigeria, Saudi Arabia).

In a strong state, especially a liberal-democratic one, there is a much stronger assumption that the government acts only as the legitimate agent of the nation-state and that its claims are subject to public scrutiny and are open to questioning. Also in the strong state, it is generally assumed that "national security can be viewed primarily in terms of protecting the components of the state from outside threat and interference" (Buzan 1991: 100), to which should probably be added "and allegedly exceptional cases of domestic activities deemed unacceptable and threatening by a great majority of the populace (e.g., terrorism)." When the state accepted a self-limitation in the form of rule of law, this was compensated by a clearer specification of the exceptional cases in which because of security the government was to be immune (Gordon 1991: 33).

A final question to be dealt with in relation to referent objects and actors is that of systemic referent objects. Appeals can clearly be made about the survival of "our unit," but security-structured arguments can also be made in relation to institutions, structures, or processes in the international system. At present, the main candidates are the institutions and organizations of international governance, which are generally valued (mostly by state and international business elites) as a precondition for continued political stability. In principle, stability can refer either to the participating units or to the relations among those units (whether on the global or the regional level). Collective institutions can stabilize units individually, or they can serve to stabilize something larger, such as a pattern among or across them.

In practice, these two functions are often combined and blurred. ASEAN, for example, was superficially about restraining conflict among the member states and creating some unity against a shared Communist threat, but it was also very much about preserving domestic stability in the member states (Acharya 1992). The EU might be seen in a similar light, as superficially about preventing conflict within the region but with a subtext of anticommunism, both internal and against the Soviet Union. NATO and the Nuclear Nonproliferation Regime are more clearly directed against international threats. Despite the apparently international orientation of the Security Council, some aspects of the UN are predominantly domestic. Many small member states would barely exist or function as states without the supporting framework of the UN, in terms of both diplomatic services and the embodying principles (self-determination, racial equality, sovereign equality) crucial for their political survival (Jackson 1990). A possible gray zone exists in the case of political unions that progress to the point at which they begin to take on statelike qualities and thus become ambiguous as to whether they are new units or forms of international regional institutions— for example, the EU.

These elements of what some call international society typically have a certain ambiguity in terms of being instrumental for securing states or being aims in themselves. The Nuclear Nonproliferation Treaty, for example, can be seen as both a self-serving move to restrict membership in the nuclear club and a system-serving move aimed at reducing the chances of nuclear war. As argued in the international society literature, such norms and institutions are not basically cosmopolitan arrangements among the human beings of the world; they are arrangements among and of the states—a society of states (Wight 1978; Bull 1977).

Somewhat in contrast to the more American, more utilitarian, and rational choice–inspired school of institutionalism, however, the international society literature also shows how these institutions carry some element of commitment. They are interwoven with classical themes of international law, ethics, and world politics and discussions of common morality and common law; thus, they carry a legitimacy not only of utility in relation to some state calculus of interests but also as manifestations of obligations beyond the nation-state or to principles held to be morally binding (Nardin and Mapel 1992; Butterfield 1965; Wight 1978; Hurrell 1993; Wæver forthcoming-c). From this dual source of collective state stability and direct commitment, various norms, principles, and institutions in the international political realm gain a stability and salience that make them possible referent objects for security action.

As a next step in defining systemic referent objects, we must recall the basic security criterion. The issue has to be a threat of a dramatic nature, portrayable as threatening the breakdown or ruin of some principle or some other irreparable effect whereby one can then legitimate extreme steps. A clear case is that of the basic principles of international society, as seen when the United States and the United Nations liberated Kuwait and attacked Iraq over Iraq's violation of an international principle—the sovereignty and territorial integrity of a recognized sovereign state.[3]

In thinking about systemic referent objects in the political sector, one must keep the distinction between securitization and politicization carefully in mind. Such referent objects must have a certain stability, be seen as pillars of the general international order, and be able to break down in some drastic (not purely gradual or incremental) sense. Concerns about the EU may well be on the political agenda. To lead to securitization, a concern has to follow the characteristic format presented in Chapter 2; some important principle—and thereby the international or regional political order—has to face an existential threat. This is exactly the scenario in the EU argument that Europe needs integration to avoid fragmentation (Buzan et al. 1990; Wæver 1993; Wæver et al. 1993, chapter 1)—an argument that has played a powerful role in post-1989 European politics, as it also did in the early postwar years. When put in the characteristic security form, the case for integration gains urgency, because its alternative is fragmentation—a self-propelling process that by definition will destroy the European project. Whether "Europe" will exist or not appears to be an either-or question. For Europe, fragmentation becomes an existential threat, because there is a risk of a development that will pass a point of no return at which the project of Europe will be irredeemably lost (Wæver 1996b). We return to this case in Chapter 9.

The UN occupies a distinctive position as systemic referent object for political security because of its central role as the repository of the basic principles of international society and international law. It represents the key idea that some (however rudimentary) international order exists, a location where some principles and norms are enshrined and upheld, and that these principles and their sanctity might have to be defended if they are violated in a way that threatens to unravel or seriously weaken them. The principles that have had this status have changed over time. At present, quite a few (although not the entire UN Charter) seem to be seen as basic, efficient, and consensual enough to legitimate action in their defense, including sovereign equality (nonintervention), human rights (nongenocide), balance of power (nonhegemony), self-determination (noncolonization), and racial equality (antiapartheid). Human rights in a broad sense is not consensual, and neither is much of the environmental agenda. The nonproliferation of weapons of mass destruction and strategic missiles and possibly nonfascism are perhaps close to achieving consensus status. This does not mean these principles are always and uniformly defended nor that each appeal to them will be effective but only that these are the principles at the international level to which one can make reference in a security way and have a chance of legitimating extraordinary action or of mobilizing strong international collective action (Mayall 1996; Roberts 1995–1996; Wheeler 1996).

The securitizing actors operating in relation to the systemic referent objects are first of all the states, because most of these principles are principles of international society—the society of states—and are often legal or semilegal in international law. But the leading international media ("the CNN factor") also plays an obvious role here, and so occasionally might NGOs and INGOs (international nongovernmental organizations). Whereas most units in the political sector have relatively clearly specified spokespersons compared to the other sectors, the systemic referent objects are usually much more open to variable securitization, to competition among different actors trying to define security for the wider international community. Such attempts to define security for a community one does not officially represent will typically be the focus of intense political struggle.

One collective actor is endowed with a formalized role as securitizing actor in a way similar to the government in the case of the state. In the UN Charter (and the interpretation that has emerged), we have a very clear instance of the logic of the speech-act function of security. If the UN Security Council acts under chapter 7 of the Charter, it has some far-reaching competences. It is able to break the otherwise inviolable sovereignty of member states by pronouncing the words "this is a threat to international peace and security." As one can see by studying the resolutions and negotiations in relation to the various major regional wars and crises that led or did not lead to UN-sanctioned interventions, the use of this formula is decisive and very conscious. As soon as these words are pronounced (from this specific position), the issue is transformed, because now the Security Council and even some members commissioned by it can legitimately do things they otherwise could not. Thus, the more skeptical members of the Security Council will be careful about crossing this line (Mayall 1991, 1996; Krause 1993).

At the level of systemic political referent objects, these formalized securitizing acts by the UN Security Council form some kind of core, but they do not exhaust the list of possible securitizations at this level. We also include cases in which this form is not adopted, but some other actors manage to establish a general acceptance that some principle or institution is threatened and can therefore act in ways they could otherwise not.

The Logic of Threats and Vulnerabilities

Starting with the sovereign state, which makes up most of the political sector, we can approach the issue of threats and vulnerabilities through the argument that a state consists of three components: idea, physical base, and institutions (Buzan 1991, chapter 2). Subtracting those issues that fall into other sectors (most threats made directly to the physical base must be military, economic, or environmental), we are left with ideas (minus identity ideas independent of institutions) and institutions as such. It is all a question of the ideas on which political institutions are built. Ideas that hold a state together are typically nationalism (especially civic nationalism but sometimes ethnonationalism) and political ideology. By threatening these ideas, one can threaten the stability of the political order. Such threats might be to the existing structure of the government (by questioning the ideology that legitimates it), to the territorial integrity of the state (by encouraging defections from the state identity), or to the existence of the state itself (by questioning its right to autonomy). As discussed in "The Political Security Agenda" section earlier, political threats take the form either of the subversion of legitimacy or of the denial of recognition (either total denial or denial of sovereign equality).

For states, there is an organizing focus for most of this—sovereignty. Existential threats to a state are those that ultimately involve sovereignty, because sovereignty is what defines the state as a state. Threats to state survival are therefore threats to sovereignty. Even minor violations of sovereignty are threats, because sovereignty is a principle that claims the ultimate right of self-government; thus, it becomes endangered if it becomes partial in any sense. Anything that can be portrayed as a violation of sovereignty (an intervention) can be presented as a security problem.

As suggested in "The Political Security Agenda," external actors probably often aim at less than sovereignty in their hostile actions, but the logic of securitization(s) that is likely to ensue will nevertheless focus on sovereignty. During the Cold War, the West generally did not question the recognition of the Soviet Union as a sovereign state in the international system but aimed at weakening its domestic legitimacy. Similarly, in South Africa, for instance, the struggle was not (and in this case neither was the outcome) about a change in sovereignty but of a reestablishment of sovereignty on a new political basis. We should, however, remember our specific way of analyzing security in this book: When is this type of action securitized and in what terms?

What did the government claim it defended? Not just its own political position but sovereignty in its external and internal senses. Almost all threats that come (or that can be presented as coming) from abroad, if designated as "threats" and "security problems," will be so with reference to their violation of sovereignty and its sister concept, nonintervention.

In some cases, the international society is able to legitimize intervention by referring to genocide, aggression, or, increasingly, simply the lack of "good governance." In such cases, a dual securitization is in play. The government will undoubtedly protest because its sovereignty has been violated (not by trying to argue its right to perform genocide but by claiming a right to do whatever is decided domestically). On the other side, international society will act with reference to some principle that has allegedly been violated; because the violation of sovereignty and nonintervention is such a drastic step in the modern state system, the intervening actor will have to make a strong and extraordinary appeal, which often means that claim will have to take a security form. The countersecuritization of the intervened upon will be with reference to one specific international principle, albeit the most powerful such principle: sovereignty.

Typically, the intervenor will try not to question the legitimacy of the unit as a unit. The U.S. invasion of Panama was different from the Iraqi invasion of Kuwait in that only the latter aimed at removing the sovereignty of the attacked. Intention is, however, not very relevant here. The EU might not intend to undermine national identities in its member countries, but the process nevertheless generates such fears (cf. Chapter 6). Similarly, the government intervened against in the political sector will not be satisfied with the qualifying rhetoric of the intervenor and will protest with reference to its sovereignty.

Our specific speech-act approach thus points toward a rather focused agenda and a typical sequence of securitization and countersecuritization. At first this will sound strange, because it differs from what are normally seen as political threats as a result of the difference between an objectivist and a speech-act approach. In objectivist (e.g., *People, States and Fear* [Buzan 1991]) terminology, one would say the state is based on the following pillars, and one of these is undermined by this action, and it is therefore a political security problem. With the speech-act approach, the focus is on the security argument, and it will be with reference to sovereignty for the securitizing state.

Such sequences can lead to intensely political situations. Different, high-profile political principles are at stake, and different actors claim different orders of priority among them while making controversial interpretations of what threatens "their" referent object. In contrast to many of the other cases of securitization explored in this book, we have here explicitly a constellation in which security is pitted directly against security. On both sides, the question of who has the competence to define security threats will typically be controversial—on the international side this is necessarily so since no formal procedure exists, and domestically, in the state defending its sovereignty, there will be oppositional forces (and often a silent majority of the population) who agree with the principle defended internationally (human rights, good governance, nonproliferation) and disagree with the priority given to sovereignty. But according to the modern state system, the government as state representative structurally has the option of invoking sovereignty.

Some confusion is bound to be produced by the relationship between state and government. The government is the usual, and usually legitimate, voice of the state. But the government can try to use rhetoric about the security of the state when more reasonably there is only a threat to the government itself. If there is a threat to the government (the ruling elite and its ideology), it is only a threat to the form of the state and not to the state as such. This, however, will qualify as a threat to the state as well if it has to violate sovereignty (self-determination) on the way. Sovereignty implies a right to decide on the political form of the state without external forceful interference, which means that even if this form is decided by undemocratic means—and thus hardly qualifies as self-determination by the people—it is self-determination in the negative sense of avoiding foreign decisions by virtue of being self-contained within the political space of the state. A government threatened from abroad therefore will always with some right be able to invoke the security of the state, because sovereignty can be claimed to be violated if the political form is suddenly to be decided or even decisively influenced from abroad.

The distinction between strong and weak states is important here, because it highlights different degrees of vulnerability to political threat. A strong state will typically be fairly invulnerable in the political sector; it will not be ethnically divided and thus not open to secessionist action. Its government will be neither divorced from the general opinions of its citizens nor dependent upon suppressing views and information and therefore will be fairly invulnerable to external actors supporting oppositional voices.

Such states may nonetheless feel politically threatened. During the Cold War, the United States perceived a political (as well as a military) threat from the Soviet Union in terms of the question of the legitimacy and efficiency of U.S. democratic capitalism raised by the existence and performance of the Communist rival. Strong states can also experience political security threats from integration projects that threaten their sovereignty (and their recognition and status). This is clearly illustrated by the political discourse within some of the EU member states (Wæver et al. 1993, chapter 4). This is a strange kind of threat, because it is substantially self-imposed. States enter a process—for economic reasons or because of regional security concerns (Buzan et al. 1990)—and this process has the potential to cut away at their sovereignty.

Depending upon what kind of weakness the state exhibits, it will be worried about different vulnerabilities and will therefore securitize differently. The ethnic case is rather straightforward. When state and nation do not correspond—as is generally the case—there is potential for destabilization. This can take the form of secession if a part of the population wants to form its own state (e.g., Eritreans, Ibos, Tibetans), of expropriation by a power that claims inclusion of what it sees as a part of its people (North and South Korea, China and Taiwan), or of irredentism in which a part of the population or territory is claimed by another state (Kashmir, the Kurile Islands, Nagorno-Karabakh). In all cases, external actors are already related to the story; thus, their action will easily be seen as inciting this threatening potentiality.

In the case of domestic divisions on ideological grounds, there can be a fear of foreign intervention in the ideological or political arena. But there can also be a fear of more structural threats from the global political order, or international society, if that order develops in the direction of a general promotion of some principle such as democracy or human rights that is not compatible with the existing political order of the state (e.g., Muslim and Asian reactions against human rights).

Since the end of the Cold War, international society has been marked by a relatively high degree of homogeneity organized as concentric circles around a dominant Western center (Bull and Watson 1983; Buzan 1993). In addition to demanding a market economy and democracy, this hegemonic set of rules prescribes self-opening if one wants to become an insider—increased interpenetration and thereby decreasing insistence upon far-reaching interpretations of sovereignty. The trend is toward interpreting sovereignty less as an attribute of individual countries within international society and more as operational within a collective relationship among insiders (international society) and between insiders and outsiders. One can become an insider, in which case one opens oneself (which means one defines more things as legitimate interaction and fewer as illegitimate intervention). Or one resists this process, thus becoming an outsider (or semi-periphery) in which one operates in the more traditional way, with more extensive use of the slogans of nonintervention and sovereignty—and thereby also with more extensive use of the label *security* to describe threats to the state (Buzan and Segal 1992; Wæver 1995a, 1996b). Outsider states face a double bind. It has become accepted as part of the emerging "standard of civilization" that a civilized state is a democratic, open-market economy. States must either accept this (and so open themselves to the center) or reject it (and face not only exclusion from the highest rank of states but also risk becoming less of a state in the eyes of international society and thereby more exposed to intervention by the center) (Buzan 1996).

Political threats to international referent objects—international law, international order, international society—are not cast in terms of sovereignty. These objects represent established orders. They can thus be threatened by nonacceptance (e.g., holdouts against the Nuclear Nonproliferation Treaty [NPT]), violation (Iraq, North Korea, and the NPT), and challenge (Mao's China and the NPT). Some of these threats, especially challengers, have traditionally been discussed in terms of revolutionary states (Kissinger 1957; Wight 1978; Skoçpol 1979; Halliday 1990; Armstrong 1993)—that is, states that challenge the international order (or do not accept its organizing principle). The revolutionary state is a power whose cooperation is necessary for a stable international order; it is a great power that denies the international order by putting forward its alternative principle (or pure power) as another vision for the system. But the revolutionary state is not the entire story. In some situations a smaller power, not viewed as a systemic challenger as such, can be seen as a threat to a political principle or principles; examples include Iraq (to self-determination and nonproliferation), Iran (to nonintervention and nonproliferation), Serbia(ns) (to ethnic equality and human rights), and South Africa under apartheid (to racial equality). Nonacquiescence, violations, and challenges often produce the distinctive security logic of domino theories: "This seemingly limited and local problem is a general one, because it will set precedents that define future behavior. Our failure here will tempt others to make aggressive challenges to the international order."

Regionalizing Dynamics?

In terms of international security, the political sector by definition is not strong on localizing trends, and the decisive issue will be the balance between unit-to-unit dynamics and actions with reference to system-level referent objects—that is, a discussion of a possibly increasing role for the UN, regional principles, or both. The regional tour (as conducted in the military and societal chapters) is therefore not obvious in this sector (it is not in the economic and environmental sectors either). First, there is no systematic distribution of one kind of security dynamics in one region and another kind in another region; instead, some basic types intermix among each other. Second, it is not immediately clear that the regional level can be the starting point, because strong dynamics exist at other levels too.

The traditional case of political security involves one state making appeals in the name of sovereignty, trying to fend off some threat from another actor that is usually external, such as another state, but that is often combined with an internal threat. Within this broad category, it would be useful to have some subdivision to clarify when the security action is focused on what kind of threat and thereby what kind of security interactions are started.

As argued earlier, states can be subdivided according to the source of their vulnerability (a state-nation split or political ideology); for some kinds of threats, we can also distinguish between intentional threats and threats caused inadvertently by the constellation of organizing and legitimizing principles of different units. (The strong-weak state distinction does not point to distinct phenomena or constitute systematic variation in this case; it is simply that most threats are more alarming to weak states.) Finally, passing out of the pure unit-to-unit cases, it is possible that the source of the threat is systemic trends or organizing principles. Before we proceed to cases other than states (system-level referent objects, as well as other units), we will examine these different types of state situations, in each case asking for their regionalizing and nonregionalizing dynamics and their geographical location—are they typical of some regions and absent from others?

1. *Intentional threats to (weak) states on the basis of their state-nation split.* Because state and nation do not line up, it is possible for some other actor—within the state or neighboring it—to raise secessionist or irredentist claims. There are numerous possible examples: Hungary against Romania, Russia against the Ukraine, Somalia against its neighbors, Kurds threatening Iraq and Turkey. This kind of threat is found in almost all regions of the world (Prescott 1987). It is endemic to Eastern Europe, and Belgium and perhaps the UK are examples in Western Europe. In the Middle East, this type of threat is relevant in relation to Palestinians, Kurds, Arabs in Iran, and Shiites in Iraq and the Gulf states. In Africa, many states are weak in this regard, but this situation mainly creates domestic security problems of a societal nature; rarely (e.g., Ibos, Eritreans) is the state as such openly challenged by a claim for different borders (although this could easily change in the future). In Asia, the major cases of this type are Tibet-China and Kashmir, the Tamils in Sri Lanka, various groups in India, self-claiming nations within China, and the opposite way around (with a nation covering more than one state) in the Korean situation. There are few examples in North America, by far the most conspicuous being Quebecois secessionism.

Most of the concrete cases also have societal dimensions and are dealt with in more detail in the chapter on that sector. In the political sector, we primarily look upon this type of threat in terms of the effects on the stability of state structures and the undermining of state-carrying national or state ideologies. Usually, these controversies generate bilateral or trilateral conflicts, and they frequently tie together different sectors—societal, political, and often military. They constitute a major chunk of international security problems.

2. *Intentional threats to (weak) states on political-ideological grounds.* Here, the ideology on which the regime operates is not widely accepted. Threats can be leveled against the state on this basis, and the regime claims these are security problems. Examples are North and South Korea and the United States against Cuba. Whereas this category could be said to capture the nature of what for around 40 years constituted the major conflict in the system—the Cold War (which also had elements of type 4)—it seems to be much more rare in the post–Cold War system. Those cases that do exist often blend into type 1, as with Korea where the national factor is obviously also at play; type 4, as with the Cold War and India-Pakistan; or type 7, where the general trend in the legitimizing principles of the system is at odds with the principles of one particular state. It is a fairly striking finding that although internal divisions and political-ideological weaknesses are often among the main concerns of regimes, it is rare for foreign actors to challenge directly the legitimacy of regimes, although it is somewhat more common for weak regimes to blame domestic unrest on foreign orchestration. The position of the Arab states toward Israel was such a case, but even this situation is changing. This surprising situation probably testifies to the continued strength of the principle of sovereignty and nonintervention: to question a regime as such is problematic. One either has a direct conflict with the country or tries to have it branded by international society as breaching more basic rules (e.g., nonapartheid, genocide), or one must abstain from major moves against the legitimacy of the regime and the state.

3. *Inadvertent, unit-based threats to state-nation vulnerable states.* Unintentional threats should be sorted into two groups. Accidental, one-time threats are not very interesting to us. Unavoidable, interlocking, inadvertent threats, however, happen when two or more states are locked into a security conflict because of incompatible organizing principles. Here, we can try out the distinction between nation-state and political-ideological vulnerabilities to see if it produces systematic variation.

Inadvertent threats based on a state-nation split could be illustrated by the case of Estonia and Russia, in which the Estonian definition of Estonia is perceived as a threat to the Russians in Estonia (and thereby in Russian politics too); simultaneously, a Russia defined in a certain way is by definition a threat to Estonia. A Croatia defined on a territorial basis (the borders of the old part-state of Yugoslavia) and a Serbia defined on an ethnic basis (the nation of Serbs) are difficult to reconcile as well (Wiberg 1993). Such security dilemmas can be handled only through processes that involve critical self-reflection by the involved parties on their own identity and concept of stateness. The political struggles within each society over how to articulate state and nation are at the heart of this type of security predicament.

Such cases are found in the same regions as type 1. They basically involve the same factors; they are simply a particularly vicious version.

4. *Unintentional threats to states on political-ideological grounds.* This type of threat constellation can be illustrated by the Cold War, as noted earlier. The clearest example, however, remains that of the India-Pakistan conflict, which hinges on competing ideas of the state—different basic political legitimizing principles that are not only mutually exclusive but are also unavoidably threatening to each other. Pakistan is based on religious exclusivity, whereas India is a continentwide, inclusive state able to accommodate ethnic and religious differences—thus also including Muslims. (Not to overdo the emphasis on abstract principles: If India were to change its self-definition toward Hindu nationalism, this would in some logical sense solve the problem vis-à-vis Pakistan; however, since in practice that situation would produce a number of local conflicts between religious and ethnic groups into which the India-Pakistan dimension would be drawn, it is unlikely to be much of a solution to the regional security dilemma.) The relationship between Israel and the Palestine Liberation Organization was another case (although with elements of type 3) in which for a long time the self-definition of each group included the negation of the possible existence of the other (or rather, of the other as that which the other wanted to be). The way in which this conflict constellation has been modified is perhaps instructive for the nature of this type of conflict: It is possible only to move the conflict out of the space of "no compromise possible" through processes that touch the heart of political identity and that therefore become of the utmost political intensity within each.

Conflicts of this type are not common. They are serious and often long-standing when they do appear but are not the typical form of political security conflict.

5. *Security of and against supranational, regional integration.* This category is not intended to distinguish between regional and global, but there is a difference between *principles* and *organization*—between the systemic political principles discussed in "The Logic of Threats and Vulnerabilities" in this chapter and in types 6 and 7 and organizations that try to take over a broad range of state functions on a regional scale. Principles are relevant mainly at the global but also at the regional level; supranational political organization is relevant mainly at the regional level, and it is primarily in the EU that such organization becomes threatening to state sovereignty. Examples beyond those of the EU threatening member-state sovereignty could be pan-Arabism in its best days and potentially the CIS in the future.

Whenever the regional formation takes on such a solid quality, one can also talk of political security the other way around: The supranational, regional integration formation can begin to have its own security discourse in which the member states and nations can be among the threats when they react against integration—for example, on the basis of their fear of the inte-grating organization. In the case of the EU, the very principle of integration (the negation of nation-based fragmentation) seems to be the equivalent of sovereignty, the principle that can be threatened; if it is violated in some specific instance, it can do so in a way that becomes self-propelling (frag-mentation and power balancing) and that thus constitutes an existential threat (Wæver 1996b; Chapter 8 in the present book).

6. *Systemic, principled threats against states that are vulnerable because of a state-nation split.* A historic instance of this type of threat is the Austrian (and Austrian-Hungarian) case vis-à-vis the nationalist move-ment in the nineteenth century; for a time, this case seemed to be mainly of historical relevance. Again, however, we are experiencing a general wave of national self-determination, of "every nation its state" thinking—a new spring of nations—and all multinational and otherwise non-nation-corre-sponding states have good reason to be worried.

7. *Structural (systemic) threats to (weak) states on political-ideologi-cal grounds.* Here, a state's political system is challenged but this time not by another state but by a general development of international society on principles that are incompatible with those of the state. The classical exam-ple, now resolved, was that of antiapartheid and South Africa. The most important contemporary cases in which security actions are taken against this type of threat are in East Asia and the Middle East—"Asian" values and national sovereignty defended against an allegedly Western universal-ism (China, Singapore, and Malaysia), and Islamic values similarly posited as threatened not only by Western culture but also by what is seen as a Western attempt to organize the international system on its principles.

These seven are the different kinds of threats to states, the main unit of this sector. We have pointed to two other major categories: other unit-level candidates, notably transnational movements, and system-level political principles and institutions.

8. *Threats to transnational movements that command supreme loyalty from their members.* No large movements of this type are very effective today; thus, they could all be seen (to the extent that they qualify as referent objects in the political sector) as experiencing severe security problems, as threatened by the sovereign states that try to command the supreme loyalty of their subjects. The Communist movement is obviously of minor rele-vance here and has not been a factor for some time—some would say not since the 1920s or 1930s when it became de facto a Soviet state–centered organization. Others would say the movement has not been a factor since the Sino-Soviet split. If one focuses on the way members in other countries felt loyalty to a transnational movement, however, one could claim the Communist movement was a reality until the end of the 1980s. The move-ment was sometimes experienced with fear by states (but that fear was most often overlaid by the fear of the Soviet Union and thus is not a category of

its own), and the movement itself acted in relation to what it saw as threats. Today, no transnational political movements of this caliber are found, perhaps only religious ones, with Islam the strongest candidate.

9. *Threats to international society, order, and law.* The most obvious recent example of this type is Iraq's invasion of Kuwait, but it is so obvious, so overused (including our own previous discussion in this chapter), and probably now perceived by many as the exception to some rule (no similar swift and determined action came in the cases of Bosnia and Rwanda) that it is not very useful. An alternative illustration could be the North Korea–nonproliferation–U.S. story. The general logic of such security actions was spelled out in the previous section. An external power, the United States, makes reference to some general principles and points to threats to international stability; by doing so, it tries to mobilize others in support of its actions toward North Korea. In this case (in contrast to Iraq), the United States uses the securitization mostly to legitimize its own acts. North Korea sees these acts as interventions in domestic affairs and violations of sovereignty, because it is the sovereign choice of states whether to leave an international treaty like the NPT or not. With reference to the emerging international principles of nonproliferation and openness, the United States claims a right to pressure North Korea both to open itself up to more extensive inspections than other states and to stay in the NPT regime. On the basis of this securitization of international principles (which was convincing because it coincided with the treaty review conference), the United States could make both official threats about (not very relevant) economic sanctions and unofficial, more drastic threats (or rumors) about possible surgical attacks.

Are these nine types of threats predominantly local, regional, or global? They are almost never local in the sense of intrastate (as we see it in, for example, the environmental sector). But they are frequently less than regional—that is, bilateral. A few are unilateral-global in the sense of one state trying to defend itself against some international trend or principle. Clearly dominant, however, are relationships between two or among a few states. Does this go against the regional perspective (i.e., is it too small or subregional)? No, regions are made up of networks of unit-to-unit threats; the small constellations could be the first steps toward larger formations.

The question therefore is, do these threats typically link up and generate chains and networks of regional conflict constellations? Not as much as is the case in the military sector, where means (power) are generally more fungible: If A threatens B, and C—weakened by its conflict with D—also fears A, C can come to the aid of B by engendering some additional threat against A, perhaps by soliciting the help of its ally E. This scheme is possible because military power is relatively easy to cumulate, calculate, and transfer. The force of C can supplement that of B and thereby counterbalance A. This is rarely the case in the political sector. Chain reactions do not occur at the level of power, although they may at the level of principles. If A threatens B by violating the principle of nonintervention (e.g., assisting secessionists), this will be of great interest to C, which also has a large minority and therefore supports B's protests against A.

The main linkages in this sector seem to be in terms of principles rather than power. Principles travel relatively more easily than (military) power. But principles occasionally have a regional component: This is unacceptable behavior in Europe, the African charter of human rights, the Asian concept of values, the unacceptable involvement of an extra-hemispherical actor in the Americas, and so forth. Simultaneously, at the level of principles is a very strong global component—international society. The balance between regional and global principles varies among regions. In all cases, the global level is in some sense the more prominent in that most international law and UN quasi-law is developed for the entire system. But if the most operative and controversial elements are given a distinctive regional twist, the regional level can still be the most powerful referent in a given political instance.

Thus, it is possible to briefly survey the different regions after all, now that the question is clearer. Are there important regional constellations of principles, violations, fears, support campaigns, and the like? For Europe yes, Africa yes, Asia not much but emerging "Asian values." For North America no, only some rules of the Organization of American States (OAS) that are close to those of the UN, amounting mostly to universal rules plus nonintervention for extra-hemispheric powers. For Latin America no, except as for North America. Thus, for all of America some. For the Middle East yes.

In cases where principles are regional to a significant extent, the smaller bilateral, trilateral, and subregional constellations will tie together at the regional level to some extent because other actors in the region will be mobilized to support one or the other side; other actors will have their own interest in taking positions because these principles are of relevance to conflicts in which they are engaged or are worried about.

Summary

There are many bilateral political security constellations, and they sometimes link up in regional patterns. The principles that create this linking are as much global as regional; therefore, some security actions—such as major UN operations—are also based on global domino theories and make cross-regional linkages. The main dynamics of this sector, however, operate at levels from bilateral to regional, with various smaller constellations included that would often register as subcomplexes in other sectors, especially the military one. If there were only this sector, these dynamics might remain bilateral or as microcomplexes. But with the interaction among sectors, such dynamics become tied into bigger complexes they rarely cut across or in other ways complicate; on their own, they do not generate such large complexes. For instance, territorial disputes (Sabah) between Malaysia and the Philippines quietly mobilize other ASEAN states, first because they threaten to weaken ASEAN as such and second because similar disputes are occurring in the area and other states therefore have views on how the Malaysia-Philippines disputes should be resolved.

Generally, issues that are typically bilateral or trilateral become regionalized because other actors within the same regime of principles will take positions because of their interest in either the specific outcome of the contest or the effect on those principles. In the case of highly visible or crucial rule-defining events (e.g., Iraq-Kuwait), the conflict can become globalized and draw in many countries, but the networks of principles have a density at the regional level that often lifts local conflicts to this plane.

Notes

1. According to Max Weber, a political unit is defined by its relationship to a specific instrument—organized violence (1972 [1922]: 30). The state is defined as one form of such political organization, one that "within a specific territory . . . (successfully) claims the monopoly on legitimate political violence" (Weber 1972 [1922]: 822, our translation; the parentheses are Weber's). The state is a specific form of *Herrschaftsverhältnis* for which the achieved legitimacy is the most remarkable. Thus, the focus is on the way otherwise fluid relations become institutionalized and authority established. With writers such as Ernesto Laclau and Claude Lefort, in contrast, the political is almost the opposite of this. Politicization means to open up petrified relationships, and the political is opposed to the social, when the latter refers to sedimented practices as unreflected "natural" ways of being and doing that can be moved into the sphere of choice and contestation by politicization. As soon as some political practice has been successful in establishing something "fixed," it stops being political—and political practice will be that which upsets this order, which dislocates its discursive underpinning (Laclau 1990: 68).

2. On this third axis, "the shaping" leans somewhat to the Weberian side with its emphasis on governing, but it is a bit more open-ended and emphasizes the attempt more than at least is commonly attributed to Weber (although Weber loved gerunds—nouns made from verbs—so the transformation into activity, process, and attempt is after all rather Weberian). We want to retain the Weberian ring to the "politics" of the political sector, whereas "politicization" refers to the Laclau side. Thus, we use "political" to describe the orders and arrangements attempted and in part achieved by people regarding the organization of political power, "the shaping of human behavior for the purpose of governing large groups of people."

3. *Principles* are much more likely to be referent objects for security action than are *values* because principles can be violated, and small cases can be depicted as of larger significance because they threaten a principle. Cases that infringe upon values will typically be more gradual—a little less, a little more—and thereby diffi-

cult to securitize. If values are made the central concept of security theory, one is more likely to end on the aggregative, individualizing road that most likely securitizes widely, because most things individuals value are "threatened" in numerous ways. By focusing on principles, we retain a conception in which referent objects can be posited as *existentially* threatened; their survival is at stake, according to securitizing actors. Values point to gradualism, individual security, and the unending expansion of securitization; principles point to either-or, to intersubjective constitution, and to a more limited security agenda.

CHAPTER 8

How Sectors Are Synthesized

People, States and Fear (Buzan 1991) led to clear-cut conclusions about the importance of regional security complexes in the military and political sectors. These complexes showed strong territorial coherence. In other words, one of the primary locations in which to find the sources of explanation and the outcomes of traditional security dynamics is the regional level. Does securitization related to the referent objects of the other sectors also result in coherent regional security complexes? If so, are these regions identical to the military-political ones?

To assess overall trends among local, regional, and global levels is complicated by the often polemical nature of the arguments. As soon as someone puts too much emphasis on localization, regionalization, or globalization, it is easy to raise counterarguments. If one, for example, stresses the increasing regionalization in economics in terms of territorial bloc formation (the EU, NAFTA, and APEC), another can counter this by pointing to globalization in terms of interaction capacity (e.g., low transportation costs, international capital) or to global regimes (the rules set by the IMF, the WTO, the World Bank, and the G7). If the global structure is emphasized, it is easy to point to the importance of regional or even national economics. In the first part of this chapter, we try to break out of this trap by decomposing the question, summing up the analysis we carried out in the previous chapters sector by sector.

One of the assumptions in our study is that we are working within an international system that is global in scale. On the face of it, one might expect that the shrinking world and globalization arguments mean the territorial factor is disappearing from politics. The revolution in interaction capacity—including intercontinental ballistic missiles (ICBMs) and jumbo jets, satellites, and the development of cyberspace—has eroded the significance of distance. Changing global regimes characterize periods in what is rightly called *world* history: the eras of imperialism, world war, decolonization, bipolarity, and global interdependence.

Despite the apparently triumphal march of globalization, the evidence from our sector chapters suggests this is only part of the story. The ability to travel worldwide does not mean everyone is doing so. The strengthening of the global level does not obliterate other levels. Tom Nierop (1994, 1995) rightly remarks that even most of the people who invented and created cyberspace are living in one place—Silicon Valley. Despite the overall global structure, there are regional differences that are too crucial to be neglected. Different rules of the game apply in various subsystems. The invisible hands, types of anarchy, and international regimes that condition the margins for cooperation and conflict in each of the sectors vary widely from region to region. This points to their relative independence.

In the postbipolar system, in many places regional dynamics are significantly less constrained than they were previously. But the end of the Cold War also lifted constraints on globalization, most notably in the economic sector, because all of the so-called Second World was now opened up. There have also been strong localizing developments, especially in the societal and environmental sectors—to some extent as the dialectical other side of globalization. The model for security analysis presented in this book is meant to be instrumental in sorting and comparing these uneven effects.

The first subsection sets up levels of analysis as a way of comparing the sectors and summarizes the five sector chapters into one matrix according to the weight of the levels at which securitization occurs. Section 2 looks at linkages across the sectors and states conclusions about what can be said at the aggregate level about the relative weights of the different levels and whether congruent regions form in the different sectors. Section 3 contrasts this approach with one that starts from the actors, with each synthesizing the different sectors in its specific weighing and possibly connecting of security concerns. Section 4 offers a brief survey of how cross-sectoral weighing of security operates for some different units (France, Japan, Third World states, Sudan, the LIEO, and the environment). In contrast to this impressionistic overview, section 5 is an empirically based case study of the EU. Space does not allow great amounts of documentation, but the case study is intended to illustrate a possible method for studying securitization. The final section discusses the merits of different forms of synthesizing sectors—aggregate, as in sections 1 and 2, or by the units, as in sections 3, 4, and 5—for different purposes.

Levels of Analysis as a Way of Comparing Sectors

In the sector chapters, we traced the globalizing, regionalizing, and localizing tendencies in the security debates about the referent objects and threats in each sector. At what level does the securitization within each of the sectors appear? Does the subsystem level show coherent regional security complexes in geopolitical terms within each and across all of the sectors? In each chapter, we have assessed the importance of securitization at the different levels of analysis, and these arguments are summed up in Figure 8.1. Globalizing dynamics operate at the *system* level. At the *subsystem*

Figure 8.1 Securitization at Different Levels of Analysis

Dynamics/ Sectors	Military	Environment	Economic	Societal	Political
Global	**	****	****	**	***
Non-regional subsystemic	**	**	**	**	*
Regional	****	***	***	****	****
Local	***	****	**	***	**

**** - dominant securitization; *** - subdominant securitization; ** - minor securitization; * - no securitization

level, there are two possible patterns: regionalization if patterns are geographically coherent and nonregional subsystemic if they are not. Finally, there are *localizing* dynamics at the subunit level.[1]

Can we add up the results and arrive at an overall conclusion about whether a dominant trend exists across the spectrum? Yes and no. Not every observer will give equal weight to each sector. There is a classical debate over whether to put politics before economics or the reverse. Environmentalists will disagree either way, and some argue that identity issues are behind everything. Traditional security studies weights the military sector so heavily that it becomes the only one worth studying.

For our purposes, the relative weight of sectors should depend primarily upon the degree of securitization but should also consider the relative importance of types of issues when sectoral concerns clash. For instance, relatively speaking, the economic sector has the least successful securitization (which is one of the major reasons the regional level continues to have a claim for primacy, because the economic sector is probably the most strongly globalized), but the degree of securitization is not the only factor to consider. In terms of relative importance, it is worth remembering an argument from traditional security studies (which is not as entirely conclusive as its proponents claim but is partly correct nevertheless): When a calculation relating to a military conflict meets a concern from one of the other sectors, military-political arguments carry the most weight. This is not always correct, however, since both identity and environment can become very strong motives. But the basic approach is correct: We should look for what counts most when different concerns conflict. This conclusion is important when we try impressionistically to balance the findings of the different sectors.

The overall picture indicates that regional security complexes dominate the military, political, and societal sectors; that they are potentially strong in the economic one; and that they are present in the environmental sector. The global level is dominant in the economic sector, but global dynamics themselves stimulate regionalization. Global-level dominance in the environmental sector refers mainly to the level of the debate. Environmental issues as such are spread across all levels; some affect local structures only, others affect the international system as such, and some fall in between and form regional clusters of interdependent issues. Most successful securitization here is local. When we draw upon the finding that the economic sector has comparatively little successful securitization, a rough weighing points to the regional level as still fairly central despite the move to a wider security agenda.

Linkages Across Sectors

It is impossible, however, to conclude on the basis of this study whether the regional security complexes are always identical in each sector. In principle, we could find that security dynamics in most sectors were regional but that the regions were different. Is military Europe the same as political Europe and societal Europe? Is economic East Asia the same as political East Asia and environmental East Asia? Whether these sectoral subsystems overlap and thus form coherent regions can be answered only tentatively and on a descriptive basis. Examples of relatively coherent regions across sectors are the Middle East, Europe, the CIS, Southeast Asia, Southern Africa, and North America. Potential cases are found in East Africa, Central and Latin America, East Asia, and perhaps the Pacific. But in all of these cases, one can always point to exceptions.

Obviously, the answers to these questions are of crucial importance, not the least for IR theory; the more the dynamics of the five sectors highlight identical regions, the more they lead to overall congruent power configurations and thereby make the regional level more powerful in explanations. One factor that supports a tendency toward congruence among sectoral regional subsystems is that in the end, the actors themselves must make up their minds as to how the securitization of different values adds up. The next three sections develop this question of how sectors are synthesized by actors.

The question of whether the regional security complexes match across sectors is answered in part by looking at the ways in which the sectors are linked to one another. Although we maintain that the disaggregated world of sectors makes analytical sense because different agenda, values, discourses, and the like can be reasonably clustered in these five sectors, it should be remembered that sectors are lenses focusing on the same world. Not surprisingly, the sector chapters are full of cross-references.

In the chapter about the military sector, for instance, it was noted that military security serves functions in the other sectors, whereas warfare tends to disrupt stability in the other sectors. This refers to the security debate with which we are so familiar: What do we see when we perceive all sectors through the lens in which military rationales (the use of, or protection against the use of, violence) ultimately dominate? But the question can also be phrased the other way around. Problems that on the surface seem to be military might, on closer inspection, turn out to be motivated by fears in the other four sectors. Wars of independence, for example, may focus on separatism and border conflicts, whereas they are better understood in terms of identity concerns; wars against a ruling government might actually represent mere frustration about deteriorating living conditions caused by environmental decline. The sector linkages resemble the ultimate consequence of Karl von Clausewitz's dictum: War is the continuation of politics with the admixture of other means.

Such linkages can be formulated for all 10 dyads among the five sectors. Military operations can be the continuation of environmental conflict or, the reverse, can be constrained by environmental limitations. Raising the "identity flag" can entail the continuation of economics with the admixture of other means—for example, legitimizing protectionism—or, the reverse, economic free trade arguments can be used as a means in rapprochement policies. It is important to know how sectoral concerns feed into one another. When do they reinforce and when do they modify each other? Chapters 3–7 contain examples for each of the sector dyads. Disaggregating security into sectors has been helpful in distilling distinctive patterns of vulnerabilities and threats, differences regarding referent objects and actors, and different relationships to territorializing and deterritorializing trends in the system. The number of cross-linkages, however, stands as a massive warning against treating the sectors as closed systems.

Cross-Sectoral Security
Connections Through the Actor's Lens

In the present book, we have dissected the world of security into five sectors. The purpose of such a disaggregating exercise is to put security back together in, it is hoped, a more transparent form. The reconnecting job can be done in two ways that are not incompatible but that serve different purposes. The section "Levels of Analysis as a Way of Comparing Sectors" weighed the findings of all the sectors both as a total picture and as a general lesson about security in its different forms. That section looked at the different pictures that emerged in the particular sectors and at the ways these five pictures could possibly be combined.

In Chapter 1, however, we asked whether one should study security sector by sector and then try to relate the different sector-specific maps of the world to one another or rather try to see all security interaction as one constellation and security as an integrated field. The section "Levels of Analysis as a Way of Comparing Sectors" viewed the five sectors from the analyst's outside perspective. The rest of this chapter does so from the inside, through the actor's perspective. In both cases, one can draw on the lessons of Chapters 3–7 because one needs an understanding of the peculiarities of security of each of the types—economic, military, and so forth.

The case for looking through the actor's lens is as follows. Sectors are not ontologically separate realms; they are not, like levels, separate subsystems (Buzan, Jones, and Little 1993: 30–33). Some units, particularly the state, appear in several or all of the sectors, although at different strengths. We see sectors as a purely analytical device, as different lenses through which to see different views of the same issues.

But although they are analytical devices, sectors exist not only in a theoretician's head but also in policy heads, where the concept of security itself is the integrating force. Actors think about economics, politics, and other areas but judge their main security problems across the board. Thus, units do not exist in sectors; sectors exist in units as different types of security concerns (political, economic, etc.). These different concerns are weighed and aggregated *by* the units.[2] One unit (say, the United States) can feel threatened mainly by military matters and will define security in narrow military terms (which, in turn, allows it to define its own uses of nonmilitary means as "ordinary interaction" rather than security issues, regardless of how others perceive them; Wæver 1989b, 1995b). Another unit (say, the former USSR) has existential fears about sociocultural penetration by a dynamic neighboring area and insists that the concept of security should be wider and should include "nonmilitary security problems." A third state (say, Latvia) might see demographic developments as existential and apply the security approach to these.

To grasp political dynamics, one needs to focus on the most dynamic interactions, the loops, the vicious circles—regardless of whether these stay within one sector. A political analysis searches for constellations of interlinking securitizations and is open about whether these interlinkages operate across sectors.[3] The sectors should not be projected *out* as a map of the world cut up into sectors (each to be filled with units, aims, threats, and dynamics); they should be sent *in,* into the actors as different kinds of security concerns.

The basic argument here is about analytical sequence: A specific security analysis does not start by cutting the world into sectors. We have done so in this book because it was necessary to do so to resolve misunderstandings about the general domain of security. But in a specific analysis, the sequence is (1) securitization as a phenomenon, as a distinct type of practice; (2) the security units, those units that have become established as legitimate referent objects for security action and those that are able to securitize—the securitizing actors; and (3) the pattern of mutual references among units—the security complex.

Looking sector by sector, there is a risk of missing even intense security dilemmas in cases where the threat of A against B lies in one sector and the threat to which A is reacting (and thereby possibly reinforcing) from B is found in another sector. Illustrations could be Estonia-Russia (military fears and security for and against minorities) and Turkey-Syria (Kurdish separatism versus water control). Therefore, one should look at all kinds of security and look unit by unit, conflict by conflict—and thereby build the complex as the constellation of main security concerns ("main" is defined by the actors).

Accordingly, our 1993 book has no "societal security complex" and only hesitantly introduces a "societal security dilemma" (Wæver et al. 1993; see further Kelstrup 1995). There is *one* European security complex; societal security plays a part in this complex if important units act according to this logic and their action is significant enough to feed into the security policy of other actors and thus to become part of the chain of security interdependencies forming the regional security complex.

A further reason for paying close attention to cross-sectoral dynamics is that doing so might solve the problem of having to deal with one or several sector-specific maps of security complexes. Where these seem to line up (and the previous section argued that they often do), the explanation will probably be found in cross-sectoral dynamics. From a functionalist perspective, one might expect that the economic security complexes would come out differently from the military ones, which again would have different borders from the environmental security complexes. The nature of environmental affairs—even the main units—differs from affairs in economics, which, in turn, differ from military matters; thus, one should expect size and constellations to be very different. Truly, there are major deviances among sectors, but there are also some surprising consistencies.

In the societal security chapter, for instance, it was noticed that strong instances of societal security were found in Europe and to some extent in the Middle East, which taken independently should have been expected to generate smaller complexes (e.g., to focus on subregions, such as the Balkans or even Transylvania). Because of cross-sectoral connections, especially with the political sector, however, the different societal conflicts were tied together, and states acted in a generalized sense in relation to minority conflicts and self-determination with a view to regional dynamics and to principles that are partly systemic, partly regional (in this case European).

In the economic chapter, it was noticed that whereas the firm is not an easily securitizable unit, the state is, which in the classical case involves the argument that some specific production is necessary for the state in an argument that draws upon other sectors, traditionally the military or at least the political sector. Furthermore, a conspicuous finding in the economic chapter was the role of system-level referent objects, notably the LIEO, which points to the securitization of *principles*. This situation has created an interaction and probably a synergy between the political and economic sectors, in which the interpretations of who are insiders and who are outsiders in the two spheres are mutually reinforcing. The degree of danger involved in a breach of principles in one sector is determined in part by judging the location of an actor in the other sector: If Japan, for example, violates a political principle, it will be of greater concern to the United States because the latter suspects Japan of evading the principles of the economic game.

Also in the economic sector, the political (and perhaps the military) sector helps to explain the peculiar phenomenon of economic regionalization. The political interpretation of who represents a strategic economic competitor seems to be involved in the formation of economic unions and blocs, which, in turn, creates an increasing rationale for political competition along these lines. As argued in Chapter 5, societal factors are also involved in the formation of regional economic blocs: "They are cultural defense mechanisms against the powerful homogenizing effects of open markets." To preserve societal security, a certain regional variation in political economic models has been necessary (cf. Helleiner 1994b).

An important reason for these elements of consistency is the way security perceptions in one field color the interpretation of what constitutes a security problem in another sector. It is important to remember that we are not mapping all environmental interaction, only the constellations of interaction relating to environmental *security* (as is true in the other sectors). When is one likely to define an environmental problem as an environmental *security* problem?

Beyond the factors that generally influence how dramatic the issue appears is often the perception of some actor connected to the problem. A water dependency on another country may be unpleasant and may cause one to be concerned about that country's pollution and overuse of water, but if one has a conflict with that country for other reasons, one is much more likely to define the water problem as a security problem. Thus, through the attachment of the security label, sectors insert themselves into each other.

Does this imply a return to the traditional idea that the military sector is, after all, the dominant one and that only when nonmilitary factors are linked to military threats are they security relevant? It could, but it does not have to. There is no necessity for one sector to be foundational to all the others, only for sectors to interconnect through the act of security labeling. In this perspective, states approach security as aggregate security, not as five separate fields. They judge which threats are most serious across sectors. As in the debate on aggregate power, in practice this may mostly involve addressing how military power can be brought to bear on nonmilitary issues, but in principle it can just as well be about economic power used in a military conflict. The principal issue is whether sectors have achieved sufficient autonomy and whether the costs of translating from one to the other sector have become so high that one can no longer aggregate security or power.

Illustrations and Devising an Empirical Investigation

What is the relevant unit for this type of analysis? At the end of Chapter 2, we discussed which of our three kinds of units—referent objects, securitizing actors, and functional actors—should be at the center of an analysis that leads to a construction of security complexes. We argued that referent objects precede securitizing actors but that for the purpose of security complex analysis, in which one should be able to connect different nodes, we have to form more general "units"—such as France, the EU, or the Baltic Sea environment—which in each case combine several slightly different but partly overlapping referent objects (such as state, nation, people, and government) and their main securitizing actors. To approach our question about cross-sectoral security definitions, we look first at some states, then move on to other kinds of units—economic and environmental—and finally turn to a more extensive analysis of the EU.

France

France is articulated as a referent object in three main forms: as (1) Europe-France, (2) as the French state, and (3) as the French nation. (See Figure 8.2.)

1. *Europe-France:* All major securitizing actors, but mainly the state elite, appeal to the defense of France in a mode in which the fate of France is tied to that of Europe. Europe is constructed as a larger France, and France is thus defended by defending this Europe. France-Europe is defended (1a) in global competition with the United States and Japan and (1b) against a return of its own past in the form of wars and power struggles (more on this in the next section). The latter includes peacekeeping in Bosnia and other efforts to avoid wars in Europe. Ideally, such operations should be shaped in a way that simultaneously maximizes the European element and thus serves to create an independent European security identity. During the early Chirac period, the (1a) argument, with its emphasis on employment and social stability, gained a prominent position, although it pointed to policy needs that could only be pursued with European partners.

Figure 8.2 The Security of France

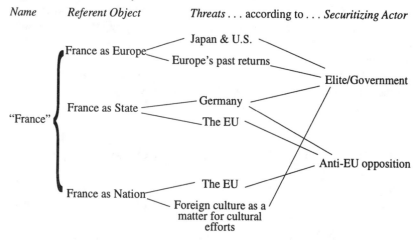

2. *The French state:* The state considered more separately as France is the second referent object. It is appealed to (2a) first by the government in the form of cautious references to a possible German problem and the rationale of French policy as handling this problem through integration and multiple balances with the UK, Spain-Italy, or even Russia. Alternative voices in France (those skeptical of the EU, more national unilateralist voices) make the Germany-related arguments even more strongly, and (2b) they project French sovereignty as threatened by EU integration.

3. *The French nation:* The nation itself is presented as threatened. Most obviously, a campaign is constructing this scenario in parallel with the sovereignty threat from the EU—Europe as a threat to identity—which often goes together with immigrants as a threat to nation and identity (3a). In more official circles, however, a cultural defense of France has also become more distinct (3b). The Chirac government upgraded this defense in parallel with its continuation of an EU-based overall strategy close to Mitterrand's.

Economic arguments are significant in French security rhetoric, and they mainly channel into (1a), the global interpretation in which France and Europe are two sides of the same coin. Societal security concerns are structured even more clearly according to an overarching pattern of definitions derived from the political setup. Virtually the same argument can end up meaning opposite things depending upon the political rationale with which it is articulated. Politically, two main programs attempt to articulate the security of France. One basically draws on the EU-France doubling of the Mitterrand era and presents security as occurring primarily at the level of the system (global competition) and as a general strategy for Europe (avoiding war and handling Germany). The new twist is to attempt to combine this program with a more segregated defense of French culture, probably as a compensatory move to take energy out of the competing program, which more clearly appeals to "France" as separate from Europe (and thereby from Germany).[4] Both of these main programs articulate threats in several sectors and integrate them narratively; thus, the separate threats are strongly colored by each other. (This interpretation of France draws heavily on Holm 1993; and Wæver, Holm, and Larsen forthcoming).

Japan

Japan is famous in the field of security studies for its concept of comprehensive security. Formally, this refers primarily to the formula delineating that security policy should operate at three levels: to influence positively the overall international environment, to cope unilaterally with threats, and to act in solidarity with "countries sharing the same ideals and interests" (Barnett 1984: 1; Tanaka 1994: 34). When one reads through actual Japanese calculations and reasoning about threats and efforts, the function of the concept seems to be mainly to stress the interconnectedness of problems to ensure that Japan does not have to deal specifically with problems that are painful (usually historical) or that demand types of action Japan wants to avoid (usually political-military). Conveniently, Japan can almost always interpret problems at least in part as economic development issues and can therefore point to a possible Japanese contribution to security policy in the form of economic assistance (e.g., Tanaka 1994: 46f). This is a very interesting case of a country constructing aggregate-comprehensive security as a general category and thereby achieving an increased ability to take action in its preferred sector regardless of the sector from which the threat emerges.

"Third World" States

Regarding what are sometimes too easily generalized as *third world states,* it has been argued as a general characteristic that domestic political concerns tend to be the lens through which other threats are judged—"although this does not mean external threats do not exist, it does imply that such threats often attain prominence largely because of the conflicts that abound within Third World states" (Ayoob 1995: 7). Mohammed Ayoob further asserts that for Third World states the definition of security should be primarily political, because other realms "must be filtered through the political realm" (Ayoob 1995: 8). Because of the general vulnerability of states and regimes, this concern will most often be the criterion by which to judge the other vulnerabilities—economic or ecological—that definitely do exist.

The relationship between internal and external factors is symbiotic (Ayoob 1995: 51), but the internal vulnerability—in Ayoob's argument, defined by the political elites—is so central that even third world states' collective concern regarding their status in the international system is largely an extension of the internal security situation as far as third world elites are concerned (Ayoob 1995: 191).

To pick a specific case from the third world, we can draw on Francis Deng's study of *Sudan* and summarize the complex analysis brutally as follows. The conflict is generally recognized as basically an identity conflict, a conflict both between identities (the northern Arab-Muslim and the southern, African Christian-Animist) and within identities, notably the contested nature of the dominant northern-Sudanese project (cf., e.g., Deng 1995: 3ff., 135ff., 348). Paradoxically, the South, which the North is trying to assimilate, is also the Other against which the North's identity is stabilized, as is also the case the other way around (Deng 1995: 402). The entire affair is unquestionably intensely securitized, but this seemingly remains within the societal sector. The conflict, however, has its focus on—and is often triggered by—the control of state structures (Deng 1995: viii, 135ff., 484ff.).

External factors are important to the conflict. As perceptively argued by Deng,

> It is important to distinguish between foreign involvement in the conflict and external systems that act as models for the perceptions of Sudanese identity. While direct foreign involvement has had minimal lasting effect, externally based models of identity have been at the core of the racial, ethnic, cultural and religious configuration of the Sudan. (1995: 347)

Thus, we see internal and external factors merged but with the domestic constellation defining the issues, and we see politics setting the scene—both of which reconfirm Ayoob's general statements. In this case, identity issues (societal security) make up most of the conflict, but they are structured largely by the political sector; otherwise, one would have expected the conflict simply to multiply within and across state borders in a network of clan, tribe, and religious conflicts. The relatively focused Sudanese conflicts testify to the importance of struggles over state power and its usage and thus to the role of the political sector in structuring extensive societal security problems, in this case organizing around a localizing—that is, intrastate—conflict.

States are typically involved in all sectors, even if their hierarchies differ among the different sectors. Also, we could expect to find the EU involved in all sectors and possibly securitizing in several, because functionally it covers all fields and has state qualities. With cases like the LIEO or the environment/Greenpeace, one might at first expect single-sector appearances, but here we also find that more sectors are usually involved, even if there is a clear or a formal focus on one sector.

The Liberal International Economic Order

Moving on to the less statelike cases, the liberal international economic order (a referent object, not an actor except in the *Wall Street Journal*) was touched upon earlier. It is appealed to mostly by the leading capitalist states, which use it both against each other in the case of alleged violations of GATT-WTO rules and against outsiders and would-be insiders who are molded into appropriate modes of behavior and, to some extent, modes of being. And as argued previously, this effort blends with the politics of international society—the concern for the principles of the political sector—where especially the definition of insiders and outsiders serves to connect the two sectors. Societal dynamics are also present in the dialectics between regionalism and liberal globalism because of the legitimation of regionalism as a defense of cultural distinctiveness.

The Environment

In the environmental sector, linkages across sectors are legion, and for the purpose of a security complex analysis it seems possible to take dense packages of referent objects and actors as a focus. When one looks to the typical environmental actors, such as environmentalist groups, their arguments often point to threats that are really societal, economic, or military. As argued in Chapter 4, the rhetoric of environmentalists seems at first to be in defense of "the environment"; when more skeptical audiences have to be convinced, the arguments are phrased in terms of threats to societal stability, long-term economic sustainability, and even the dangers of wars over scarce resources. The intersection of environmental problems with threats from other sectors forms the basis of much successful securitization by environmental activists.

Thus, even in the more challenging sectors, we find that security actors do not function in separate sectors. States appear in all sectors, and even when some referent objects or actors are clearly rooted in one specific sector, there are links to other sectors. This finding does not substantiate, although it does support, the far-reaching thesis presented in "Cross-Sectoral Security Connections Through the Actor's Lens" that security functions mostly as aggregate security for actors and that therefore *they* weigh the different sectors against each other. We as analysts therefore do not have to connect fully packaged, separate sectors—they are interrelated in the securitization process. The credibility of this theory demands more detailed empirical studies of the way units securitize. To what extent do their securitizations in one sector influence, and become influenced by, those from other sectors? Only if such linkages exist can aggregate security be at play. Space does not allow a full range of case studies here, so we present one relatively systematic case with somewhat more complete documentation than those surveyed so far.

The case(s) should also serve to investigate whether cross-sectoral connections mean one specific sector is always dominant (the military one, as traditionally claimed, or the political sector as considered in Chapter 7 and, for example, in Jahn, Lemaitre, and Wæver 1987, and Ayoob 1995) or whether the connection is one of mutual coloring—that is, all sectors are interpreted in light of the general security issue: overdetermination. In part, the issue of aggregate versus sector-specific security is about bureaucratic-institutional questions: To what extent is security centralized in a specific organ (e.g., a national security council) or decentralized? Aggregate security does not demand that actors view all security issues through some grand conception of the total situation, only that there is a kind of ranking at the top with which actors perceive some issue(s) as primary instances of security as such. This is exactly what we should expect because of the nature of security: Since security is about priority, about elevating issues to absolute priority, it is natural that different candidates will battle it out (politically) with each other. If an issue has not pushed almost all other issues aside, it has not been fully securitized. Therefore, it is in the nature of security as conceived here (securitization) that the five sectors can not remain separate but must vie for primacy.

We need to investigate whether this mechanism of cross-sectoral interpretation actually operates and, if so, how (for instance, whether the military sector does dominate all others or the sectors influence each other in more complex ways). We must also investigate how it is possible to conduct security complex analysis in a cross-sectoral mode instead of building sector-specific complexes. To find the answers requires an empirical study of some units that define security and, preferably, also of security interaction among units. This entails three questions: (1) choice of units, (2) choice of method, and (3) choice of material and sources.

1. *The unit chosen is the EU.* We have made a number of impressionistic comments on various other cases, but we want to study at least one systematically. Choosing a state would be problematic in a book that wants to show that other units can be referent objects and actors. But some of the more extreme cases are too obviously dominated by one sector to be worth an entire study (cf. Greenpeace, described previously). The EU is a nonstate but with some statelike features and is interesting because of its involvement in complex, multilayered politics.

2. *How should we study our cases?* The obvious method is discourse analysis, since we are interested in when and how something is established by whom as a security threat. The defining criterion of security is textual: a specific rhetorical structure that has to be located in discourse.

We will not use any sophisticated linguistic or quantitative techniques. What follows is discourse analysis simply in the sense that discourse is studied as a subject in its own right, not as an indicator of something else. By this method we will not find underlying motives, hidden agenda, or such. There might be confidential sources that could reveal intentions and tactics, but the purpose of discourse analysis is not to get at something else. One of its weaknesses is that it is a poor strategy for finding real motives. If one's theory points toward questions at another level than intentions, however, this critique is irrelevant. Discourse analysis can uncover one thing: discourse. Whenever discourse and the structures thereof are interesting in themselves, discourse analysis makes sense. This is the case if one has reason to believe discourse has structures that are sufficiently rigid to shape possible policy lines (Wæver 1994; Wæver, Holm, and Larsen forthcoming) or if one wants to locate a phenomenon that is defined by a characteristic discursive move (e.g., this book). The technique is simple: Read, looking for arguments that take the rhetorical and logical form defined here as security.

Discourse analysis is not the exclusive method of securitization studies. A complete analysis will also include more traditional political analysis of units interacting, facilitating conditions, and all of the other dimensions of security complex theory. But to see whether securitizations are separate or are defined by each other, a study of the actual phrasing of the securitizing moves seems appropriate. Furthermore, this small case study has a second purpose beyond the specific Chapter 8 question: to see whether our Chapter 2 definitions are operational. Is it possible to recognize securitization when one meets it? Are the criteria so vague that there will be too many cases, making the entire exercise meaningless, or are the demands too high and instances therefore extremely rare? The study of the EU discourse aims to show whether the rhetorical structure of securitization is sufficiently distinct that a close reading of texts can lead to a relatively indisputable list of instances.

3. *The analysis should be conducted on texts that are central* in the sense that if a security discourse is operative in this community, it should be expected to materialize in this text because this occasion is sufficiently important (cf. Wæver 1989a: 190ff.). The logic is that if a securitization is socially empowered in a given society (when "a" argues that all of A is threatened by B, this is generally accepted as valid and powerful, and "a" thereby gains acceptance for doing x), we should expect "a" to use this argument whenever a debate is sufficiently important. Since the security argument is a powerful instrument, it is against its nature to be hidden. Therefore, if one takes important debates, the major instances of securitization should appear on the scene to battle with each other for primacy; thus, one does not need to read everything, particularly not obscure texts.

We have selected texts of an overall nature.[5] Although the choice of general debates rather than more specific debates on concrete measures has the advantage of structurally including the criterion of importance—actors have to prioritize which issues and arguments to select in a general "free" session—it has the disadvantage of being less clear about what the measure advocated or legitimated is. Often, it will therefore be easier to find the first part of the securitization move—arguing for existential threats and urgency—and less clear whether this points to specific emergency measures and a violation of normal politics or established rules. Therefore, an aftercheck is carried out in the form of reading a wide selection of texts that relate specifically to the different sector subjects.[6] Because of the limited space available in the present context, findings from these texts are reported only when they deviate significantly from the main analysis. The texts were chosen from a limited period—1995—both to maximize possible structural cross-determination and to minimize arbitrariness in the selection of instances. It is better to have a limited set of texts and a complete representation of securitization instances than a large set from which the authors pick at liberty. In each document, a search for security arguments is carried out, and each finding is investigated as to its context, the referent object, the threat, and—not least—its connection to other sectors, that is, whether the security nature of the issue is derived from the fact that the source of the threat is already securitized in another sector.[7]

If this were a case study of a region, of a security complex, it would have to include several referent objects, their securitizations, and—not least—the interaction among them. After reading the EU case, it might seem impossible to do this for all parties to a complex. Will security complex analysis always have to involve that much discourse analysis, that much close reading of texts? No! It is simply a question of the level of detail in a case study.

In CSCT, the security complex was also built from the concerns and perceptions of the actors, but rarely did a security complex analysis involve a formalized, empirical study of these factors (Buzan and Rizvi et al. 1986 probably comes the closest). Most analyses of regional security complexes would concentrate on the aggregation, on pulling together the regional story, and would—much in the tradition of security studies—base themselves on a rather impressionistic interpretation of the different actors. Security experts usually draw upon a varied repertoire of sources, newspapers, conversations, theories, and other academic writings on the case, which all come together in their skillful judgment about the nature of Russian security concerns or what is most central to Indian security. The documentation is rarely spelled out in any formal way. (The judgment of the security expert—where formal evidence ends—is found relevant exactly because he or she is an expert and the evidence is inconclusive. In this, the security expert is more like a management consultant, who is asked to evaluate a situation, than like a traditional scientist whose argument counts only as far as the evidence is conclusive.)

The following, rather detailed investigation of the micrologic of one node in a security complex is thus the corollary to other studies of actors that in CSCT should be done in a book-length analysis of a complex but that would be left out and replaced with qualified judgment in a more brief analysis that concentrates on that which is particular to security complex analysis—the regional totality. With the revised security complex analysis, one can still do the regional analysis without engaging in discourse analysis on each actor. But it is probably useful to try it a few times to get an understanding of the microdynamics of regional security.

The European Union: A Reading

On his final step to becoming president of the *Commission,* Jacques Santer, in his 17 January 1995 speech (Santer 1995a: 14), used security arguments in a few contexts. First:

> Europe has witnessed great events over the past five years: Germany has been reunited, Communism has fallen. But, as Vaclav Havel has said, everything is possible but nothing is certain any more. We are experiencing once again the resurgence of rabid nationalism, erupting in some cases into bloody conflict, as in what was the former Yugoslavia. This tragedy teaches us one fundamental lesson: it is more important than ever that the Union remain an axis of peace and prosperity for the continent of Europe. First of all, we must preserve and develop what we have built over the past fifty years. It is something of a miracle that war between our peoples should have become unthinkable. To squander this legacy would be a crime against ourselves. Secondly, the Union cannot be a haven of peace in a troubled sea. Hence the importance of future enlargements. Hence, too, the importance of developing a genuine foreign and security policy.

The fact that this legacy can possibly be "squandered" implies that the miracle of the Western European security community is a precarious achievement and that integration as such has to be defended to preserve peace.[8] This points to the general conclusion of keeping the process of integration alive and to the specific inferences that enlargement and common foreign and security policy are mandatory.

Second, "our venture will fail" if it remains "the prerogative of a select band of insiders" (Santer 1995a). Ordinary Europeans want to participate, and they want clear signs that the EU will act on matters of importance to them. So far, it is difficult to know what conclusions to draw from this argument—more and more often heard—although it is often strongly dramatized. Thus, it cannot yet be seen as a clear securitization.

Equally weak, and thus below the threshold of security, are references to the threat from new technologies potentially dominated by others (the United States and Japan)—"I want to see European traffic on the global information highways"—and the use of terms such as securing the survival of the European social model, environmental problems with their potential of "jeopardizing future generations' chances of meeting their needs," and protection of "rural areas and smaller towns." Although here they do not take clear security forms, each of the subjects returns later in other contexts with the next step more clearly indicated.

The word *security* is mentioned in the fixed expression "common foreign and security policy"[9] and beyond this—and more distinctly—in the context of internal security, of legal and internal cooperation to combat crime, drugs, and illegal immigration. In the work program (section 4), a similar reference is made to internal security, even stating that "criminal organizations have already shown that they can and will exploit weak points in the defence of the Union." Therefore, it is argued, the Commission will be using its competencies to the limit (European Commission 1995: section 4; Santer 1995a: 16, 1995b: 107), and there is at least a tone here of "we can do this because it is about security" or "you must understand that we have to do this."

The other documents from the Commission and from Santer repeat variations on these themes, although they differ in sometimes giving a more dramatic expression of the environmental argument or more dramatic expressions regarding internal security. We will visit the two other institutions in turn—first the Council, then the European Parliament—then sum up and analyze the findings.

The Cannes Declaration (June 1995) from the *European Council*—summits of heads of states and governments—is almost free of security arguments (European Council 1995a). There are hints of such arguments in formulations about a currency crisis, about stability (in relation to Russia), and perhaps most strongly on police cooperation (in the annex on Euro-Mediterranean cooperation). The Madrid Declaration (December 1995) is totally free of securitization (European Council 1995b). Given its composition—member states—it is understandable that this body securitizes less for Europe, that is, that it hesitates to give "Europe" extraordinary powers. A little more securitization is found in the other Council documents.

The other form in which the Council appears in our material is as the president of the Council (the head of state or government representing the country chairing the EU for that half year). This situation is more complex in the sense that a Spanish prime minister speaks according to both Spanish and Council logic; he speaks differently from, say, a German chancellor and also differently from the way he would speak if he were not in the EU chair (for instance, he is more positive about Eastern enlargement). Technically, he represents the Council, although the collective "check" is fairly loose. There is nevertheless a certain role framing, and especially on occasions such as the ones we are dealing with here, the prime minister or president speaks with the knowledge that his speech must be tolerable to all of the states. Of this type we have François Mitterrand's grand farewell speech of 15 March 1995 and Felipe Gonzáles Márquez's as part of the State of the Union debate in November 1995.

Mitterrand's speech contained two parts—a normal presentation of the program of the French presidency and a personal part, his European testament. In the normal part, he is most dramatic in the section on internal security, which is given as the first example of the need for citizens to feel concretely the utility of the EU.

> I am thinking firstly . . . of the EUROPOL Convention . . . the general rule that we must all move forward together—in particular, in the area of security. As far as the right of asylum and immigration is concerned, a great deal remains to be done. . . . Europe will be a people's Europe only if our people feel secure in Europe, and because of Europe. I could say as much . . . about cooperation on justice, or about coordinated action to combat terrorism and organized crime. (Mitterrand 1995: 48)

The other remarkable element in that part of the speech which was picked up the most often by the parliamentarians, was his argument about Europe's need for "a soul, so that it can give expression—and let us use more modest language here—to its culture" (Mitterrand 1995: 48). This leads to an argument for the specifically French position, which also became, however, EU policy—the cultural exception in the GATT. "It [the principle of cultural exception] stems from the belief that the cultural identity of our nations, the right of each people to develop its own culture, is in jeopardy. It embodies the will to defend freedom and diversity for all countries, to refuse to cede the means of representation—in other words, the means of asserting one's identity—to others" (read: the United States) (Mitterrand 1995: 48). The arguments point to relatively innocent policies such as more education about Europe, multilingual teaching, and the like; more controversially, the French-led policy in the audiovisual sector is presented as "a matter of urgency" (Mitterrand 1995: 49). All of this builds toward arguments for refusing "the logic of a blind market—or the blind logic of the market" and thus for maintaining GATT-WTO exceptions and resistance against the general trend toward opening and deregulation.

In the personal part of the speech (1995: 51), Mitterrand tells the story of his relationship to World Wars I and II and the task of his generation to pass on the experience and memory and thus the motivation for the reconciliation and peace-building functions of the EU. In effect, this is the same argument as Santer's first—the peace-integration argument—only more dramatic:

> What I am asking you to do is almost impossible, because it means overcoming our past. And yet, if we fail to overcome our past, let there be no mistake about what will follow: ladies and gentlemen, nationalism means war! [loud applause] War is not only our past, it could also be our future! And it is us, it is you, ladies and gentlemen, the Members of the European Parliament, who will henceforth be the guardians of our peace, our security and our future! (Mitterrand 1995: 51)

Gonzáles used some of the same arguments, especially regarding the unstable continent after the Cold War and Euro-skepticism as a threat to fragment the European continent. After unemployment, which is given first priority although not in a security form, "the second great challenge lies in security policy—that is, action to make it possible for us to resist organized international crime, the drugs traffic, terrorism and so on—of immediate concern to our citizens" (Gonzáles 1995: 155). Therefore, he argues more strongly here than anywhere else the need to give the EU additional tools (Gonzáles 1995: 142).

With the field of internal security, one could argue that this is a different kind of security, that there has always been talk about internal security that should be kept separate from our concept of international security. Didier Bigo (1996), however, has shown how internal and external security merge during these years; especially in the Europeanization of internal security, this concept is used to link a diversity of issues (terrorism, drugs, organized crime, transnational crime, and illegal immigration) and, with reference to this new political entity, to empower certain security agencies to operate freely across a European space. It should be noticed that these arguments are actually in a mode more analogous to international security than to the "law and order for the safety of the individual" logic of internal security. They are about distinct threats, alien and malignant actors such as terrorists, organized crime, and drug traffickers.

Finally, there are hints in many places that the project of European Monetary Union (EMU) has been securitized. Because of its embeddedness in the volatile global financial system, EMU can fall in a speculative rush; furthermore, it is of principled importance to the EU. Mitterrand said "the introduction of a single currency is the only means of ensuring that Europe remains a great economic and monetary power, and it is the best means of ensuring the sustained growth of our economies" (1995: 46). Still, the Council is generally careful with this: On the one hand, it appeals for more consistency in policies enabling the introduction of the single currency and the third phase of EMU, but on the other hand, there is a hesitancy to say too clearly that the whole thing falls if EMU falls. Everybody knows it is distinctly possible that this goal will not be reached, and there is no reason to risk pulling everything down with EMU in that case.

In the debates in the *European Parliament,* eight distinct themes for securitization appeared.

1. The biggest threat, many argue, is the complex of unemployment, social marginalization, and—linked to this—xenophobia (e.g., MEP Lilli Gyldenkilde, European Parliament 1995a: 24): "These are the real challenges if we are to achieve a secure Europe." In itself, this threat can point to several contrary lines of action; therefore, its articulation with other arguments is decisive. It is sometimes offered as an argument against the dominant Euro-construction in which growth and new technology are seen as the solution. This argument is advanced both by people like

Gyldenkilde, who are skeptical of European integration, and by some who support integration, such as MEP Alexander Langer (in European Parliament 1995a: 26)—who argues, however, that growth and competition destroy regional and social roots, the very identities of European citizens. The technogrowth people, of course, present their line as the way to master the threat. In between these views, the leaders of the largest group in Parliament—the socialists—merge competitiveness with social argument. MEP Pauline Green, for instance, (in European Parliament 1995a: 21) makes the connection gender equality => utilize all qualifications => compete globally => protect the European social model. And MEP Wilfried A. E. Martens argues that social policy, the environment, research, and new technology are necessary because "at the same time, the union must preserve its model of development with a human face and invest in its intellectual capital, so as to remain in the vanguard of the world's great technological powers into the twenty-first century" (European Parliament 1995a: 22).

2. *The European social model* is the term used to refer to the welfare state, which varies greatly among European states and can appear as "the European model" only in a comparison with non-Europe, which is exactly what happens. The European social model is defined in contrast to the United States and Japan and is to be defended against these others, as well as against those among its own reformers who, to compete globally, will sacrifice this model (and thereby a part of what is "Europe"). This construction has the political merit of linking a sociopolitical issue to the fate of "Europe" as such.

3. MEP Klaus Hänsch, in contrast, who is also rather dramatic in discussing unemployment (it "undermines people's faith in justice and democracy, and therefore in the stability of our societies in Europe"; European Parliament 1995c: 135), wants Europe to do more to improve competitiveness and especially to fend off the threatening perspective of "other economic regions of the world—Japan, USA, all of South East Asia—dominating key technologies. We should not allow that in the Europe of our children all TV-sets are Japanese and all TV-programmes American and we Europeans only observers. We should not allow this to happen" (European Parliament 1995c: 135). In this case, the argument supports the mainstream policy of flexibilization, reform of social systems, and investment in new technologies.

4. In the case of those emphasizing unemployment, that problem is often linked to the frequently heard argument (cf. also Santer 1995a, quoted earlier) that without the support of Europe's people the process will fail. Thus, the issue is dramatic because it is the main threat to individual Europeans and, not least, because it is one of the major threats to the European project (e.g., Green in European Parliament 1995c: 46).

These first four lines—unemployment, the European social model, new technology, and popular support for the EU—and the relevant defenses are potentially in tension with each other but are also potentially closely linked. Therefore, much of the politics of the Parliament is about attempts to articulate these lines, to interpret one in the light of the others—for example, the necessity of new technology to compete but thereby also to solve unemployment and save the European social model.

The first three lines have an element of the issue itself being almost of security quality—unemployment at the social or individual level, competitiveness as economic security, the European social model as an identity issue—but when rhetoric must reach the highest levels and existential élan has to be achieved, the specific argument is given the twist that it is the fate of *integration* that is at stake. Therefore, the EU has to make progress in those areas "closest to the citizen"—the economy.

Still, all of this is only the first step in a securitization. It establishes an existential threat and probably also gets some acceptance of this—it is close to a consensus position in the Parliament, as well as in the other two institutions dealt with here (therefore, struggle sets in about how to articulate it and we get the competing programs of the different political wings). But we have not yet seen attempts to suggest specific measures of a radical nature. For the purpose of this chapter, however, it is interesting to see how the cross-sectoral connections work out: The securityness of economic issues is multiplied by a political argument (about the survival of integration).

5. More in line with the peace-integration argument presented by Santer, it is argued by, for example, Martens (European Parliament 1995a: 22) that the dialectics of deepening and enlargement will be decisive for the success or failure of the European political project. And MEP Gijs M. De Vries argues (in European Parliament 1995a: 23) that "security has become the major assignment of the Union"; the Union has to be the "accuser of nationalism and provincial suspicion." Both these arguments draw on the general picture of a potential weakening of integration—because of either enlargement or growing nationalism—and therefore of a need to insist on deepening. Langer argued more dramatically that nationalism is on the march, and ethnic cleansing appears in many forms; therefore, Europe "needs high and positive examples of a road leading to integration, democracy, peace, social justice and conservation of the environment" (in European Parliament 1995a: 26). The citizens must notice that integration is preferable to breakup. This argument was put even more bluntly by the German chair and president of the Parliament, Hänsch, at the State of the Union session:

> In this new climate of opinion a new nationalism is emerging, which often also appears in disguised form and alleges, in tones of political correctness, that although it may be for Europe it is against political union. Let us not be fooled. The new nationalism, which has little regard for what we have managed to build up in Western Europe over the past fifty years or even wants to destroy it, that new nationalism leads straight back to pre-

war Europe! [applause] Not for years has anyone put it as clearly as François Mitterrand did in his farewell speech in this House in January this year, when he said that nationalism is war, and in the new [applause] undivided Europe that has existed since 1990 it is still the case that no state must ever again be allowed to become so sovereign that it can decide alone on war and peace and on the weal and woe of its neighbours. (Hänsch 1995: 135)

The threat is not only nationalism, it is also sovereignty. The various new dangers Hänsch further mentions—to the East and the South—are serious because they threaten to bring the EU countries back into rivalry.

Security logic is used by MEP Eolo Parodi when he argues that the EU is in a crisis of power and therefore he abstains from a showdown with the Commission, as he thinks one should otherwise have aimed. This cannot be risked due to the crisis and the potential for unraveling of the EU (European Parliament 1995a: 29).

6. In foreign policy, the parliamentarians criticize the other institutions for not doing enough to defend human rights (European Parliament 1995a: 24, 27, 41). At one level, the argument is that security ultimately stems from the inside, that the only true basis for solid security is the state of law and respect for human rights (e.g., European Parliament 1995a: 23). This looks like the general liberal, missionary idea of security, but it also has a specific twist because "human rights" are seen as a European idea. By conducting a human rights–based foreign policy, the EU not only defends the rights of concrete people around the world or a general universal principle; it also defends its own values and distinctiveness. Human rights are significant, because "despite national and political frontiers, we have succeeded in finding a common language" (MEP Jannis Sakellariou in European Parliament 1995a: 41).

This argument is especially characteristic of European Parliament logic. It has to be something European that is threatened. The Parliament's securitizations are most often attempts to define the specific object threatened as linked to Europe as such. As with the "unraveling" arguments (number 4 and 5), this argument manages to place the EU (or even "Europe") as at stake but this time less through a political-IR argument and more through an identity argument. Argument 2 (the European social model) had elements of this, too.

7. In the field of internal security, there is a general (and fairly logical) pattern in which the Council and the Commission use more classical securitization to obtain more powers, police cooperation (including secrecy and monitoring), and the Europeanization of competences, whereas the Parliament also wants attention to the issue but equally for the purpose of observing the observers and policing the police—that is, of trying to profile the rights of citizens in the name of European values (e.g., Martens in European Parliament 1995b: 111; MEP Alonso José Puerta in European

Parliament 1995b: 113; Hänsch in European Parliament 1995c: 136f).
Parliamentarians press mostly for a Europeanization of internal security but
do not want this to lead to secrecy and loss of parliamentary control. Parties
vary on this issue largely along a left-right axis. But the leading voices in
the Parliament that speak on behalf of the major groups seem very much
aware of the difference between their position and that of the other institutions. From the Commission, the Council, and those parliamentarians who
push mainly for more attention to internal security, the case is often bol-
stered by giving internal security a second-order security importance:
"Citizens will not see the benefits of the frontier-free area unless the Union
can demonstrate its capacity to *guarantee their security* and combat the
drugs traffic and organized crime" (Santer 1995b: 107).

    8. Finally, the environment is often mentioned as an area of great
importance when serious threats are present (more on this later).

    There are a number of single-instance security hints of less signifi-
cance.

    An analysis of these instances of securitization shows that one security
argument is shared across institutional settings: the peace argument. In
addition, the different actors have some smaller securitizations.

    Interestingly, the Council has few securitizations. One reason could be
that it ultimately works from national perspectives and therefore does not
want systematically (only in limited, ad hoc instances) to equip the EU with
emergency powers or automaticity. Another reason could be that the
Council is the most powerful institution; if it says something is a security
problem it must act on it, whereas the Parliament especially uses its arguments mostly to criticize the inaction of others.

    In the Parliament, the use of a wide range of securitizations (although
mostly in rather mild form) should be seen as part of a more general search
for priority areas wherein because it is a parliament, it tries to find issues
closer to "the citizen"—that is, concrete matters on which people can register the value of EU action. In this search, there are two criteria; one is
importance to ordinary people, the other is that the theme should somehow
have a specific European quality. Therefore, arguments tend to converge
around slogans such as "the European social model" and "human rights (a
European idea)," as well as the peace argument: European integration is the
alternative to European wars and power balancing. Except for the latter, it
is not clear that all these cases should overrule normal politics or principled
reservations. But the peace argument is central in arguments vis-à-vis
national politics (not least in Germany) in upholding an integration-orient-
ed policy and thus overruling concerns about sovereignty and identity. The
environmental argument also has some peculiar features. These are notable
in the arguments of the Parliament but also in those of the Commission.
Section 1.12 of the Work Programme for 1995 says: "At the international

level, the EU should follow up on the Rio summit by striving for a leading position in global questions about the environment and sustainable development and by walking in the front on issues."[10]

What is at play here has been shown by Markus Jachtenfuchs in his dissertation on the EU and the greenhouse effect (Jachtenfuchs 1994). The concept of leadership, in which the EU is endowed with a special role in international environmental politics, was originally invented in the greenhouse case but was later "transferred to the totality of EC [European Community] environmental policy" (Jachtenfuchs 1994: 245). Especially for the Commission, environmental leadership forged a link to integration as such and to an international role for the Community.

> Environmental leadership conveys the image of the EC as a new type of power, dealing with contemporary problems in appropriate terms, and contrasts this image to that of the United States as a traditional military power neglecting problems that cannot be solved with traditional means of foreign policy. "Leadership" underlines the EC's aspiration to become a superpower, but a modern one. By promoting the leadership concept, the Commission could enhance its own role and status as the representative and speaker of the Community. (Jachtenfuchs 1994: 275)

This case brings out clearly what has also been seen in fragments on other issues: The specific issue is articulated with the general issue of "integration" as such, and typically this is where the security quality is added.

The arch example of this is, however, the most clearly securitized issue in EU discourse: the peace argument of integration as the bulwark against a return to Europe's past of balance of power and wars. This argument is the one used the most consistently in all instances in the EU and the one that is the most strongly securitized. Europe as a project, as history, is at a crossroads, and security is at play as the question of integration versus fragmentation (Wæver 1996a, b; de Wilde 1996). Integration is made an aim in itself (because the alternative is fragmentation).[11] Thereby security legitimacy is obtained for the rationale the EU Commission and bureaucracy have used all along: that any specific policy question should always be subject to a dual estimate, that of the issue itself and of its effects in terms of strengthening or weakening integration (Jachtenfuchs and Huber 1993). By adding the security argument, integration gains urgency because its alternative is a self-propelling process that by definition will destroy "Europe" as a project and reopen the previous insecurity caused by balance of power, nationalism, and war. Integration gains a grammatical form closer to security logic. Whether "Europe" exists or not appears as a "to be or not to be" question (for a more elaborate analysis, see Wæver 1996b).

This is Europe's or the EU's unique security argument, which is likely the reason it very often structures other, more tentative security questions. It is basic because it defines the EU's existence. In interaction with other securitizations, it narratively fuses societal, economic, environmental, political, and military arguments into one specific plot. Has this situation shown multi- and cross-sectoral dynamics, or could it be argued to have one dominant sector because it is basically political? This argument is cross-sectoral and thus constitutes "aggregate security" because it draws on arguments from the other sectors. In the case of the economy, for example, competitiveness is reconfigured as a question of Europe's quality as global actor and is thereby merged with the political "existence" (international presence) argument. Threats such as new technologies, unemployment, and U.S. and Japanese competition become increasingly central to the motivation for the *necessity* of integration—for Europe.

It is possible to reach conclusions from this brief case study, first in terms of the possibility of reading for security and second in relation to the aggregation of sectors by actors. Methodologically, the results were fairly encouraging. It would have been problematic if no instances of securitization had been found, but it would have been even more so if there had been hundreds of examples in each text. Actually, we found a limited, manageable, and meaningful list: four instances by the Commission, of which one was clearly primary, and eight by the Parliament, although most of these were only tentative securitizing moves with little sign of what extraordinary action should follow. The Council, revealingly, used very little securitization. Clearly, the lesson is that it is possible to read with the securitization gauge whether arguments take the specific form of presenting existential threats (and, if they constitute full securitization, to point toward extraordinary steps that possibly violate normal procedures). It is possible to judge which cases qualify and which do not. The criteria are not formalized enough to send hundreds of students into the coding laboratory in the style of 1960s behavioralist IR. The criteria are a little more interpretative, but it does not seem farfetched to conclude that people working with an understanding of securitization theory would have reproducible findings.

In relation to the other purpose of this chapter—the sector aggregation issue—we have three findings.

1. The securitizations in different sectors are connected. The main instances of securitization are narratives that draw upon elements from several sectors to produce images of existential threats and necessary action—typically, sustained integration.
2. Just as nations have identity and states sovereignty as their organizing principle and security focus, the different securitizations around the EU seem to converge on integration as the equivalent generalized measure.[12]
3. Not only different national and party political origins produce variation in securitizations; the different institutional settings also differ in themes and emphasis. This makes sense because of their different

positions in relation to long-term integration and, concretely, in terms of their different degrees of responsibility for action and implementation. Securitizing actors make a difference, even when they appeal to the same referent object.

Conclusion: Purposes

The different ways of aggregating sectors set out in this chapter are not a question of finding *the* superior form of security analysis; they point instead to the different purposes a security analysis might have. The sector-by-sector approach ties into a logic of complexity, which can be found in a superficial form as a craving for complexity and in a more sophisticated macrohistorical version. The units-as-synthesizers approach is attached to a logic of constellations that is oriented toward analyzing contemporary political situations.

For many wideners, security analysis functions as a proof of complexity. The inclusion of more sectors says the traditionalist's military story is too simple, too narrow. And more actors serve to counter a state-based account. Whether the new image becomes simple enough to render another story is not the main issue; it is used primarily to counter excessively narrow conceptions: "Don't forget the environment," and "This is not the whole story—security is also about . . ." The image becomes a kind of checklist, a large matrix on which one can put sectors along one side and units along the other and then say, "There are all these types—see how the establishment only looks at the small corner up there (at best 4 boxes), but there are 25" (cf. de Wilde 1995).

In contrast, the focus on constellations and dynamics is aimed at reduction, at finding the turning points that might decide the way the future will unfold and thus function as a political analysis—one that could be of help in political choices. The main difference is simply what kind of analysis one is interested in—complexity versus constellations.[13]

The first type—the matrix with many boxes—functions as a political argument only at an aggregate level, because it rarely comes to any conclusions or sums up in any way that makes it much of an analysis of a specific situation. This type can be used as a critique of established policies as too narrow. But unless one assumes that because there are 25 boxes each should receive 4 percent of political attention, it says little about what could constitute good policy. A general problem with this method, as with much liberalist IR theory, is that it only complicates matters in an attempt to give detailed one-to-one maps of the world instead of trying to simplify, as realist theories are at least (some would say more than) willing to do.

The matrix approach is also useful for macrohistory (e.g., Buzan 1995a; Buzan and Little 1994, 1996; Buzan and Segal 1997), which aims at a global, theoretical analysis of trends and wants to disaggregate and aggregate in the analysis: What is the general trend regarding the relative importance of sectors; what are the relations between economic security and political security that explain large trends in global developments? Here, a number of events and decisions are summed up, and it is noticed that, for example, more and more security struggles are over environmental issues. This summary can become part of a grand narrative on the direction of the international system at the end of the twentieth century (and the second millennium).

But if one's aim is to conduct a concrete contemporary political analysis, the second approach is superior. In such an analysis, one wants to grasp a political constellation, the main lines of struggle, the crucial decisions, the cross-pressures operating on key actors, and the likely effects of different moves. One cannot, for example, look at Europe sector by sector—the units are the nodes, and the way they balance sectoral threats will be included in a constellation made up of units. The actual security concerns— the securitizations—of the actors are the basic building blocks of such constellations.

This chapter has shown that actors do act in terms of aggregate security—that is, they let security concerns from one sector color their security definitions in other sectors, or they add everything up and make a judgment on the basis of some overarching narrative that structures security as such. For example, whether an economic issue is labeled a security problem is not unrelated to how the actors involved perceive their general relationship with each other. If Turkey changes some regulations in the economic field in relation to Syria, for example, this is likely to be perceived as a security affair because Turkey also controls the water tap, which Syria depends on, and the Turkish-Syrian relationship is tense because of the Kurdish issue, which Syria uses to counterbalance these other threats. If Poland makes the same change in regulations vis-à-vis the Czech Republic, this is more likely to be framed simply as an economic issue—perhaps heavily criticized but not considered a security issue, a threat, an aggressive action.

With this confirmation of cross-sectoral securitization and that described in "Linkages Across Sectors," which holds that the regional-territorial subsystemic level is still an important level of security interaction, it seems possible to reformulate security complex theory in a postsovereign form. Security complex analysis was originally formulated for states only (a security complex consisted of states) and mainly for the political and military sectors. Although we employed security complex analysis, we also subverted it through our attempts to broaden the concept of security to both new actors beyond the state and new sectors beyond the political and military. In our work on the new sectors, we further found it necessary and useful to change the overall perspective to a constructivist understanding of security, in which security becomes a specific social practice rather than some objective question of threats or psychological spirits. It was unclear for a time whether the concept of security complexes could be restated on this more multifarious basis. On the basis of this chapter, it seems we can still identify both the securitizing actors and the referent objects they securitize and will therefore be able to complete the mapping of how the processes of securitization interact: the security complex.

Notes

1. The unit and subunit levels are collapsed into one, because in interaction terms there is no unit level proper. If units interact with each other, they either produce subsystems (nonregional subsystems or regional security complexes) or their interaction is part of the system-defining structure. If the interaction occurs within the unit, it is an interaction among subunits and is treated as "localizing." Complicated border cases are boundary-crossing interactions among subunits on a scale approximately like the unit. This will be classified as localizing.

2. The use of the term *security unit*—with some ambiguity in comparison with the previous precision regarding referent object or actor—is motivated in the argument at the end of Chapter 2 about which units are the building blocks of security complexes.

3. The word *constellation* is used here to emphasize that it is not the units themselves in a static way that make up the whole; it is the way their movements, actions, and policies relate to each other that forms a truly political pattern at the level of relations of relations (cf. Elias 1978 [1939]; Lasswell 1965 [1935]). A security complex consists not simply of India and Pakistan; it consists of an Indian set of perceptions and policies as they form a specific constellation with Pakistani perceptions and policies. This is even more complicated for all larger regions.

4. This is paradoxical in relation to the normally expected pattern of state and nation (sovereigny and identity) (cf. Chapter 7; Wæver et al. 1993, chapter 4; Wæver 1995a, forthcoming-a). The logic of the different referent objects operates as it should—nation is defended as identity, the state as sovereignty—but the securitizing actors are surprising because the state elite uses a distinct reference to the nation-culture, whereas the competing voice claims to represent the true state interest. (A possible explanation could be the one we give in Wæver et al. 1993, chapter 4, and Wæver forthcoming-a, that long-term integration demands increasing separation between state security and societal security. We imagined this, however, as implying increasingly separate voices, whereas in France the state tries to articulate both—separately but by the state.)

5. Specifically, the texts (all from 1995) are the speech by President (chairman of the Commission) Jacques Santer to the Parliament and the ensuing debate in Parliament on the question of accepting the new Commission, 17 January; President Mitterrand's speech to the Parliament that same day and debate on the plans of the French presidency; the Commission's Work Programme for 1995, its presentation speech by Santer to the Parliament on 15 February and debate hereon in Parliament 15 February and 15 March; the conclusions from the meetings of the European Council in Cannes, 26–27 June, and Madrid, 15–16 December; and the declarations of the three "presidents" on "the state of the European Union" and debate on these in Parliament, 15 November (a new tradition, practiced for the first time in 1995).

This list includes some key occasions for the three most relevant institutions:—the Council, the Parliament, and the Commission—ignoring here the powerful Court, which is subject to a different kind of political rationale that is not impossible to include but that raises new questions that go beyond the present context.

6. At least one text has been selected from each area: military (a, the WEU-defense; b, Yugoslavia), environmental (a, *general* environmental policy; b, one specific case), societal (European culture and citizenship), economic (a, general state of the economy; b, foreign economic policy), and political (general politics is covered by the overall debates listed in note 5; a more specific area is citizenship). This has been done for each of the three institutional contexts: the European Parliament (debates), the European Commission (reports, White or Green Books), and the Council (declarations).

7. The full analysis is printed as Ole Wæver, COPRI *Working Paper* no. 1997: 25.

8. Elsewhere, Santer has made this point, stressing "that the unification of Europe is a daily effort, a permanent struggle against centrifugal forces and the temptations of the past." And "the cost of non-Europe would be exorbitant" (Santer 1995c: 138).

9. The arguments about "foreign and security policy" are mostly very vague about how these issues actually constitute serious threats to Europe(ans) and thus are unclear as to whether "security policy" is "security" according to our criteria (cf. Chapter 3 about nonsecurity defense matters). Foreign and security policy, however, begins to take on security importance in a different sense than the classical one of being about military threats. Santer argues that through foreign policy, through external relations (especially among large, regional groups), we are "affirming our collective identity on the world scene and encouraging others to overcome the traditional approach of every man for himself" (Santer 1995c: 139). Thus, in relation to security arguments about whether Europe "exists" (Wind 1992; Furet 1995)—truly an existential matter—the identity question becomes less the internal one of "how alike" Europeans are and more the external issue of appearing as one on the international scene. In this sense, foreign and security policy is of primary security importance to the EU (cf. Wæver 1996b, forthcoming-e).

10. A parallel case is found in Santer (1995a) in relation to development and aid: "The Union must continue to play its leading role in development cooperation and humanitarian aid, for they both contribute to peace and stability in certain areas of the world. It is essential to be active out in the field and the Commission will be doing just that" (p. 15). From here the text leads on to: "Nobody could deny that the Union is an economic giant and yet this is not reflected in the political role it plays. This is why the Maastricht Treaty set out to lay the foundations for a more ambitious political approach by developing a common foreign and security policy" (p. 15). Thus, development has been tied into the reasoning about the EU achieving a voice and an international presence.

11. Europe's Other is not Russia, not Muslims, not even East Asian competitiveness; Europe's Other is Europe itself, Europe's past (Baudrillard 1994 [1992]; Derrida 1992 [1991]; Rytkønen (1995); Wæver 1996b, forthcoming-e). Ideas such as balance of power that have been seen as quintessential Europeanness (Boer 1993) are now transformed so that anti–balance of power (integration) comes to be seen as a European value.

12. It is not "us Europeans unified in our state" that has to be defended; there is no project to defend a sovereignty (which is not established) or a communal identity (which would be self-defeating because it would challenge the member nations). The fact that something as unusual as a process or a project and a large

historical narrative emerges as a referent for security illustrates the novel and experimental character of the EU beyond our usual political categories (cf. Wæver 1995a, 1996b, forthcoming-e).

13. On the two approaches, see also Kostecki 1996, chapter 3. He labels them integrative and aggregative approaches.

CHAPTER 9

Conclusions

Security Studies: The New Framework for Analysis

The new framework results from the expansion of the security agenda to include a wider range of sectors than the traditional military and political. Expanding the security agenda is not a simple or a trivial act, nor is it without political consequences. It is not just about tacking the word *security* onto *economic, environmental,* and *societal.* Pursuing the wider security agenda requires giving very careful thought to what is meant by security and applying that understanding to a range of dynamics, some of which are fundamentally different from military-political ones. As argued earlier, this approach does not exclude traditional security studies. Indeed, we hope it will largely lay to rest the rather scholastic argument between traditionalists and wideners. More important, we hope it will dissolve the unhelpful boundary between security studies and the international political economy (IPE). Much of the agenda that emerges from the new framework lies in the realm of IPE, not least because of the propensity of liberal economics to spill security issues over into other sectors. Consequently, security studies needs to draw upon the expertise available in IPE. In return, this linkage will allow IPE to confront the security aspects of its agenda rather than pushing them into the sterile and unfriendly boundary zone between IPE's "zone of peace" and security studies's "zone of conflict."

In the previous eight chapters, we set out a new framework for security studies. In Chapter 2, we presented a method for understanding the process of securitization in any sector. Without a general method for distinguishing security issues from merely political ones, it is impossible to pursue the wider agenda coherently. The danger is that all things seen as problems will unthinkingly be classified as security issues. By defining security almost exclusively in terms of one sector (the military), traditional security studies has avoided ever having to think very hard about what security actually means. As argued in Chapter 3, it is possible to conceive of some aspects of military policy as not constituting security.

In Chapters 3 through 7, we applied this method to the five principal sectors of the subject. The sectoral approach is crucial to the new framework for three reasons. First, it maintains a strong link to traditional security studies. Although traditional security studies is more or less monosectoral, that fact enables it to be fitted easily into the wider scheme of a multisectoral approach. The use of sectors thus maintains interoperability between the old and new approaches, enabling the latter to incorporate smoothly the insights of the former.

Second, the sectoral approach reflects what people are actually doing with the language by adding "security" onto sector designators (economic, environmental, and the like). This behavior is a vital part of the securitization process despite the fact that in the discourse it often reflects impulsive or superficially tactical moves designed to raise the priority of a given issue in the general political melee. These moves can, if successful, nevertheless generate deeper political consequences. Sectors are distinctive arenas of discourse in which a variety of different values (sovereignty, wealth, identity, sustainability, and so on) can be the focus of power struggles. The rhetoric of sectors generates a need for analytical follow-up to get some handles on how these consequences might unfold.

This points to the third reason for using sectors, which is that they provide a way of understanding the different qualities of security that are features of the wider agenda. Although some qualities of security are common across sectors, each sector also has its own unique actors, referent objects, dynamics, and contradictions that need to be understood in their own terms. The first task of these five chapters was therefore to identify the new or different security qualities that will be added into security studies as a consequence. Their second task was to explore the consequences of widening the agenda for the place of regional formations in security analysis.

Disaggregation into sectors opens up a wealth of insight, but it also poses the problem of how security studies is to be organized. Does the sectoral approach simply create four new subfields to be placed alongside traditional security studies and dealt with largely in isolation from each other, or can the sectors be reintegrated into a single field? Chapter 8 noted that the patterns within the different sectors sometimes did line up in layer-cake complexes (i.e., with regional security patterns in different sectors fitting into the same geographical space) but that in general there was too much overlap and interplay among the sectors to warrant treating them in isolation. The chapter built on this conclusion by arguing that units integrate the sectors both in their policymaking processes and in the way they relate to each other. Therefore, in political terms, there is one integrated field of security.

This new framework raises a number of questions: (1) What are the implications of the new framework for classical security complex theory? (2) What are the problems associated with the social constructivist methodology we have employed? (3) How do the new framework and traditional security studies compare in terms of costs and benefits? Addressing these questions is the substance of this chapter.

Implications of the New Security
Studies for Classical Security Complex Theory

We started this project with a question about how to combine the regional focus of CSCT with the wider agenda of security studies. Since we have set out what we think is a compelling case for the new framework, we have not escaped this obligation. On the face of it, we appear to have made life difficult for ourselves by throwing a lot of awkward complications into what was a fairly neat and clear-cut theory. CSCT was a product of thinking in the mode of traditional security studies—state centric and organized around military-political security concerns. Within the military-political nexus, CSCT gave reasons to expect regional formations, explained how those formations were structured and how they mediated intervention by outside powers, and offered ways of specifying and, to a point, predicting outcomes. Since we have attacked traditional security studies (TSS), have we not also attacked CSCT?

This question can be answered yes and no. In favor of "no" is the fact that although we have rejected the method of TSS, we have not rejected its subject matter, which we have located as one part of our larger picture. Our focus on socially constructed rather than objective security does not affect CSCT, because that element was already strongly built into it with the role given to amity-enmity as a key structuring variable and the consequent spectrum of conflict formation, security regime, and security community. The idea of intersubjective constructions of securitization and desecuritization processes fits comfortably into the idea of security interdependence, which lies at the heart of CSCT. One has only to think of how the Cold War ended, how desecuritization has occurred in southern Africa, or how the process of securitization continues to be sustained in the Middle East and between India and Pakistan to see how comfortable this fit is. From this perspective, CSCT remains relevant when appropriate conditions obtain.

It would, however, be boring to leave it at that. From the arguments in Chapters 3–7, it is clear that interesting regional dynamics are found in all of the new sectors. But only exceptionally will it be appropriate to treat these as self-contained, homogeneous "security complexes" within a single sector. Sometimes, but not always, the regionalizing dynamics in different sectors will line up to produce a layer-cake formation that can be treated as a single complex. Although sectoral analysis may be a clarifying way to begin analysis, the logic of overspill is strong almost everywhere, and as argued in Chapter 8, actors will generally reintegrate sectors in their own processes of securitization. Threat perceptions in one sector are shaped by a unit's primary fears, even if these stem from other sectors. Given this more diverse and more complicated conception of security, can security complex theory be reformulated to operate in a world in which the state is no longer the only referent object and the military-political sector is no longer the only arena for security relations?

Recall the basic definition of a security complex from Chapter 1:

> Security interdependence is markedly more intense among the states inside such complexes than with states outside them. Security complexes are about the relative intensity of interstate security relations that lead to distinctive regional patterns shaped by both the distribution of power and historical relations of amity and enmity. A security complex is defined as *a set of states whose major security perceptions and concerns are so interlinked that their national security problems cannot reasonably be analyzed or resolved apart from one another.* The formative dynamics and structure of a security complex are generated by the states within that complex—by their security perceptions of, and interactions with, each other.

In light of the arguments in this book, this definition has to change to be compatible with the new framework. One issue is that the original formulation of security complex theory was based on the logic of regions being generated purely by interactions among states (see Chapter 1, "'Classical' Security Complex Theory" and "Moving Beyond Classical Security Complex Theory"). In the political and military sectors, it was the projection of power by states that led to regional complexes, with their specific security dilemmas, balances of power, and patterns of enmity and amity. With the new framework, security complexes cannot be limited to state and interstate relations and to politico-military issues; they must make room for other types of security units and issues.

A second problem is the question of whether the idea of exclusively bottom-up (or inside-out) construction can be retained. Although that form of regional construction remains the dominant one, we have also identified regions created by top-down processes. In the environmental and, more arguably, the economic sectors, regions can be created as patterns within system-level processes, such as a group of countries finding themselves sharing the local effects of a climate change or a cluster of countries all finding themselves in the periphery.

This second difficulty can be handled in terms of the spectrum from conflict formation through security regime to security community. CSCT instead assumed that security complexes had their origins as conflict formations (thus forming from the bottom up) and that they might or might not evolve toward more amity-based types of security interdependence (still working in the bottom-up mode). This was the story in Europe and seemed also to be the case elsewhere (e.g., Southeast Asia, Southern Africa,

North America). In the military-political realm, history offered little evidence of any other pattern, and to a very considerable extent this assumption will remain valid. In Chapter 1, "Regions," this regionalizing dynamic was explained by the immobile character of the dominant political unit—the state.

This logic is not confined to the military and political sectors. It can also be found in the environmental sector; some environmental issues have strong geographical fixtures. The logic of hydropolitics, for example, is largely about subsets of actors that are highly interdependent in the face of one river system or sea or pollution problem. In such cases, the regional security complex is the upper limit of the politics related to environmental issues in that specific geographical location. The bottom-up formulation can be found in the other sectors as well. In the societal sector, we find territorially based identity groups interacting with their neighbors. In the economic sector, we find states clustering together to produce regional free trade associations (FTAs), common markets, or unions. When, as in this latter case, the interaction is more that of a security regime or a security community (rather than a conflict formation), it may well reflect, and have repercussions on, security relations outside the complex. When units enter into the amity half of the spectrum, cooperating over their security, this may be a way to both resolve security dilemmas between them and present some form of common front to outside actors. This line of thinking provides the key to dealing with security regions formed from the top down.

With the wider agenda, it is possible to envisage regional security interdependence arising less from interactions between units than from collective responses to shared fates arising from outside systemic pressure. One could imagine, for example, the formation of regional security interdependence on the basis of shared concerns about the (in)stability of the LIEO or about the interplay of climate change and water supply. When security interdependence comes top down rather than bottom up, it seems highly likely that the resultant security complex will be found at the amity end of the spectrum (a security regime or community) rather than at the enmity end (conflict formation). Although common threats could set units against each other, they are more likely to bring them together. One danger to watch out for here is mistaking subregional security regimes for security complexes. The Gulf Cooperation Council constitutes a security regime but is nevertheless part of the Gulf subcomplex and is not a security complex in its own right.

Thus, in all sectors the logic of regionalization can be the result of bottom-up processes that find their upper limit at the subsystem level. But regionalization can also result from top-down processes when the subsystem is triggered by global structures, interaction capacities, and processes. In the first case, the leading methodological question is, what is the minimum scale, or the lowest level, at which sources of explanation can be located without creating incoherent analyses? Do we need arguments that are located at a higher level of analysis? In other words, what is the smallest environment of a specific security issue? This is the method behind classical security complex theory.

In the second case, the global level *is* the smallest environment. The leading methodological question here is, does the location of the sources of explanation at the global level provide a coherent analysis of security issues throughout the system? And if not, do the differences show coherent patterns that allow us to conclude the presence of specific regional or non-regional subsystems? The difference is that the bottom-up regions exist independently within the international system and the top-down regions exist because of the international system. Given the overall condition of a global international system, regions will generally be a mixture of bottom-up and top-down processes but usually with one process clearly dominant.

As explained in Chapter 1, "'Classical' Security Complex Theory," security complexes are ultimately defined by the interaction among their units; thus, the top-down–bottom-up question is only one about the causes behind that process: The security complex as such *is* the pattern of security interaction. This means that already in CSCT the constructivist element was that a security complex is what states actually do (not what they say they do—we do not ask, for example, if Arafat thinks there is a Middle East security complex—but the pattern of fears and actions they act upon). For instance, if an analyst found that in terms of "objective" threats the Middle East was the wrong scale by which the actors should define their horizon— they ought to join together against their *real* threat, the West—this would be of little importance. In actuality, the states would still be locked into patterns of rivalry and alliances that constituted a regional security complex. Similarly, for sea pollution the real factor that defines the security complex is the actions taken by the units and thus the constellations they form.

The novelty is that in CSCT it was also assumed that the causality behind the formation of the security complex was bottom up, that the interaction of mutual security concerns *within* the region had produced the complex. Now we open up the possibility that causation can be top down; thus, it is sometimes necessary to start from the system level to explain the formation of the complex. Still, the complex itself is defined by the actions and relations in the region; if it was not, if it was defined solely by global-level considerations and actions, it would not be a regional security complex. Arguments about the nature of joint problems (top down) can therefore never exhaust the explanation of security complexes; they are only facilitating conditions. The very act of securitization always has autonomy; therefore, the security complex is defined by the securitizations that take place inside it.

With these thoughts in mind, the definition of security complexes can be reformulated as follows:

Security interdependence is markedly more intense among the units inside such complexes than with units outside them. Security complexes are about the relative intensities of security relations that lead to distinctive regional patterns shaped by both the distribution of power and relations of amity and enmity. A security complex is defined as *a set of units whose major processes of securitization, desecuritization, or both are so interlinked that their security problems cannot reasonably be analyzed or resolved apart from one another.* The formative dynamics and structure of a security complex are normally generated by the units within it—by their security perceptions of, and interactions with, each other. But they may also arise from collective securitizations of outside pressures arising from the operation of complex metasystems, such as the planetary environment or the global economy.

Armed with this revised definition, we still have to resolve security complex theory with the arguments about security constellations made in Chapter 8. How relevant does the particular regional formation remain when actors are synthesizing security across a range of sectors, each of which may have rather different dynamics? Does it remain relevant only when military-political security dynamics dominate, or can it be applied to other aspects of the wider security agenda?

Security constellations is a much wider concept than security complexes, reflecting as it does the totality of possible security interrelationships at all levels. One needs to think about the concept not just in relation to security complexes but in relation to the entire framework of which they were a part. CSCT located security complexes at the regional level within a four-tiered framework that ran from substate through regional and interregional to system. Each of these tiers represented a distinctive level of interaction: within states (focusing especially on weak states), between states (linking them into regional complexes), between complexes (a minor or residual category except in places where the boundaries between complexes were unstable), and between great powers (defining the system level or, in neorealist terms, the polarity of the system). The idea was to separate these four tiers for purposes of analysis and to put them back together to get the whole picture, emphasizing one or another tier depending on the objective of the analysis (whether a particular state, a region, or the international system as a whole).

Security constellations can be fitted into a similar sort of framework, albeit probably a more complicated one. They reflect the entire range of security relations we looked at in Chapters 3–7 in terms of localizing, regionalizing, subglobalizing, and globalizing dynamics. As in CSCT, there is no reason to expect that territorially coherent regions should involve more than one subset of security constellations. The reason for focusing on them is because of their relative neglect as a structuring feature of international security and their importance in mediating relations between local units and outside powers. Compared with the CSCT framework, security constellations will almost certainly generate a much fuller set of nonregional subglobal patterns (such as those created by the sets of countries that export copper or those countries vulnerable to sea-level rises).

The politico-military focus of CSCT allowed little room for nonregional subglobal patterns. Because politico-military relations are strongly mediated by distance, adjacency is a main element that determines interaction capacity. Threats are expected to travel more easily over shorter distances; thus, security interdependence among neighbors is, in general, more intense than that with more remote actors. Moreover, the dominant units of the system—states—owe much of their identity, as well as their political, military, and economic power, to their territorial sovereignty rights. In the original formulation of security complex theory, therefore, the international system consisted of geopolitical building blocks: states, regional security complexes, and global structures. In this sector, nonregional subsystemic patterns would be unusual, if not wholly absent.

But once other sectors and units are added in, the picture changes. Relations in the economic and environmental sectors in particular are much less mediated by distance, which opens more possibility for nonregional security formations. Nonregional subsystems consist of units bound by common interests that are unrelated to adjacency. An example is AOSIS, the Alliance of Small Island States—the potential victim states of a sea-level rise. These 35 states will disappear if politics fails to deal with the causes of global warming and the disaster scenarios hold true. AOSIS is clearly a subset, to be located at the subsystem level, but it is not a region. Nonregional subsystems are typically issue specific and are defined top down. The chance that the AOSIS states have something more in common than a shared fate under global warming is virtually nil. This means that unlike regional subsystems, the chances of cross-sectoral congruence in nonregional subsystems are low.

Thus, as with CSCT, the regional level still plays a distinctive role in security constellations. There may be times and places in which it does not, as there were for CSCT, and with the wider agenda there may well be nonregional as well as regional security formations at the subsystem level. In understanding the absence of security complexes, one would now have to add sectoral considerations to the two existing explanations (overlay and states with too little power to interact sufficiently to create a regional formation). When the security agenda is dominated by economic or environmental concerns, regionalizing tendencies *may* be weak (although not necessarily so, depending on the type of issue). But there are three good reasons for thinking the regional level will remain an important focus of security analysis within the new framework.

1. As long as political life is structured primarily by states, territoriality will continue to be important and will be predisposed toward regional

formations. States, in other words, will tend to construct political responses in their own territorial image. As noted in Chapter 7, the political sector does in some senses permeate all of the others. Only if political life became truly neomedieval, with authority divided in partly nonterritorial ways, would the regional imperative be greatly weakened.

2. On current evidence, regional security dynamics remain strong in many parts of the world in the sectors in which security relations are the most strongly mediated by distance (i.e., political, military, and societal). New security complexes, such as those in the Balkans, the Caucasus, and West Africa, and ongoing ones, such as those in South Asia and Southern Africa, clearly contain mixtures of politico-military and societal security dynamics, actors, and referent objects. As long as that remains the case, regional formations will be a natural and expected outcome. A spillover effect is that these formations influence the way in which less obviously territorial issues in the economic and environmental sectors are seen. Once the regional formation is present, it acts as a lens through which to focus other issues into its own structure. This situation is perhaps most obvious in Europe, where the EU represents a fusion of economic with military-political concerns. The opposite case will unfold in East Asia, where the possibilities for economic regionalism face the obstacle of a possible conflict formation in the security complex emerging in the military-political sphere (Buzan 1997).

3. Some environmental and economic issues are structured so as to reinforce existing regional security complexes. Thus, water-sharing issues in the Middle East and pipeline questions in the CIS both add to existing regionalizing imperatives.

The Constructivist Approach

At stake here is where to locate oneself analytically on a spectrum that ranges from constructivist to objectivist. On this issue, we will compare our securitization approach to two other approaches: traditional security studies (TSS) and critical security studies (CSS). This approach is complex because the axis has to be used twice—once regarding "security" (how socially constituted is the security nature of issues) and also in regard to social relations in general. Especially in the comparison between CSS and our position, one is more constructivist on one axis and the other is more constructivist on the other axis; therefore, this must be differentiated to grasp the differences.

Traditional security studies is usually objectivist regarding security in the sense that security studies is about telling what the real threats are, how best to deal with them, and—as a second-order question—how actors manage or mismanage security policy because of intellectual or bureaucratic failures. Usually, TSS is also generally objectivist. It sees states as the given, eternal form of units; it views interests as something objective; and it has rules about the behavior of states that take on something close to natural science status, such as balance of power and arms race theory.

Critical security studies, in contrast, views the system very much in constructivist terms. If states dominate the arena, this is a feat of power politics repressing other dimensions of reality that could potentially replace the states if an emancipatory praxis could—with the help of critical theory—empower other subjectivities than those that dominate at present.[1] The social world does not exhibit any iron laws, all regularities can be broken, and it is the task of critical theory to show this—as well as to expose how some logics came to be seen as necessary when in fact they are contingent.

On the issue of security, however, CSS is often less constructivist than one would expect. As part of the argument against established discourses of security, CSS will often try to mobilize other security problems—environmental problems, poverty, unemployment—as more important and more threatening, thereby relativizing conventional wisdom. By this method, CSS often ends up reproducing the traditional and objectivist concept of security: Security is about what *is* a threat, and the analyst can tell whether something really is a security problem and for whom. Also, this approach will often contribute to the general securitization of ever larger spheres of social life (Wæver 1995b). First-generation security wideners such as Scandinavian peace research, as discussed in Chapter 1, often fall very close to the upper left corner (objective security, constructed social relations). Critical security studies stretches from this view toward the more poststructuralist parts of the movement, which emphasize the politics of defining what constitutes security, in the upper right quadrant of Figure 9.1.

Our securitization approach is radically constructivist regarding security, which ultimately is a specific form of social praxis. Security issues are made security issues by acts of securitization (cf. Chapter 2). We do not try to peek behind this to decide whether it is *really* a threat (which would reduce the entire securitization approach to a theory of perceptions and misperceptions). Security *is* a quality actors inject into issues by securitizing them, which means to stage them on the political arena in the specific way outlined in this book and then to have them accepted by a sufficient audience to sanction extraordinary defensive moves.

Defining security as a self-referential praxis must constitute radical constructivism—on the security axis. Regarding general social relations, however, we are less constructivist than most authors of CSS. When one has adopted a basically constructivist position that assumes social relations are not laws of nature but the contingent product of human action and always potentially open for restructuration, one can emphasize the contingency of a construction (for instance, the state or an identity) and then base one's analysis on the possibility that it could change in part by one

Figure 9.1 Schools of Security Studies

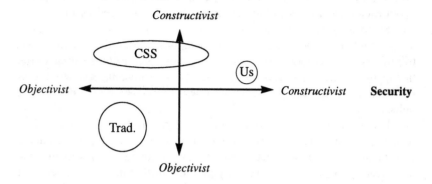

exposing the processes that made it what it is. Or one can assume that this construction belongs among the more durable and keep it as constant throughout one's analysis (to focus variation on other dimensions).

The latter approach does not imply that one has to take the construction as *necessary,* as in principle and forever unchangeable (Buzan and Wæver 1997). Structures are sedimented practices that are not currently politicized and thereby not widely seen as a matter of choice. One can therefore take them as likely frameworks for some discussions, but it is also possible—more critically—always to conclude that since they are in principle contingent, we should talk about how they could change.

This is probably what has caused most of the critique of our previous book: Since we studied security conducted in the name of identities (societal security), we must be objectifying identities (see, most strongly, McSweeney 1996). We *do* take identities as socially constituted but not radically moreso than other social structures. Identities as other social constructions can petrify and become relatively constant elements to be reckoned with. At specific points, this "inert constructivism" enables modes of analysis very close to objectivist—for example, Waltzian neorealism, as long as one remembers that in the final instance the ontology is not Waltz's naturalism and atomism but some form of constructivism or even, in line with classical realism, rhetorical foundations (Dessler 1989; Buzan, Jones, and Little 1993, part 3; Wæver 1994, forthcoming-b).

We try to reinsert continuity (and in other contexts even structures) within constructivism; therefore, we do not want to create a security theory that can only tell how everything could be different. We also want to understand why actors operate the way they do, both now and very likely also tomorrow. Transformation is one but not always the most reasonable strate-gy for improving security; in many cases, as analyst one can help more by grasping the patterns of action among units as they are and thereby help to avoid escalations, to steer vicious circles toward managed security com-plexes and eventually security communities.

Our relative objectivism on social relations has the drawback of con-tributing to the reproduction of things as they are, of contributing to the taking for granted that CSS wants to upset. The advantage is—totally in line with classical security studies—to help in managing relations among units.

The advantages and disadvantages of our radical constructivism regarding security are probably more controversial. The main disadvantage is our inability to counter securitizations (say, of immigrants) with an argu-ment that this is not really a security problem or that the environment is a bigger security problem. We can engage in debates over factual matters relating to the securitization (are projections for future immigrants realistic; do cultures lose coherence if they live together with foreigners, or are they more likely to be strengthened), but since the meaning of security is to lift it to a different kind of politics, we cannot contest this in terms of truth; only pragmatically or ethically can we ask, what are the likely effects of securitizing this issue? Will doing so be a helpful way of handling this issue, and what are the side effects of doing it in a security mode? We can expose the unnecessary nature of the securitization but not its falsity.

A major part of our attempt to engage critically with securitizations will be—since we are international relationists and undertake security stud-ies—to point to likely effects on interactions with other units. If we securi-tize this way, we will create fears in B, and then we have a security dilem-ma. A desecuritization of the issue, in contrast, will leave it to other procedures. It is possible to participate in the debate over the likely events if the situation is left desecuritized but not to close this debate by giving a scientific measurement about whether the situation constitutes a threat, which would demand a deterministic social universe.

Most of the comments we have had so far are about this kind of issue, about the role of the analyst and thus about essentially political issues—which is revealing in a discipline that previously saw itself as engaging in value-free social science. A gain from raising the securitization debate will be to involve other schools of security studies more openly in debates about the political role of security analysts.

A second kind of advantage and disadvantage of the debate relates to the kinds of analytical questions that can or cannot be dealt with. The major new opening is probably an ability to historicize security, to study transfor-mations in the units of security affairs. Traditional security studies defines the units (states) and the instruments (military) that by definition make any security phenomena elsewhere invisible. Much of critical security studies has an individualist, reductionist ontology and therefore also translates everything into a homogeneous currency—individual security. Securitization studies can analyze how and when new referent objects attain the status of something in the name of which one can successfully undertake security and can study the degree to which the new sectors actually exhibit politics in the form of security. It becomes possible to draw a map of security in between the closed, predefined world of traditionalists, the everything-is-security of the wideners, and the everything-could-be-different of CSS. To the traditionalist, this map will seem transient because it is not founded on material factors but only on sedimented patterns of security practice; to the critical theorist, it will be reactionary in reproducing the world as it is and not as it could be.

Contrasting Our New
Framework with the Traditional Approach

The most obvious difference between our new framework and the traditional approach to security studies is in the choice of a wide (multisectoral) versus a narrow (monosectoral) agenda. Wideners must keep an open mind about the balance among the sectors, the cross-linkages between them, and the types of threat, actor, and referent object that might be dominant in any given historical time. By contrast, traditional security studies gives permanent priority to one sector (the military) and one actor (the state) plus any links or crossovers from other sectors that relate directly to the use of force. The two approaches are also incompatible methodologically to the extent that our definition of security is based on the social construction of threats and referent objects, whereas traditionalists take an objectivist view of these factors. In principle, this difference of method could lead to rather different understandings of security, even in the military sector and relating to the state. In practice, traditionalists cannot afford to get too far out of line with socially constructed threats without risking marginalization. The danger here is that the traditionalists' objectification of threat and referent object will push them into the role of securitizing actors. This danger has been a part of long-standing peace research and more recent CSS warnings about TSS.

Apart from this methodological difference, the general subject matter of TSS can be seen as one subset of our new framework. Both share a methodological collectivism that leads them to draw a boundary between international security and a wider political theory of security. Unlike some peace research and parts of its recent spin-off, critical security studies, our framework, and TSS reject reductionism (giving priority to the individual as the ultimate referent object of security) as an unsound approach to international security. This does not mean they reject the validity of individual-level security, only that they see it as relatively marginal to understanding international security. By international security, we mainly mean relations between collective units and how those are reflected upward into the system. We keep the term *international* despite its ambiguities, both because it is an established usage and because its ambiguities hint at multisectorality ("nation" rather than "state").

In weighing the costs and benefits of the two approaches, at least two different qualities need to be taken into account: their relative intellectual coherence and the way in which they handle the potent rhetorical power of the security concept.

In terms of intellectual coherence, there is perhaps little to choose. We think we have answered the traditionalists' charge set out in Chapter 1. By making the use of sectors explicit and differentiating between politicization and securitization, it is possible both to retain a distinctive subject area and to restore intellectual coherence to the wider agenda. Traditional security studies is not immune to the charge of intellectual incoherence itself (Buzan 1987). Although its concentration within a single sector does give it the superficial appearance of intellectual (and sociological) coherence, its boundaries are by no means well-defined. The "use of force" criterion, the most common delineation of the field, cannot be (or has not yet been) used to set clear boundaries. Any attempt to do so quickly finds the subject extending into large areas of peace research and into much of the general study of international relations. It would be extremely difficult to differentiate TSS from either realist approaches to international relations or substantial swaths of international political economy (such as hegemony theory). The new framework may be more complicated than the traditional method, but it has equal claim to intellectual respect, and its complexity is open and accessible rather than hidden and undiscussed.

The second comparison between the new framework and TSS is in terms of how well they handle the potent rhetorical power of the security concept. For both approaches, security is an empowering word—setting political priorities and justifying the use of force, the intensification of executive powers, the claim to rights of secrecy, and other extreme measures. The way security is understood and used profoundly affects the way political life is conducted. As is well-known, excessive securitization produces the international equivalents of autism and paranoia. Closed states, such as the erstwhile Soviet Union, Iran, and North Korea, that are trying to promote distinctive development projects securitize everything from nuclear missiles and opposing armies to miniskirts and pop music. Such wide-ranging securitization stifles civil society, creates an intrusive and coercive state, cripples (eventually) the economy, and maximizes the intensity of the security dilemma with neighbors that do not share the ideological project. Avoiding excessive and irrational securitization is thus a legitimate social, political, and economic objective of considerable importance.

The academic debate about how to constitute security studies cannot responsibly proceed in isolation from this real-world political context.

The question is how best to limit claims to security so the costs and benefits of securitization are reasonably balanced. Progress on this question is closely linked to the much wider sense of progress attached to the development of Western international society as a whole. It perhaps begins with the construction of the Hobbesian state in the eighteenth century. The creation of the Leviathan was aimed at opening a sphere of public economic and political life, and this could not be done without pushing the use of force back into a contained space controlled by the state. Under the Leviathan, citizens could not draw swords over economic grievances or political disagreements, which were to be handled by the rule of law and the market. The logic of existential threat and the right to use force over economic or political relationships were reserved to the state and thus were largely desecuritized among the citizens (Williams 1996, forthcoming).

This domestic development pointed the way to the wider sense of progress as desecuritization, inherent in the liberals' project since the nineteenth century of attempting the intellectual and political separation of economics from politics. To the extent that this separation can be achieved, it desecuritizes the international economic realm to leave people, firms, and states freer to pursue efficiency without the constraints of self-reliance and the need to consider calculations of relative gain. Paradoxically, this separation and the interdependence that follows from it are then supposed to allow desecuritization to spill over into military-political relations.

The desecuritization of economics is central to the ideology of capitalism. This project has been taken the furthest in the "zone of peace" that now characterizes Western international society (Goldgeier and McFaul 1992; Singer and Wildavsky 1993; or in an earlier version, Keohane and Nye 1977). With the demise of the Communist counterproject and the closed states and societies associated with it, the prospect exists for a more widespread dissolving of borders, desecuritizing most kinds of political, social, and economic interaction. This development is the most advanced within the EU, but it is also inherent in the shift from modern to postmodern states and from more closed to more open political constructions that is going on in many parts of the world.

On the face of it, this project to limit the scope of securitization would seem to argue in favor of the traditionalists, with their narrow agenda, and against the wideners. It is indeed rather surprising that such a line of attack has not been used against the wideners, except in a limited way by Daniel Deudney (1990) (and in our own previous reflections; see Buzan 1995b, and Wæver 1995b). The wider agenda seems to be more vulnerable to excesses of securitization than the traditional military one (which is vulnerable enough by itself if taken to the extreme). Reserving security for the military sector has a pleasing "last resort" ring about it and fits comfortably with the broadly liberal ideology that is now enjoying its post–Cold War ascendance. In this perspective, widening the security agenda can be cast as a retrograde move. It threatens the hard-won desecuritizing achievements of liberalism and perhaps even those of the Hobbesian Leviathan over the past three centuries and is out of line with the imperatives toward more openness in the post–Cold War world.

We do not wish to question the general progress of Western international society, and we are on record here and elsewhere arguing in favor of desecuritization as the long-range political goal. But note that the liberal approach to desecuritization is primarily about detaching and freeing other sectors from the use of force and thus eventually reducing and marginalizing the military sector itself. Demilitarization by sector has been the characteristic liberal approach to desecuritization, and in that sense traditional security studies is, surprisingly, one of its products (rather than a product of conservatism, as one might first think). For what is TSS about if not the isolation of the military sector as embodying "security" (and for some of its more liberal practitioners, it is hoped, then, its eventual marginalization in international relations).

This liberal approach has costs as well as benefits. It is one way of understanding desecuritization but arguably not the best and certainly not the most appropriate in current circumstances. Ironically, the very success of the liberal project is now giving rise to the demand for a wider security agenda, for a reinvention of security in terms other than military. Rather than an atavistic assault on the three-century liberal project, we see the new framework as a constructive and necessary response to that project.

Even during the Cold War, two costs of the liberal approach that equated demilitarization with desecuritization were already evident. One was its ideological role in international power politics, and the second was its vulnerability to politico-military logics of oversecuritization.

Whether intentionally or not, liberal desecuritization legitimized the post-1945 U.S.-Western imperium, which operated on the demand for access rather than in the traditional European style of direct control. The desecuritization of economic relations facilitated this imperium of access. It made economic penetration by the strong legitimate and threw political obstacles in the way of the weak, who viewed their security in much wider terms than just military relations. For many states and peoples on the periphery of the international system, the attempted liberal desecuritization of the political economy was itself a security issue. The self-serving qualities of liberal choices about defining the security agenda were seen as invidious, whatever their merits elsewhere. Liberal states were able to delegitimize the nonmilitary security claims of other actors, in the process subordinating them to the "normal" politics of the market economy and pluralist politics. By itself, this situation justified a wider perspective on security, but only the voices of the weak calling for a new international economic order supported it, and it was largely drowned out by the titanic military confrontation of the superpowers.

This confrontation can be seen as evidence of the vulnerability of politico-military logics to oversecuritization. By equating "security" with "military," the Western—particularly the U.S.—political establishment exposed itself to an objectivist, externally determined definition of security that was extraordinarily difficult to break. That definition drove the logic of nuclear parity with the Soviet Union, paved the way for the disaster in Vietnam, and legitimized the self-mutilation of McCarthyism. This objectivist, military understanding of security all but forecloses the option of fundamentally questioning any securitization. When locked into a military sector defined as "security" and faced with a military threat, it is difficult to do more than argue about how dangerous the threat is. In this mode of thinking, asking whether something military should be securitized is extremely difficult, since it requires not only making a case for the issue at hand but also redefining the terms of the discourse. One advantage of the securitization approach advocated here is that it points to the responsibility involved in talking about security (or desecuritization) for policymakers, analysts, campaigners, and lobbyists. It is a *choice* to phrase things in security (or desecurity) terms, not an objective feature of the issue or the relationship itself. That choice has to be justified by the appropriateness and the consequences of successfully securitizing (or desecuritizing) the issue at hand.

With the end of the Cold War, the extension of the market economy into nearly all of the formerly Communist world, and the intensification of global finance, investment, and production, the case for a wider security agenda has become stronger. The demise of the Cold War has, at least for the time being, greatly reduced military rivalries among the great powers. Security concerns are more about the consequences of how the open international system operates—a set of issues that affects the strong actors as much as it does the weaker ones. This development is most obvious in the case of the international economy (Rosenau 1990; Ruggie 1993; Cerny 1995; Strange 1994). The rise of economic security is not just a throwback to classical mercantilism. It is a reaction against the various dangers of global liberalization—the risk of becoming a loser; the general hazard of system instability, especially financial; and the dark side of trade in the form of criminal activities in drugs, weapons, and other banned products (e.g., CFCs). The rise is also about the crossover effects of the global economy on environmental issues, domestic political autonomy and stability, and military self-reliance. As we argued in our 1993 book (Wæver et al.), some of the postmodern liberal moves in the international system—most notably the integration of the EU—were also crucial to the generation of societal security problems.

In the post–Cold War world, therefore, it can be argued that a wider security agenda is a necessary response to the global success of the liberal project. Among other things, this can be seen in the number of system- and subsystem-level referent objects uncovered in Chapters 3 through 7. In some central ways, the liberal project does seem to have succeeded in marginalizing military security and along with it the approach of traditional security studies. But in so doing it has raised new security problems that can only be handled in a multisectoral framework. The danger of excessive securitization remains, and a core part of the new framework must therefore be to provide the means of identifying and criticizing counterproductive claims to securitization (including military ones).

But to assume that the post–Cold War world has been successfully desecuritized or that only military security issues remain would risk misunderstandings equal to or greater than those associated with the wider agenda. Our approach has the basic merit of conceptualizing security as a labeling for which actors can be held responsible rather than an objective feature of threats. Thus, although the multisectoralism of the approach enables a proliferation of securitization, its constructivism delivers the means for questioning and politicizing each specific instance. This contrasts with the approach of TSS, which puts a firm sectoral limit on what constitutes security but which has objectified, depoliticized, and indeed naturalized it as the only allowable understanding of security. On this test as well, the new framework can hold its own against the traditional one.

Note

1. In this respect, critical security studies is more closely linked to critical theory and parts of poststructuralism in IR than to what passes for constructivism in the larger discipline. What is probably the dominant strand of constructivism in IR is affiliated with names such as Alexander Wendt (1992, 1994, 1995), Peter Katzenstein (1996a, 1996b), Emanuel Adler (1992, 1995), and Michael Barnett (1995; Adler and Barnett 1996, forthcoming). For various reasons, these authors are often deliberately state centric and want to show how constructivism can explain state action better than traditional realist or liberalist explanations. One of the reasons for this tendency could be the birth of this constructivism in the agent-structure debate (Wendt 1987), which was translated into IR as agent-state, structure-international structure (Wæver 1994). Also, this constructivism is usually very careful to distinguish itself from anything sounding poststructuralist (cf. Wæver 1996c). The term *constructivist,* however, could easily cover a much wider range of possible positions and probably will increasingly as authors in the part of the spectrum that could be called either nonconfrontational poststructuralism or radical constructivism launch their works. Within security studies, we have only recently seen a systematic attempt to launch "mainstream constructivism" as an approach to security (Katzenstein's weighty edited volume [1996b] is the flagship), whereas the school we discuss here, critical security studies, has been emerging gradually and consistently over the last several years, drawing upon mixtures of critical theory

(Marx, Gramsci, Habermas), poststructuralism, and mainstream constructivism (Booth 1979, 1991, 1994, 1995; Dalby 1988, 1990; Klein 1990, 1994; Krause 1992, 1993; Krause and Williams 1997; Luke 1989; Walker 1988, 1990; Wynn-Jones 1995; for a critical discussion of some of these works, see Hansen 1994).

Bibliography

Acharya, Amitav (1992) "Regionalism and Regime Security in the Third World: Comparing the Origins of the ASEAN and the GCC," in Brian Job (ed.), *The Insecurity Dilemma*. Boulder: Lynne Rienner, pp. 143–164.

Adams, W. M. (1990) *Green Development: Environment and Sustainability in the Third World*. London: Routledge.

Adler, Emanuel (1992) "The Emergence of Cooperation: National Epistemic Communities and the International Evolution of the Idea of Nuclear Arms Control," *International Organization*, 46:2, pp. 101–146.

——— (1995) "Seizing the Middle Ground," unpublished manuscript.

Adler, Emanuel, and Michael J. Barnett (1996) "Governing Anarchy: A Research Agenda for the Study of Security Communities," *Ethics and International Affairs*, 10, pp. 63–98.

Adler, Emanuel, and Michael J. Barnett (eds.) (forthcoming) *Governing Anarchy: Security Communities in Theory, History and Comparison*. Cambridge: Cambridge University Press.

Allison, Graham (1971) *The Essence of Decision: Explaining the Cuba Missile Crisis*. Boston: Little, Brown.

Anderson, Benedict (1983) *Imagined Communities—Reflections on the Origins and Spread of Nationalism*. London: Verso Publishers.

Anderson, Kim, and Richard Blackhurst (1993) *Regional Integration and the Global Trading System*. Hemel Hempstead: Harvester Wheatsheaf.

Appiah, Kwame Anthony (1994) "Identity, Authenticity, Survival: Multicultural Societies and Social Reproduction" in Amy Gutmann (ed.), *Multiculturalism: Examining the Politics of Recognition*. Princeton: Princeton University Press, pp. 149–163.

Arendt, Hannah (1958) *The Human Condition*. Chicago: University of Chicago Press.

——— (1959) "On Humanity in Dark Times: Thoughts About Lessing," an address on accepting the Lessing Prize of the Free City of Hamburg (originally in German), Reprinted in *Men in Dark Times*. New York: Pelican Books, 1973.

Ariff, Mohammed (1996) "Institutionalisation of Economic Cooperation in the Asia-Pacific Region with Special Reference to APEC," *Dokkyo International Review*, 9, pp. 177–192.

Armstrong, David (1993) *Revolution and World Order: The Revolutionary State in International Order*. Oxford: Clarendon Press.

Austin, J. L. (1975 [1962]) *How To Do Things with Words*. 2d ed. Oxford: Oxford University Press.

Ayoob, Mohammed (1995) *The Third World Security Predicament: State Making, Regional Conflict, and the International System*. Boulder: Lynne Rienner.

Baldwin, David A. "The Concept of Security," *Review of International Studies* 23:1 (1997), pp. 5–26.

Barnett, Michael (1995) "Sovereignty, Nationalism, and Regional Order in the Arab States System," *International Organization,* 49:3, pp. 479–510.

Barnett, Robert W. (1984) *Beyond War: Japan's Concept of Comprehensive National Security.* Washington, D.C.: Pergamon/Brassey's.

Baudrillard, Jean (1994 [1992]) *The Illusion of the End* (translation of *L'Illusion de la fin: ou La greve des evenenments.* Paris: Galilee, 1992), translated by Chris Turner. Stanford: Stanford University Press. (An alternative translation by Charles Dudas, York University, Canada, was made available chapter by chapter during 1993–1994 on the internet through CTHEORY.)

Benedick, Richard Elliot (1991) *Ozone Diplomacy—New Directions in Safeguarding the Planet.* Cambridge: Harvard University Press.

Bigo, Didier (1994) "The European Internal Security Field: Stakes and Rivalries in a Newly Developing Area of Police Intervention," in Malcolm Anderson and Monica den Boer (eds.), *Policing Across National Boundaries.* London: Pinter Publishers, pp. 161–173.

——— (1996) *Polices en réseaux: l'expérience européenne.* Paris: Presses de Sciences Po.

——— (forthcoming) "The New Field of Security in Europe: Mixing Crime, Border and Identity Controls," in Anne-Marie Le Gloannec and Kerry McNamara (eds.), *Le Désordre Européen.* Paris: Presses de Sciences Po.

Blaikie, Piers, Terry Cannon, Ian Davis, and Ben Wisner (1994) *At Risk: Natural Hazards, People's Vulnerability and Disasters.* London: Routledge.

Böge, Volker (1992) "Proposal for an Analytical Framework to Grasp Environmental Conflicts," *Zurich: ENCOP (Environment and Conflicts Project) Occasional Paper.*

Booth, Ken (1979) *Strategy and Ethnocentrism.* London: Croom Helm.

——— (1991) "Security and Emancipation," *Review of International Studies,* 17:4, pp. 313–327.

——— (1994) "Dare Not to Know: International Relations Theory Versus the Future," in Ken Booth and Steve Smith (eds.), *International Political Theory Today.* London: Polity Press, pp. 328–350.

——— (1995) "Human Wrongs and International Relations," *International Affairs,* 71:1, pp. 103–122.

Bourdieu, Pierre (1991 [1982]) *Language and Symbolic Power.* Cambridge: Harvard University Press (mostly a translation of *Ce que parler veut dire*). Paris: Libreire Arthème Fayard, 1982.

——— (1996) Response at seminar on "Fin-de-Siecle Intellectuals: Looking Back, Looking Forward," University of California at Berkeley, April.

Brock, Lothar (1991) "Peace Through Parks: The Environment on the Peace Research Agenda," *Journal of Peace Research,* 28:4, pp. 407–422.

Brown, Lester R., et al. (1993) *State of the World 1993: A Worldwatch Institute Report on Progress Toward a Sustainable Society.* New York: W. W. Norton.

Brown, Neville (1989) "Climate, Ecology and International Security," *Survival,* 31:6, pp. 519–532.

Bull, Hedley (1977) *The Anarchical Society: A Study of Order in World Politics.* London: Macmillan.

Bull, Hedley, and Adam Watson (eds.) (1983) *The Expansion of International Society.* Oxford: Clarendon.

Bureau of the Census (1996) "U.S. Population Projections." Washington, D.C.: U.S. Department of Commerce.

Butler, Judith (1996a) "Performativity's Social Magic" in Theodore R. Schatzki and Wolfgang Natter (eds.) *The Social and Political Body,* New York: Guilford Press.

───── (1996b) "Anti-Intellectualism" Presentation with Pierre Bourdieu at seminar "Fin-de-siecle Intellectuals: Looking Back, Looking Forward," University of California at Berkeley, April.

Butterfield, Herbert (1965) "The Historic States-Systems," unpublished paper for the British Committee for the Theory of International Politics.

───── (1975) "Raison d'État," Martin Wight Memorial Lecture, University of Essex.

Buzan, Barry (1983) "Regional Security as a Policy Objective: The Case of South and Southwest Asia," in A. Z. Rubinstein (ed.), *The Great Game: The Rivalry in the Persian Gulf and South Asia.* New York: Praeger, chapter 10.

───── (1984) "Economic Structure and International Security: The Limits of the Liberal Case," *International Organization,* 38:4, pp. 597–624.

───── (1987) *An Introduction to Strategic Studies: Military Technology and International Relations.* London: Macmillan.

───── (1988) "The Southeast Asian Security Complex," *Contemporary Southeast Asia,* 10:1, pp. 1–16.

───── (1991) *People, States and Fear: An Agenda for International Security Studies in the Post–Cold War Era.* 2d ed. Boulder: Lynne Rienner; Hemel Hempstead: Harvester Wheatsheaf.

───── (1993) "From International System to International Society: Stuctural Realism and Regime Theory Meet the English School," *International Organization,* 47:3, pp. 327–352.

───── (1994a) "National Security in the Post–Cold War Third World," *Strategic Review for Southern Africa,* 16:1, pp. 1–34.

───── (1994b) "The Post–Cold War Asia-Pacific Security Order: Conflict or Cooperation," in Andrew Mack and John Ravenhill (eds.), *Pacific Cooperation: Building Economic and Security Regimes in the Asia-Pacific Region.* St. Leonards: Allen and Unwin Australia; Boulder: Westview Press, pp. 130–151.

───── (1994c) "The Level of Analysis Problem in International Relations Reconsidered," in Ken Booth and Steve Smith (eds.), *International Political Theory Today.* London: Polity Press, pp. 198–216.

───── (1995a) "Focus On: The Present as a Historical Turning Point," *Journal of Peace Research,* 32:4, pp. 385–399.

───── (1995b) "Security, the State, the 'New World Order' and Beyond," in Ronnie D. Lipschutz (ed.), *On Security.* New York: Columbia University Press, pp. 187–211.

───── (1996) "International Security and International Society," in Rick Fawn and Jeremy Larkin (eds.), *International Society After the Cold War: Anarchy and Order Reconsidered.* London: Macmillan, pp. 261–287.

───── (1997) "The Asia Pacific: What Sort of Region in What Sort of World?" in Anthony McGrew and Chris Brook (eds.), *A Pacific Community? Perspectives on the Pacific Rim in the Contemporary World Order.* Milton Keynes: Open University, Chapter 4.

Buzan, Barry, Gowher Rizvi, et al. (1986) *South Asian Insecurity and the Great Powers.* London: Macmillan.

Buzan, Barry, Morten Kelstrup, Pierre Lemaitre, Elzbieta Tromer, and Ole Wæver (1990) *The European Security Order Recast: Scenarios for the Post–Cold War Era.* London: Pinter Publishers.

Buzan, Barry, and Gerald Segal (1992) "Introduction: Defining Reform as Openness," in Gerald Segal (ed.), *Openness and Foreign Policy Reform in Communist States*. London: Routledge, pp. 1–17.

Buzan, Barry, and Ole Wæver (1992) "Framing Nordic Security—European Scenarios for the 1990s and Beyond," in Jan Øberg (ed.), *Nordic Security in the 1990s: Options in the Changing Europe*. London: Pinter Publishers, pp. 85–104.

Buzan, Barry, Charles Jones, and Richard Little (1993) *The Logic of Anarchy: Neorealism to Structural Realism*. New York: Columbia University Press.

Buzan, Barry, and Richard Little (1994) "The Idea of 'International System': Theory Meets History," *International Political Science Review*, 15:3, pp. 231–255.

Buzan, Barry, and Gerald Segal (1994) "Rethinking East Asian Security," *Survival*, 36:2, pp. 3–21.

Buzan, Barry, and Richard Little (1996) "Reconceptualising Anarchy: Structural Realism Meets World History," *European Journal of International Relations*, 2:4, pp. 403–438.

Buzan, Barry, and Gerald Segal (1997) *Anticipating the Future*. London: Simon and Schuster.

Buzan, Barry, and Ole Wæver (1997) "Slippery? Contradictory? Sociologically Untenable? The Copenhagen School Replies," *Review of International Studies*, 23:2, pp. 143–152.

Buzan, Barry, and Eric Herring (forthcoming 1998) *Pandora's Box: Military Security, Technology, and World Politics*. Boulder: Lynne Rienner.

Cable, Vincent (1995) "What Is International Economic Security?" *International Affairs*, 71:2, pp. 305–324.

Campbell, David (1993) *Writing Security: United States Foreign Policy and the Politics of Identity*. Manchester: Manchester University Press.

Carr, E. H. (1939) *The Twenty Years' Crisis 1919–1939: An Introduction to the Study of International Relations*. London and Basingstoke: Macmillan.

Carroll, John E. (ed.) (1988) *International Environmental Diplomacy: The Management and Resolution of Transfrontier Environmental Problems*. Cambridge: Cambridge University Press.

Carson, Rachel (1962) *Silent Spring*. Harmondshire: Penguin, 1991.

Cerny, Phil (1995) "Globalization and Structural Differentiation," unpublished paper, European Consortium for Political Research-Standing Group on International Relations (ECPR-SGIR) Conference, Paris.

Chipman, John (1992) "The Future of Strategic Studies: Beyond Grand Strategy," *Survival*, 34:1, pp. 109–131.

Clausewitz, Karl von (1983 [1832]) *Vom Kriege*. Berlin: Verlag Ullstein.

Conze, Werner (1984) "Sicherheit, Schutz" in Otto Brunner, Werner Conze, and Reinhart Koselleck (eds.) *Geschichtliche Grundbegriffe: Historisches Lexicon zur politisch-sozialen Sprache in Deutschland, vol. 5*, Stuttgart: Klett-Cotta.

Cox, Robert (1994) "Global Restructuring: Making Sense of the Changing International Political Economy," in Richard Stubbs and Geoffrey Underhill (eds.), *Political Economy and the Changing Global Order*. Toronto: McClelland and Stewart, pp. 45–59.

Crawford, Beverly (1993) *Economic Vulnerability in International Relations—The Case of East-West Trade, Investment and Finance*. New York: Columbia University Press.

——— (1995) "Hawks, Doves, But No Owls: International Economic Interdependence and Construction of the New Security Dilemma," in Ronnie D. Lipschutz (ed.), *On Security*. New York: Columbia University Press, pp. 149–186.

Crawford, Neta C. (1991) "Once and Future Security Studies," *Security Studies,* 1:2, pp. 283–316.

Dalby, Simon (1988) "Geopolitical Discourse: The Soviet Union as Other," *Alternatives,* 13:4, pp. 415–443.

—— (1990) *Creating the Second Cold War: The Discourse of Politics.* New York: Guilford.

den Boer, Pim (1993) "Europe to 1914: The Making of an Idea," in Pim den Boer, Peter Bugge, and Ole Wæver, *The History of the Idea of Europe.* Milton Keynes: Open University (republished by Routledge, 1995), pp. 13–82.

Delumeau, Jean (1986) *Rassurer et protéger: le sentiment de sécurité dans l'Occident d'autrefois,* Paris: Fayard.

Deng, Francis M. (1995) *War of Visions: Conflict of Identities in the Sudan.* Washington, D.C.: Brookings Institution.

Der Derian, James (1987) *On Diplomacy.* Oxford: Basil Blackwell.

—— (1992) *Anti-Diplomacy: Spies, Terror, Speed and War.* Oxford: Basil Blackwell.

—— (1993) "The Value of Security: Hobbes, Marx, Nietzsche and Baudrillard," in David Campbell and Michael Dillon (eds.), *The Political Subject of Violence.* Manchester: Manchester University Press, pp. 94–113.

Derrida, Jacques (1977a [1972]) "Signature Event Context," *Glyph,* 1, pp. 172–197.

—— (1977b) "Limited Inc a b c," *Glyph,* 2, pp. 162–254; reprinted in Derrida, *Limited Inc.* Evanston, Ill.: Northwestern University Press, 1988, pp. 29–110.

—— (1988) "Afterword: Toward an Ethic of Discussion," in Derrida, *Limited Inc.* Evanston, Ill.: Northwestern University Press, pp. 111–154.

—— (1992 [1991]) *The Other Heading: Reflections on Today's Europe.* Bloomington: Indiana University Press.

Dessler, David (1989) "What's at Stake in the Agent-Structure Debate?" *International Organization,* 43:3, pp. 441–473.

Deudney, Daniel (1990) "The Case Against Linking Environmental Degradation and National Security," *Millennium,* 19:3, pp. 461–476.

—— (1995) "The Philadelphian System: Sovereignty, Arms Control and Balance of Power in the American States Union, circa 1789–1861," *International Organization,* 49:2, pp. 191–229.

Deutsch, Karl, et al. (1957) *Political Community and the North Atlantic Area.* Princeton: Princeton University Press.

de Wilde, Jaap (1991) *Saved from Oblivion: Interdependence Theory in the First Half of the 20th Century: A Study on the Causality Between War and Complex Interdependence.* Dartmouth: Aldershot.

—— (1994) "The Power Politics of Sustainability, Equity and Liveability," in Phillip B. Smith, Samuel E. Okoye, Jaap de Wilde, and Priya Deshingkar (eds.), *The World at the Crossroads: Towards a Sustainable, Liveable and Equitable World.* London: Earthscan, pp. 159–176.

—— (1995) "Security Levelled Out: The Dominance of the Local and the Regional," in Pál Dunay, Gábor Kados, and Andrew J. Williams (eds.), *New Forms of Security: Views from Central, Eastern and Western Europe.* Dartmouth: Aldershot, pp. 85–102.

—— (1996) "The Continuous (Dis)Integration of Europe: A Historical Interpretation of Europe's Future" in Jaap de Wilde and Håken Wiberg (eds.), *Organized Anarchy in Europe: The Role of States and Intergovernmental Organizations,* London: I. B. Taurus, pp. 85–106.

Dibb, Paul (1995) "Towards a New Balance of Power in Asia," *Adelphi Paper 295.* London: International Institute for Strategic Studies (IISS).

Dieren, Wouter van (ed.) (1987) *Taking Nature into Account. Towards a Sustainable*

National Income: A Report to the Club of Rome. (Dutch translation: De natuur telt ook mee. Naareen duurzaam nationaal inkomen.) Utrecht: Spektrum.

Does, René A. H., and André W. M. Gerrits (1994) "'Eurazië': milieu als *casus belli*. Over ecologie, nationalisme en nationale veiligheid in het GOS," *Transaktie*, 23:4, pp. 399–429.

Dorff, Robert H. (1994) "A Commentary on Security Studies for the 1990s as a Model Curriculum Core," *International Studies Notes*, 19:3, pp. 23–31.

Ehrlich, Anne (1994) "Building a Sustainable Food System," in Phillip B. Smith, S. E. Okoye, Jaap de Wilde, and Priya Deshingkar (eds.), *The World at the Crossroads: Towards a Sustainable, Liveable and Equitable World*. London: Earthscan, pp. 21–38.

Elias, Norbert (1978 [1939]) *The Civilizing Process*, vols. 1 and 2. New York: Urizen Books.

Ember, Carol, Melvin Ember, and Bruce Russett (1992) "Peace Between Participatory Polities: A Cross-Cultural Test of the 'Democracies Rarely Fight Each Other' Hypothesis," *World Politics*, 44:4, pp. 573–599.

European Commission (1995) *Work Programme*. Bulletin of the European Union, Supplement 1/95 (Danish and English).

European Council (1995a) *Cannes European Council 26 and 27 June 1995: Presidency Conclusions*. SN 211/2/95 (English and Danish).

——— (1995b) *Madrid European Council 15 and 16 December 1995: Presidency Conclusions*. SN 400/95 (English).

European Parliament (1995a) *Debates of the European Parliament*. 17 January, no. 4–456, Brussels, pp. 13–45 (on the Commission), 45–68 (on the program of the French presidency).

——— (1995b) "Debate on 1995 Commission Work Programme," *Debates of the European Parliament*. 15 February, no. 4–457, Brussels, pp. 105–128, continued 15 March, no. 4–460, pp. 88–99.

——— (1995c) "State of the Union Debate," *Debates of the European Parliament*. 15 November 1995, no. 4–470, Brussels, pp. 144–156.

Fawcett, Louise, and Andrew Hurrell (eds.) (1995) *Regionalism in World Politics*. Oxford: Oxford University Press.

Feshbach, Murray, and Alfred Friendly, Jr. (1992) *Ecocide in the USSR: Health and Nature Under Siege*. New York: Basic Books.

Flavin, Christopher, and Odil Tunali (1995) "Getting Warmer: Looking for a Way Out of the Climate Impasse," *World Watch Paper*, pp. 10–19.

Foucault, Michel (1979) *Discipline and Punish: The Birth of Prison*. New York: Vintage Books.

——— (1991 [1978]) "Governmentality," in Graham Burchell, Colin Gordon, and Peter Miller (eds.), *The Foucault Effect: Studies in Governmentality*. Chicago: University of Chicago Press, pp. 87–104.

Furet, François (1995) "Europe After Utopianism," *Journal of Democracy*, 6:1, pp. 79–89.

Galtung, Johan (1971) "A Structural Theory of Imperialism," *Journal of Peace Research*, 8:2, pp. 81–118.

Gilpin, Robert (1981) *War and Change in World Politics*. Cambridge: Cambridge University Press.

——— (1987) *The Political Economy of International Relations*. Princeton: Princeton University Press.

Goldgeier, James M., and Michael McFaul (1992) "A Tale of Two Worlds: Core and Periphery in the Post–Cold War Era," *International Organization*, 46:2, pp. 467–491.

Gong, Gerrit W. (1984) *The Standard of "Civilisation" in International Society.* Oxford: Clarendon Press.

Gonzáles Márquez, Felipe (1995) "State of the Union," speech by the president-in-office of the Council, *Debates of the European Parliament.* 15 November, no. 4–470, pp. 140–144.

Gordon, Colin (1991) "Governmental Rationality: An Introduction," in Graham Burchell, Colin Gordon, and Peter Miller (eds.), *The Foucault Effect: Studies in Governmentality.* Chicago: Chicago University Press, pp. 1–52.

Gorz, Andre (1977) *Écologie et liberté.* Paris: Editions Galilee.

Gowa, Joanne S. (1994) *Allies, Adversaries and International Trade.* Princeton: Princeton University Press.

Gray, Colin S. (1992) "New Directions for Strategic Studies: How Can Theory Help Practice?" *Security Studies,* 1:4, pp. 610–635.

———— (1994a) "Global Security and Economic Wellbeing: A Strategic Perspective," *Political Studies,* 42:1, pp. 25–39.

Gray, Colin S. (1994b) *Villains, Victims and Sheriffs: Strategic Studies and Security for an Inter-War Period.* Hull: University of Hull Press.

Gutmann, Amy (1994) "Preface and Acknowledgment" and "Introduction," in Gutmann (ed.), *Multiculturalism: Examining the Politics of Recognition.* Princeton: Princeton University Press, pp. ix–xv, 3–24.

Haas, Peter M. (1992) "Introduction: Epistemic Communities and International Policy Coordination," *International Organization,* 46:1, pp. 1–35.

Haas, Peter M., Robert O. Keohane, and Marc A. Levy (eds.) (1993) *Institutions for the Earth—Sources of Effective International Environmental Protection.* Cambridge, Mass.: MIT Press.

Hacker, Andrew (1992) *Two Nations: Black and White: Separate, Unequal, and Hostile.* New York: Scribners.

Haftendorn, Helga (1991) "The Security Puzzle: Theory-Building and Discipline-Building in International Security," *International Studies Quarterly,* 35:1, pp. 3–17.

Halliday, Fred (1990) "The Sixth Great Power: On the Study of Revolution and International Relations," *Review of International Studies,* 16:3, pp. 207–222.

Hänsch, Klaus (1995) "State of the Union," speech by the president of the European Parliament, *Debates of the European Parliament.* 15 November, no. 4–470, Luxembourg, Office 4, Official Publications of the European Community. pp. 135–137.

Hansen, Lene (1994) *The Conceptualization of Security in Poststructuralist IR Theory.* M.A. thesis, University of Copenhagen, Institute of Political Science.

Hansenclever, Andreas, Peter Mayer, and Volker Rittberger (1996) "Interests, Power, Knowledge: The Study of International Regimes," *Mershon International Studies Review,* 40:2, pp. 177–228.

Hart, Thomas G. (1978) "Cognitive Paradigms in the Arms Race: Deterrence, Détente and the 'Fundamental Error' of Attribution," *Cooperation and Conflict,* 13:3, pp. 147–162.

Hassner, Pierre (1996) *La violence et la paix: De la bombe atomique au nettoyage ethnique.* Paris: Éditions Esprit.

Healey, Denis (1989) *The Time of My Life.* London: Michael Joseph.

Helleiner, Eric (1994a) "From Bretton Woods to Global Finance: A World Turned Upside Down," in Richard Stubbs and Geoffrey Underhill (eds.), *Political Economy and the Changing Global Order.* Toronto: McClelland and Stewart, pp. 163–175.

Helleiner, Eric (1994b) *Regionalization in the International Political Economy: A*

Comparative Perspective, East Asia Policy Papers no. 3. University of Toronto–York University, Joint Center for Asia-Pacific Studies.

Herz, John H. (1950) "Idealist Internationalism and the Security Dilemma," *World Politics,* 2:2, pp. 157–180.

——— (1959) *International Politics in the Atomic Age,* New York: Columbia University Press.

Hirsch, Fred, and Michael Doyle (1977) "Politicization in the World Economy: Necessary Conditions for an International Economic Order," in Fred Hirsch, Michael Doyle, and Edward L. Morse (eds.), *Alternatives to Monetary Disorder.* New York: McGraw-Hill, pp. 11–66.

Hirschman, Albert O. (1991) *The Rhetoric of Reaction: Perversity, Futility, Jeopardy.* Cambridge: Belknap Press of Harvard University Press.

Hollis, Martin, and Steve Smith (1991) *Explaining and Understanding International Relations.* Oxford: Clarendon Press.

Holm, Ulla (1993) *Det Franske Europa.* Århus: Århus Universitetsforlag.

——— (1997) "Mitterrand's French Garden Is No Longer What It Used to Be," in Knud-Erik Jørgensen (ed.), *A Reflectivist Approach to European Institutions.* London: Macmillan, pp. 128–145.

Holzgrefe, J. L. (1989) "The Origins of Modern International Relations Theory," *Review of International Studies,* 15:1, pp. 11–26.

Homer-Dixon, Thomas (1991) "On the Threshold: Environmental Changes and Acute Conflict," *International Security,* 16:2, pp. 76–116.

Horsman, Matthew, and Andrew Marshall (1995) *After the Nation State: Citizens, Tribalism and the New World Disorder.* London: HarperCollins.

Huntington, Samuel P. (1993) "The Clash of Civilizations?" *Foreign Affairs,* 72:3, pp. 22–49.

——— (1996) *The Clash of Civilizations and the Remaking of World Order.* New York: Simon and Schuster.

Hurrell, Andrew (1993) "International Society and the Study of Regimes: A Reflective Approach," in Volker Rittberger (ed.), *Regime Theory and International Relations.* Oxford: Clarendon Press, pp. 49–72.

——— (1995) "Explaining the Resurgence of Regionalism in World Politics," *Review of International Studies,* 21:3, pp. 331–358.

Hurrell, Andrew, and Benedict Kingsbury (1992) *The International Politics of the Environment—Actors, Interests and Institutions.* Oxford: Oxford University Press.

Huysmans, Jef (1996) *Making/Unmaking European Disorder: Metatheoretical and Empirical Questions of Military Stability After the Cold War.* Katholieke Universiteit Leuven, Faculteit der Sociale Wetenschappen, Departement Politieke Wetenschappen, Niuewe Reeks van Doctoraten in de Sociale Wetenschappen, no. 26.

Ifversen, Jan (1987) "Det Politiske, Magten og Samfundet," *Den Jyske Historiker,* 47, pp. 7–28.

Jachtenfuchs, Markus (1994) *International Policy-Making as a Learning Process: The European Community and the Greenhouse Effect.* Ph.D. thesis, European University Institute, Florence.

Jachtenfuchs, Markus, and Michael Huber (1993) "Institutional Learning in the European Community: The Response to the Greenhouse Effect," in J. D. Lifferink, P. D. Lowe, and A. P. J. Mold (eds.), *European Integration and Environmental Policy.* London: Belhaven, pp. 36–58.

Jackson, Robert H. (1990) *Quasi-States: Sovereignty, International Relations, and the Third World.* Cambridge: Cambridge University Press.

Jahn, Egbert, Pierre Lemaitre, and Ole Wæver (1987) *Concepts of Security:*

Problems of Research on Non-Military Aspects. Copenhagen Papers no. 1. Copenhagen: Centre for Peace and Conflict Research.

Jervis, Robert (1976) *Perception and Misperception in International Relations.* Princeton: Princeton University Press.

———— (1978) "Cooperation Under the Security Dilemma," *World Politics,* 30:2, pp. 167–214.

———— (1982) "Security Regimes," *International Organization,* 36:2, pp. 357–378.

Joenniemi, Pertti (ed.) (1993) *Cooperation in the Baltic Sea Region.* New York: Taylor and Francis.

———— (ed.) (1997) *Neonationalism or Regionality? The Restructuring of Political Space Around the Baltic Rim.* Stockholm: Nordrefo.

Joenniemi, Pertti, and Ole Wæver (1992) *Regionalization Around the Baltic Rim—Background Report to the 2nd Parliamentary Conference on Co-operation in the Baltic Sea Area,* Oslo, 22–24 April, Nordic Seminar and Working Group Report no. 1992: 521. Stockholm: Nordic Council.

Käkönen, Jyrki (ed.) (1992) *Perspectives on Environmental Conflict and International Politics.* London: Pinter.

———— (ed.) (1994) *Green Security or Militarized Environment.* Aldershot: Dartmouth.

Kaplan, Robert (1994) "The Coming Anarchy," *Atlantic Monthly,* February, pp. 44–76.

Katzenstein, Peter J. (1996a) *Cultural Norms and National Security: Police and Military in Postwar Japan.* Ithaca, N.Y.: Cornell University Press.

———— (ed.) (1996b) *The Culture of National Security: Norms and Identity in World Politics.* New York: Columbia University Press.

Kaufmann, Franz-Xavier (1970) *Sicherheit als soziologisches und sozialpolitisches Problem: Untersuchungen zu einer Wertidee hochdifferenzierter Gesellschaften.* Stuttgart: Ferdinand Enke Verlag.

Kelstrup, Morten (1995) "Societal Aspects of European Security," in Birthe Hansen (ed.), *European Security—2000.* Copenhagen: Copenhagen Political Studies Press, pp. 172–199.

Kennedy, Paul (1989) *The Rise and Fall of the Great Powers.* London: Fontana.

Keohane, Robert O. (1980) "The Theory of Hegemonic Stability and Changes in International Economic Regimes," in Ole Holsti, R. Siverson, and A. L. George (eds.), *Change in the International System.* Boulder: Westview Press.

———— (1984) *After Hegemony: Cooperation and Discord in the World Political Economy.* Princeton: Princeton University Press.

Keohane, Robert O., and Joseph S. Nye (1977) *Power and Interdependence.* Boston: Little Brown.

Kindleberger, Charles P. (1973) *The World in Depression 1929–39.* London: Allen Lane.

———— (1981) "Dominance and Leadership in the International Economy," *International Studies Quarterly,* 25:2/3, pp. 242–254.

Kissinger, Henry (1957) *A World Restored: From Castlereagh, Metternich and the Restoration of Peace, 1812–1822.* Boston: Houghton Mifflin.

Klein, Bradley (1990) "How the West Was Won: Representational Politics of NATO," *International Studies Quarterly,* 34:3, pp. 311–325.

———— (1994) *Strategic Studies and World Order: The Global Politics of Deterrence.* Cambridge: Cambridge University Press.

Kostecki, Wojciech (1996) *Europe After the Cold War: The Security Complex Theory.* Warsaw: Instytut Studiów Politycznych PAN.

Krause, Keith (1992) *Arms and the State: Patterns of Military Production and Trade.* Cambridge: Cambridge University Press.

———— (1993) "Redefining Security? The Discourses and Practices of Multilateral Security Activity," paper presented at British International Studies Association (BISA) Conference December, University of Warwick (Coventry).

Krause, Keith, and Michael C. Williams (1996) "Broadening the Agenda of Security Studies: Politics and Methods," *Mershon International Studies Review,* 40, supplement 2, pp. 229–254.

———— (1997) "From Strategy to Security: Foundations of Critical Security Studies," in Krause and Williams (eds.), *Critical Security Studies.* Minneapolis: University of Minnesota Press.

Laclau, Ernesto (1990) *New Reflections on the Revolution of Our Time.* London: Verso.

Lake, David A. (1992) "Powerful Pacifists: Democratic States and War," *American Political Science Review,* 86:1, pp. 24–37.

Lasswell, Harold (1965 [1935]) *World Politics and Personal Insecurity.* New York: Free Press.

Lebow, Richard N. (1988) "Interdisciplinary Research and the Future of Peace and Security Studies," *Political Psychology,* 9:3, pp. 507–543.

Lefort, Claude (1986) *The Political Forms of Modern Society: Bureaucracy, Democracy, Totalitarianism.* Cambridge: Polity.

Levy, Marc A. (1995a) "Is the Environment a National Security Issue?" *International Security,* 20:1, pp. 35–62.

———— (1995b) "Time for a Third Wave of Environment and Security Scholarship," in P. J. Simmons (ed.), *Environmental Change and Security Project Report,* no. 1. Princeton: Woodrow Wilson Center, pp. 44–46.

Lodgaard, Sverre (1992) "Environmental Security, World Order and Environmental Conflict Resolution," in Nils Petter Gleditsch (ed.), *Conversion and the Environment.* Oslo: International Peace Research Institute (PRIO), pp. 115–136.

Lodgaard, Sverre, and Anders H. af Ornäs (eds.) (1992) "The Environment and International Security," *PRIO Report,* 3.

Luciani, Giacomo (1989) "The Economic Content of Security," *Journal of Public Policy,* 8:2, pp. 151–173.

Luke, Timothy (1989) "What's Wrong with Deterrence? A Semiotic Interpretation of National Security Policy," in James Der Derian and Michael Shapiro (eds.), *International/Intertextual Relations.* Lexington, Mass.: Lexington Books, pp. 207–229.

MacNeill, Jim, Pieter Winsemius, and Taizo Yakushiji (1991) *Beyond Interdependence: The Meshing of the World's Economy and the Earth's Ecology.* New York: Oxford University Press.

Mann, Michael (1986) *The Sources of Social Power: A History of Power from the Beginning to AD 1760.* Cambridge: Cambridge University Press.

Manning, C. A. W. (1962) *The Nature of International Society.* London: London School of Economics.

Mansfield, Edward D. (1994) *Power, Trade and War.* Princeton: Princeton University Press.

Maoz, Zeev, and Bruce Russett (1993) "Normative and Structural Causes of Democratic Peace," *American Political Science Review,* 87:3, pp. 624–638.

Matthew, Richard A. (1995) "Environmental Security: Demystifying the Concept, Clarifying the Stakes," in P. J. Simmons (eds.), *Environmental Change and Security Project Report,* no. 1. Princeton: Woodrow Wilson Center, pp. 14–23.

Matthews, Jessica Tuchman (1989) "Redefining Security," *Foreign Affairs,* 68:2, pp. 162–177.

Mattingly, Garett (1955) *Renaissance Diplomacy.* Boston: Houghton Mifflin.

Mayall, James (1991) "Non-Intervention, Self-Determination and the 'New World Order,'" *International Affairs,* 67:3, pp. 421–430.

——— (ed.) (1996) *The New Interventionism, 1991–1994: United Nations Experiences in Cambodia, Former Yugoslavia, and Somalia.* Cambridge: Cambridge University Press.

McKinlay, R. D., and Richard Little (1986) *Global Problems and World Order.* London: Pinter.

McSweeney, Bill (1996) "Buzan and the Copenhagen School," *Review of International Studies,* 22:1, pp. 81–93.

Meadows, Donella H., Dennis L. Meadows, and Jørgen Randers (1992) *Beyond the Limits: Confronting Global Collapse, Envisioning a Sustainable Future.* Mills, Vt.: Chelsea Green Publishers.

Meadows, Donella H. et al. (1972) *The Limits to Growth: A Report for the Club of Rome's Project on the Predicament of Mankind.* New York: Potomac Associates.

Mintz, Alex, and Nehemia Geva (1993) "Why Don't Democracies Fight Each Other? An Experimental Study," *Journal of Conflict Resolution,* 37:3, pp. 484–503.

Mitterrand, François (1995) "Programme of the French Presidency," speech in the European Parliament, *Debates of the European Parliament,* 17 January, no. 4–456, Luxembourg, Office 4, Official Publications of the European Community, pp. 45–52.

Møller, Bjørn (1991) *Resolving the Security Dilemma in Europe: The German Debate and Non-Offensive Defense.* London: Brasseys.

Morgenthau, Hans J. (1966) "Introduction," in David Mitrany (eds.), *A Working Peace System.* Chicago: Quadrangle Books, pp. 7–11.

Mouritzen, Hans (1980) "Selecting Explanatory Levels in International Politics: Evaluating a Set of Criteria," *Cooperation and Conflict,* 15, pp. 169–182.

——— (1995) "A Fallacy of IR Theory: Reflections on a Collective Repression," unpublished manuscript. Copenhagen: Centre for Peace and Conflict Research.

——— (1997) "Kenneth Waltz: A Critical Rationalist Between International Politics and Foreign Policy," in Iver B. Neumann and Ole Wæver (eds.), *The Future of International Relations: Masters in the Making?* London: Routledge, pp. 66–89.

Myers, Norman (1993a) *Ultimate Security—The Environmental Basis of Political Stability.* New York: W. W. Norton.

——— (ed.) (1993b [1984]) *The GAIA Atlas of Planet Management.* London: Gaia Books.

Nardin, Terry, and David R. Mapel (1992) *Traditions of International Ethics.* Cambridge: Cambridge University Press.

Neumann, Iver B. (1994) "A Region-Building Approach to Northern Europe," *Review of International Studies,* 20:1, pp. 53–74.

Nierop, Tom (1994) *Systems and Regions in Global Politics: An Empirical Study of Diplomacy, International Organization and Trade, 1950–1991.* Chichester, N.Y.: John Wiley and Sons.

——— (1995) "Globalisering, internationale netwerken en de regionale paradox," in John Heilbron and Nico Wilterdink (eds.), *Mondialisering: de wording van de wereldsamenleving.* Groningen: Wolters-Noordhoff, pp. 36–60.

Nye, Joseph S., Jr. (1989) "The Contribution of Strategic Studies: Future

Challenges," *Adelphi Paper* no. 235. London: International Institute for Strategic Studies (IISS).

Nye, Joseph S., Jr., and Sean M. Lynn-Jones (1988) "International Security Studies," *International Security,* 12:4, pp. 5–27.

Ohlsson, Leif (ed.) (1995) *Hydropolitics: Conflicts over Water as a Development Constraint.* London: Zed Books.

Onuf, Nicholas J. (1995) "Levels," *European Journal of International Relations,* 1:1, pp. 35–58.

Owen, John (1994) "How Liberalism Produces Democratic Peace," *International Security,* 19:2, pp. 87–125.

Paye, Jean-Claude (1994) "Merciless Competition: Time for New Rules?" *International Economic Insights,* 5:1, pp. 21–24.

Peña, Félix (1995) "New Approaches to Economic Integration in the Southern Cone," *Washington Quarterly,* 18:3, pp. 113–122.

Polanyi, Karl (1957 [1944]) *The Great Transformation.* Boston: Beacon Press.

Ponting, Clive (1991) *A Green History of the World.* London: Sinclair Stevenson.

Porter, Gareth, and Janet W. Brown (1991) *Global Environmental Politics.* Boulder: Westview Press.

Poulsen-Hansen, Lars, and Ole Wæver (1996) "Ukraine," in Hans Mouritzen, Ole Wæver, and Håkan Wiberg (eds.), *European Integration and National Adaptations: A Theoretical Inquiry.* New York: Nova Publishers, pp. 231–260.

Prescott, J. R. V. (1987) *Political Frontiers and Boundaries.* London: Unwin Hyman.

Prins, Gwyn (ed.) (1993) *Threats Without Enemies: Facing Environmental Insecurity.* London: Earthscan.

Reich, Robert (1991) "What Is a Nation?" *Political Science Quarterly,* 106:2, pp. 193–209.

——— (1992 [1991]) *The Work of Nations: Preparing Ourselves for 21st Century Capitalism* (with a new afterword). New York: Vintage Books.

Rex, John (1995) "Multiculturalism in Europe and America," *Nations and Nationalism,* 1:2, pp. 243–260.

Roberts, Adam (1995–1996) "From San Francisco to Sarajevo: The UN and the Use of Force," *Survival,* 37:4, pp. 7–28.

Romero, Federico (1990) "Cross-Border Population Movements," in William Wallace (ed.), *The Dynamics of European Integration.* London: Pinter, pp. 171–191.

Rosenau, James N. (1989) "Subtle Sources of Global Interdependence: Changing Criteria of Evidence, Legitimacy, and Patriotism," in James N. Rosenau and Hylke W. Tromp (eds.), *Interdependence and Conflict in World Politics.* Aldershot: Avebury, pp. 31–47.

——— (1990) *Turbulence in World Politics: A Theory of Change and Continuity.* New York: Harvester Wheatsheaf.

Rosenberg, Emily R. (1993) "The Cold War and the Discourse of National Security," *Diplomatic History,* 17:2, pp. 277–284.

Rothschild, Emma (1995) "What Is Security?" *Dædalus,* 124:3, pp. 53–98.

Ruggie, John G. (1982) "International Regimes, Transactions and Change: Embedded Liberalism in the Postwar Economic Order," *International Organization,* 36:2, pp. 379–415.

——— (1983) "Continuity and Transformation in the World Today: Toward a Neo-Realist Synthesis," *World Politics,* 35:2, pp. 261–285.

——— (1993) "Territoriality and Beyond: Problematizing Modernity in International Relations," *International Organization,* 47:1, pp. 139–175.

Rytkønen, Helle (1995) "Securing European Identity—Identifying Danger," paper presented at the annual conference of the International Studies Association, Chicago, April.

Santer, Jacques (1995a) "Speech to the European Parliament—January 17, 1995," *Debates of the European Parliament,* no. 4–456, Luxembourg, Office 4, Official Publication of the European Community, pp. 13–20.

——— (1995b) "Speech to the European Parliament: Presentation of the Work Programme of the Commission—February 15, 1995," *Debates of the European Parliament,* no. 4–457, pp. 105–107.

——— (1995c) "State of the Union," speech by the president of the European Commission, *Debates of the European Parliament,* 15 November, no. 4–470, pp. 137–140.

Schulz, Michael (1995) "Turkey, Syria and Iraq: A Hydropolitical Security Complex," in Leif Ohlsson (ed.), *Hydropolitics: Conflicts over Water as a Development Constraint.* London: Zed Books, pp. 91–122.

Schweller, R. (1992) "Domestic Structure and Preventive War: Are Democracies More Pacific?" *World Politics,* 44:2.

Segal, Gerald (1994) "China Changes Shape: Regionalism and Foreign Policy," *Adelphi Paper no. 28.* London: IISS.

Senghaas, Dieter (1988) *Konfliktformationen im Internationalen System.* Frankfurt: Suhrkamp Verlag. This book includes a reprint of his first (1973) attempt at global analysis in terms of conflict formations.

Singer, Max, and Aaron Wildavsky (1993) *The Real World Order: Zones of Peace/Zones of Turmoil.* Chatham: Chatham House Publishers.

Sjöstedt, Gunnar (ed.) (1993) *International Environmental Negotiation.* London: Sage.

Skoçpol, Theda (1979) *States and Social Revolution.* Cambridge: Cambridge University Press.

Skodvin, Tora (1994) "Structure and Agent in Scientific Diplomacy: Institutional Design and Leadership Performance in the Science-Politics Interface of Climate Change," *Working Paper 1994:14.* Oslo: Centre for International Climate and Energy Research (CICERO).

Smith, Phillip B., S. E. Okoye, Jaap de Wilde, and Priya Deshingkar (eds.) (1994) *The World at the Crossroads: Towards a Sustainable, Liveable and Equitable World.* London: Earthscan.

Spence, Jack (1994) "Entering the Future Backwards: Some Reflections on the Current International Scene," *Review of International Studies,* 20:1, pp. 3–13.

Strange, Susan (1984) "The Global Political Economy, 1959–84," *International Journal,* 39:2, pp. 267–283.

——— (1994) "Rethinking Structural Change in the International Political Economy: States, Firms and Diplomacy," in Richard Stubbs and Geoffrey Underhill (eds.), *Political Economy and the Changing Global Order.* Toronto: McClelland and Stewart, pp. 103–115.

Stubbs, Richard, and Geoffrey Underhill (1994) "Global Issues in Historical Perspective," in Stubbs and Underhill (eds.), *Political Economy and the Changing Global Order.* Toronto: McClelland and Stewart, pp. 145–162.

Tanaka, Akihiko (1994) "Japan's Security Policy in the 1990s," in Yoichi Funabashi (ed.), *Japans' International Agenda.* New York: New York University Press, pp. 28–56.

Taylor, Charles (1992) *Multiculturalism and "the Politics of Recognition."* Princeton: Princeton University Press.

Taylor, Paul (1993) *International Organization in the Modern World: The Regional and the Global Process.* London: Pinter.

Thomas, Caroline (1992) *The Environment in International Relations.* London: Royal Institute of International Affairs.

Tickner, J. Ann (1992) *Gender in International Relations: Feminist Perspectives on Achieving Global Security.* New York: Columbia University Press.

Tilly, Charles (1990) *Coercion, Capital, and European States: AD 990–1992.* Oxford: Basil Blackwell.

Tönnies, Ferdinand (1926 [1887]) *Gemeinschaft und Gesellschaft (Sechte und siebente Auflage).* Leipzig: Fue's Verlag.

Tromp, Hylke (1996) "New Dimensions of Security and the Future of NATO," in Jaap de Wilde and Håkan Wiberg (eds.), *Organized Anarchy: The Role of Intergovernmental Organizations.* London: I. B. Tauris, pp. 323–338.

Ullman, Richard (1983) "Redefining Security," *International Security,* 8:1, pp. 129–153.

Underhill, Geoffrey (1995) "Keeping Governments Out of Politics: Transnational Securities Markets, Regulatory Cooperation, and Political Legitimacy," *Review of International Studies,* 21:3, pp. 251–278.

UNRISD (United Nations Research Institute for Social Development) (1995) *States in Disarray: The Social Effects of Globalization.* March, New York: UNRISD.

Väyrynen, Raimo (1984) "Regional Conflict Formations: An Intractable Problem of International Relations," *Journal of Peace Research,* 21:4, pp. 337–359.

——— (1988) "Domestic Stability, State Terrorism, and Regional Integration in the ASEAN and the GCC," in Michael Stohl and George Lopez (eds.), *Terrible Beyond Endurance.* New York: Greenwood Press, pp. 194–197.

Wæver, Ole (1988) "Security, the Speech Act," unpublished manuscript.

——— (1989a) "Conceptions of Détente and Change: Some Non-Military Aspects of Security Thinking in the FRG," in Ole Wæver, Pierre Lemaitre, and Elzbieta Tromer (eds.), *European Polyphony: Perspectives Beyond East-West Confrontation.* London: Macmillan, pp. 186–224.

——— (1989b) "Conflicts of Vision: Visions of Conflict," in Ole Wæver, Pierre Lemaitre, and Elzbieta Tromer (eds.), *European Polyphony: Perspectives Beyond East-West Confrontation.* London: Macmillan, pp. 283–325.

——— (1990) "Politics of Movement: A Contribution to Political Theory in and on Peace Movements" in Katsuya Kodama and Unto Vesa (eds.), *Towards a Comparative Analysis of Peace Movements,* Aldershot: Dartmouth 1990, pp. 15–44.

——— (1993) "Europe: Stability and Responsibility" in *Internationales Umfeld, Sicherheitsinteressen und nationale Planung der Bundesrepublik. Teil C: Unterstützende Einzelanalysen. Band 5. II.A Europäische Sicherheitskultur. II.B Optionen für kollektive Verteidigung im Kontext sicherheitspolitischer Entwicklungen Dritter.* Ebenhausen: Stiftung Wissenschaft und Politik, SWP-S 383/5, February, pp. 31–72.

——— (1994) "Resisting the Temptation of Post Foreign Policy Analysis," in Walter Carlsnaes and Steve Smith (eds.), *European Foreign Policy: The EC and Changing Perspectives in Europe.* London: European Consortium for Political Research/Sage, pp. 238–273.

——— (1995a) "Identity, Integration and Security: Solving the Sovereignty Puzzle in E.U. Studies," *Journal of International Affairs,* 48:2, pp. 389–431.

——— (1995b) "Securitization and Desecuritization," in Ronnie D. Lipschutz (ed.), *On Security.* New York: Columbia University Press.

——— (1995c) *Concepts of Security,* Ph.D. dissertation, Institute of Political Science, University of Copenhagen.

——— (1995d) "Power, Principles and Perspectivism: Understanding Peaceful

Change in Post–Cold War Europe," in Heikki Patomäki (ed.), *Peaceful Change in World Politics.* Tampere: Tampere Peace Research Institute (TAPRI), pp. 208–282.

———— (1996a) "Europe's Three Empires: A Watsonian Interpretation of Post-Wall European Security," in Rick Fawn and Jeremy Larkin (eds.), *International Society After the Cold War: Anarchy and Order Reconsidered.* London: Macmillan, pp. 220–260.

———— (1996b) "European Security Identities," *Journal of Common Market Studies,* 34:1, pp. 103–132.

———— (forthcoming-a) "Insecurity and Identity Unlimited," in Anne-Marie Le Gloannec and Kerry McNamara (eds.), *Le Désordre Européen.* Paris: Presses de Sciences Po; second draft printed as *Working Paper,* 1994/14. Copenhagen: Centre for Peace and Conflict Research (Finnish translation in *Kosmopolis,* 1995/1).

———— (forthcoming-b) *The Politics of International Structure.*

———— (forthcoming-c) "Four Meanings of International Society—A Transatlantic Dialogue," in B. A. Roberson (ed.), *International Society and the Development of International Relations.* London: Pinter.

———— (forthcoming-d) "Insecurity, Security and Asecurity in the West European Non-War Community," in Emanuel Adler and Michael Barnett (eds.), *Governing Anarchy: Security Communities in Theory, History and Comparison.* Cambridge: Cambridge University Press.

———— (forthcoming-e) "Security as Integration: European International Identity and American Domestic Discipline," in Charles Kupchan (ed.), *Transatlantic Security: Three Visions.* New York: Council on Foreign Relations.

Wæver, Ole, Barry Buzan, Morten Kelstrup, and Pierre Lemaitre (1993) *Identity, Migration and the New Security Order in Europe.* London: Pinter.

Wæver, Ole, Ulla Holm, and Henrik Larsen (forthcoming) *The Struggle for "Europe": French and German Concepts of State, Nation and European Union.*

Walker, R. B. J. (1988) *One World, Many Worlds: Struggles for a Just World Peace.* Boulder: Lynne Rienner.

———— (1990) "Security, Sovereignty, and the Challenge of World Politics," *Alternatives,* 15:1, pp. 3–28.

———— (1993) *Inside/Outside: International Relations as Political Theory.* Cambridge: Cambridge University Press.

Wallerstein, Immanuel (1993) "The World System After the Cold War," *Journal of Peace Research,* 30:1, pp. 1–6.

Walt, Stephen M. (1991) "The Renaissance of Security Studies," *International Studies Quarterly,* 35:2, pp. 211–239.

Waltz, Kenneth N. (1979) *Theory of International Politics.* Reading, Mass.: Addison-Wesley.

Warner, Jeroen (1996) "De drooglegging van de Jordaanvallei," *Transaktie,* 25:3, pp. 363–379.

Watson, Adam (1992) *The Evolution of International Society.* London: Routledge.

WCED (World Commission on Environment and Development) (1987) *Our Common Future.* Oxford: Oxford University Press.

Weart, Spencer R. (1994) "Peace Among Democratic and Oligarchic Republics," *Journal of Peace Research,* 31:3, pp. 299–316.

Webb, Michael (1994) "Understanding Patterns of Macroeconomic Policy Coordination in the Postwar Period," in Richard Stubbs and Geoffrey Underhill (eds.), *Political Economy and the Changing Global Order.* Toronto: McClelland and Stewart, pp. 176–189.

Weber, Max (1972 [1922]) *Wirtschaft und Gesellschaft.* Tübingen: J. C. B. Mohr.

Wendt, Alexander (1987) "The Agent-Structure Problem in International Relations Theory," *International Organization,* 41:3, pp. 335–370.

———— (1992) "Anarchy Is What States Make of It: The Social Construction of Power Politics," *International Organization,* 46:2, pp. 391–425.

———— (1994) "Collective Identity Formation and the International State," *American Political Science Review,* 88:2, pp. 384–396.

———— (1995) "Constructing International Politics," *International Security,* 20:1, pp. 71–81.

Westing, Arthur H. (ed.) (1988) *Cultural Norms, War and the Environment.* Oxford: Oxford University Press.

———— (ed.) (1990) *Environmental Hazards of War: Releasing Dangerous Forces in an Industrialized World.* London: Sage (International Peace Research Institute Oslo [PRIO], United Nations Environment Program [UNEP]).

Wheeler, Nicholas (1996) "Guardian Angel or Global Gangster: A Review of the Ethical Claims of International Society," *Political Studies,* 44:1, pp. 123–135.

White, N. D. (1996), *The Law of International Organizations,* Manchester: Manchester University Press.

Wiberg, Håkan (1993) "Societal Security and the Explosion of Yugoslavia," in Ole Wæver, Barry Buzan, Morten Kelstrup, Pierre Lemaitre, et al., *Identity, Migration and the New Security Agenda in Europe.* London: Pinter, pp. 93–109.

Wight, Martin (1978) *Systems of States.* Leicester: Leicester University Press.

———— (1986) *Power Politics.* 2d rev. ed., London: Penguin.

Williams, Marc (1993) "Re-Articulating the Third World Coalition: The Role of the Environmental Agenda," *Third World Quarterly,* 14:1, pp. 7–29.

Williams, Michael C. (1996) "Hobbes and International Relations: A Reconsideration," *International Organization,* 50:1, pp. 213–236.

———— (forthcoming) "Identity and the Politics of Security."

Wills, Garry (1995) "The New Revolutionaries," *New York Review of Books,* 10 August, pp. 50–54.

Wind, Marlene (1992) "Eksisterer Europa? Reflektioner over forsvar, identitet og borgerdyd i et nyt Europa," in Christen Sørensen (ed.), *Europa Nation-Union—efter Minsk og Maastricht.* København: Fremad, pp. 23–81.

Wolfers, Arnold (1962) *Discord and Collaboration: Essays on International Politics.* Baltimore: Johns Hopkins University Press.

Wolfson, Ze'ev, and Henry Spetter (1991) "Ecological Aspects of East-West Integration Trends," *Environmental Policy Review,* 1, pp. 14–20.

World Bank (1993) *World Development Report 1993: Investing in Health. World Development Indicators.* New York: Oxford University Press.

Wriggins, W. Howard (ed.) (1992) *Dynamics of Regional Politics: Four Systems on the Indian Ocean Rim.* New York: Columbia University Press.

Wynn-Jones, Richard (1995) "Message in a Bottle? Theory and Praxis in Critical Security Studies," paper presented at the annual conference of the International Studies Association, Chicago, April.

Acronyms

AFTA	ASEAN Free Trade Area
AIDS	Acquired Immune Deficiency Syndrome
ANC	African National Congress
AOSIS	Alliance of Small Island States
APEC	Asia-Pacific Economic Cooperation
ASEAN	Association of Southeast Asian Nations
CCAMLR	Convention on the Conservation of Antarctic Marine Living Resources
CFCs	chlorofluorocarbons
CIS	Commonwealth of Independent States
COPRI	Copenhagen Peace Research Institute
CSCT	classical security complex theory
CSS	critical security studies
EC	European Community
ECOWAS	Economic Community of West African States
EMU	European Monetary Union
EP	European Parliament
ERM	exchange rate mechanism
EU	European Union
FTA	free trade association
GATT	General Agreement on Tariffs and Trade
GDR	German Democratic Republic
GNP	gross national product
G7	Group of Seven
IBM	International Business Machines
ICBM	intercontinental ballistic missile
ICI	Imperial Chemical Industries
IGO	intergovernmental organization
IMF	International Monetary Fund
INGO	international nongovernmental organization
IPE	international political economy
IR	international relations
ITT	International Telephone and Telegraph Corporation

LIEO	liberal international economic order
MEP	Member of the European Parliament
MERCOSUR	Southern Cone Common Market
MFN	most-favored nation
NAFTA	North American Free Trade Agreement
NATO	North Atlantic Treaty Organization
NGO	nongovernmental organization
NIEO	New International Economic Order
NPT	Nuclear Non-Proliferation Treaty
OAU	Organization of African Unity
OAS	Organization of American States
OECD	Organization for Economic Cooperation and Development
OPEC	Organization of Petroleum Exporting Countries
PFP	Partnership for Peace
PKO	peacekeeping operation
R&D	research and development
SAARC	South Asian Association for Regional Cooperation
SADC	Southern African Development Community
TNC	transnational corporation
UK	United Kingdom
UN	United Nations
UNCED	United Nations Conference on Environment and Development
UNEP	United Nations Environment Program
U.S.	United States
USSR	Union of Soviet Socialist Republics
WEU	Western European Union
WTO	World Trade Organization

Index

About the Book

Two schools of thought now exist in security studies: traditionalists want to restrict the subject to politico-military issues; while wideners want to extend it to the economic, societal, and environmental sectors. This book sets out a comprehensive statement of the new security studies, establishing the case for the broader agenda.

The authors argue that security is a particular type of politics applicable to a wide range of issues. Answering the traditionalist charge that this model makes the subject incoherent, they offer a constructivist operational method for distinguishing the process of securitization from that of politicization. Their approach incorporates the traditionalist agenda and dissolves the artificial boundary between security studies and international political economy, opening the way for a fruitful interplay between the two fields. It also shows how the theory of regional security complexes remains relevant in today's world.

Barry Buzan is research professor of international studies at the University of Westminster and project director of the European Security Group at the Copenhagen Peace Research Institute (COPRI). His numerous publications include *People, States, and Fear: The National Security Problem in International Relations* and (with Ole Wœver et al.) *Identity, Migration, and the New Security Agenda in Europe.* **Ole Wœver** is senior research fellow at COPRI. He is author (with Pim den Boer and Peter Brugge) of *The History of the European Idea.* **Jaap de Wilde** is lecturer in international relations at the University of Twente (the Netherlands). He is author of *Saved from Oblivion: Interdependence Theory in the First Half of the 20th Century* and editor (with Hakan Wiberg) of *Organized Anarchy: The Role of States and Intergovernmental Organizations.*